Gloster Meteor

Meteor T.7s of the Central Flying School aerobatic team, sometimes referred to as the 'Meteorites', practising over their Little Rissington airfield in 1953, contribute to a typical Russell Adams photograph. Derek N. James.

Gloster
METEOR
Barry Jones

The Crowood Press

First published in 1998 by
The Crowood Press Ltd
Ramsbury, Marlborough
Wiltshire SN8 2HR

© Barry Jones 1998

British Library Cataloguing-in-Publication Data
A catalogue record for this book is available from the British Library.

ISBN 1 86126 162 4

Dedication
To my children, Mike, Sue, Tricia and Graham.

Acknowledgments

During the compiling of this book I have been fortunate in receiving information and photographs generously supplied by many sources. In particular I would like to express my gratitude to David Birch of Rolls-Royce Heritage, Capt Eric Brown RN, Colin Cruddas of Flight Refuelling Ltd, Bill Gunston, Ron 'Jock' Harvey, Del Holyland of Martin Baker Aircraft, Mike Hooks, Derek N. James, Philip Jarret, Ian Mantaggart, Jim Morrow, NBS Aviation, Michael Oakey of *Aeroplane Monthly*, George Pennick, Richard Riding, Bob Rose, W.H.Sleigh, Glen Surtees of GEC Marconi, Ted Whitley and Ray Williams. I trust they will feel the result justifies their assistance.

Typeset by Phoenix Typesetting, Ilkley, West Yorkshire

Printed and bound in Great Britain by Butler & Tanner, Frome

CONTENTS

PREFACE

On a late afternoon in June 1943, two ATC-uniformed teenagers scrambled off their bicycles and crouched in a hedge on the boundary of Barford-St John airfield. Today we have had jet-powered aircraft for longer than at that time there had been aeroplanes at all, and so it is rather difficult to portray our wonderment – used as we were to the Wellington IIIs of the base's No16 OTU – at the scene before us. With a Gloster Gladiator parked nearby, brown-overalled fitters were busy placing cowling panels over a strange-looking engine on the starboard side of a green- and grey-camouflaged aircraft with a vivid yellow underbelly. When in place, a large opening was left in the front of the nacelle which had us contemplating the size of the propeller that we were convinced would be brought from the T2 hangar in the background. (In our naivety, we did not stop to think how it would fit, with a great wing spar clearly visible ahead of the engine, which did not have a propeller boss anyway!) This aircraft stood on a tricycle undercarriage, and the serial DG205 had an oblique stroke followed by a 'G', which

was also something that we had not yet come across. A pilot was sitting in the cockpit, and the low-pitched whistle that had drawn our attention to the scene in the first place increased to a roar such as we had never heard before.

No propellers appeared, but the fitters hurriedly dragged chocks away from the main wheels. The aircraft started to move onto the peritrack that we had often taxied along ourselves when scrounging flights in 'Wimpys' or the odd Anson, and a red Very star shot up from the control tower as we watched the plane's progress away to the runway threshold; here it turned, and after a long holding, started a slow take-off run towards us that seemed to go on for ages. Eventually this exciting aeroplane lifted into the Oxfordshire sky above our heads and, with a bank to starboard, disappeared behind the collection of mellow sandstone cottages that make up the village of Bloxham. Turning our wide-eyed gaze back to the hangar, we perceived that another, similar aircraft was being pushed out into the sunshine; but discipline decreed that there was homework to be

done, so we returned to our bicycles – furthermore, even more important, we had an ATC squadron meeting that evening!

Such was our introduction – and one for which my friend and I, who thought we knew all the current aircraft, were totally unprepared – to the Gloster Meteor, which would be one of the mainstays of RAF Fighter and Training Commands for well over a decade, and which would also become one of Britain's most durable trials and testbed aircraft. However, in June 1943 it had not even appeared in the aircraft recognition 'bible', *Air Publication 1480X* – but my friend Bob and I had seen it, and our stature at No. 25F Air Training Corps squadron's meeting in the evening was such that, had we been of drinking age, we would have had doubles lined up for us all night!

Barry Jones
Hatton Green
Warwickshire
March 1998

INTRODUCTION

The fighter has always been the glamorous aircraft in the layman's assessment of aviation, an opinion generated because it seems to exhibit all that appeals to the eye and ear. However, a performance acquired through a combination of beauty and power, allied with the designated ability to destroy the aggressor, has maybe placed it on a peak of universal esteem higher than it merits. Having said that, the history of the Royal Air Force shows that it has been fortunate in operating some remarkable aircraft, truly outstanding examples of the aircraft designer's proficiency in this sphere.

Between the two world wars, the design office of the Gloster Aircraft Company, under the leadership of Harry P. Folland, provided the RAF with such distinguished aircraft as the Nighthawk, Grebe, Gamecock and Gauntlet; indeed the latter was still in service when hostilities between Britain and Germany were resumed in 1939. The successor to these classics was the Services' last biplane fighter, the Gladiator, which was built as a private venture to meet the ambitious Specification F.7/30's demand for a single-seat, day- and night-fighter, with a maximum speed exceeding 250mph (402.3km/h), while fitted with a four-gun armament. Harry Folland's penultimate design for Glosters, which introduced an enclosed cockpit for the pilot, was the most advanced biplane fighter operated by the RAF, whose No. 72 Squadron at Tangmere was the first to receive production examples, in February 1937.

The arrival of more heavily armed monoplane fighters from Hawker and Supermarine reduced Gladiator production to 747 aircraft. But their operational efficiency in the Middle East in the early 1940s, and in particular the actions of a handful of Sea Gladiators in the defence of the Mediterranean island of Malta, although given a certain amount of glamorizing, was such as to ensure that Gloster's last biplane featured large in the annals of the Royal Air Force.

Folland's last Gloster design, to Specification F.5/34, was their first landplane monoplane (their previous having been the Gloster VI twin-float racing seaplanes built for the 1929 Schneider Trophy contest at Cowes; this design had to be withdrawn because the engines couldn't be kept running at full throttle). Only two F.5/34s were made, as no production order materialized, again because of the arrival of the Hurricane and Spitfire.

In 1937 Harry Folland left Glosters to form his own company. The new chief designer, W.G. Carter, tendered a twin-engined, two-seat fighter for Specification F.9/37, two of which were built; but a landing accident at Boscombe Down involving the first prototype brought the project to an end. Gloster Aircraft had been taken over by Hawker Aircraft in 1934, and when the great expansion programme started in 1938, they were given the responsibility of building a new shadow factory at Hucclecote, in order to increase production for the parent company.

Carter was introduced to Frank Whittle in August 1938, and a feeling of mutual appreciation was formed between the two engineers. Wartime production of Hurricanes and Typhoons at Hucclecote was to keep the shop-floor well occupied, but the design office was under-employed. Thus when in August 1939 the Air Ministry ordered an aircraft to be designed

A picture that epitomizes the association between Gloster Aircraft and the Royal Air Force in the mid-1930s. Five Gauntlet MkIIs of No. 56 Squadron, in formation up from their base at North Weald. Author's collection.

powered by Whittle's new jet engine, Carter and his design team were available to commence such a project almost immediately.

Whitehall raised Specification E.28/39, and within fifteen months from receiving a contract, Gloster's had completed W4041/G, the first of two aircraft built, and it made its maiden flight on 15 May 1941. With World War II already under way, the advantages of Whittle-type engines relative to operational aircraft had been clearly recognized, and with their existing experience, Carter's team was entrusted to produce a design for a jet-engine-powered fighter to meet Specification F.9/40.

Thus were the seeds sown for the manufacture of the only Allied jet aircraft to see service in the 1939–45 conflict, the Meteor, which was also to constitute a large element of the RAF's fighter strength for the following decade. Both the Netherlands and Belgium assembled variants for their respective air forces, while the inventories of a further fourteen overseas countries included the Gloster aircraft in both single- and two-seat versions.

Many aircraft designs have dissolved into memories without attaining anything like the record of the Meteor, both as an operational fighter and a trainer. However, George Carter's design has been highly instrumental in the advancement of world aviation: it was the flying testbed for six new British jet engines, many thousands of which were produced and saw service with other air forces; it was the trials airframe for over 90 per cent of British radar and electronics research, which again has benefited international aeronautics; but possibly its greatest contribution to military aviation was its use by Martin-Baker Aircraft to prove the validity of James Martin's concept for an ejection seat, which to date has enabled over 7,000 aircrew to walk away from disaster.

Over 3,500 Meteors of all Marks came off the lines in the thirteen years that it was in production, with modifications for additional utilization carrying on for a further decade. As a fighter it had its limitations, and the respective merits of a tandem-seat layout for a trainer, compared with side-by-side seating, has advocates on both sides. However, a basic twin-engined, single-seat aircraft that has endured being stretched and enlarged by over fifty per cent of its original dimensions; that was fitted with more than a dozen different nose profiles without this adversely affecting its handling; that took a 450 per cent increase in engine power in its stride, as well as flying successfully with three and four engines, besides serving with weapons not even contemplated at its conception: all of this must indisputedly be proof of a reasonably sound design.

The following narrative traces the Meteor's history which, at the time of writing, is still being actively pursued in the heart of the English county of Buckinghamshire. It is periodically presented on the air show circuit – never a glamorous filly, but a great and successful work-horse.

CHAPTER ONE

Gladiators, Ancient and Modern

The legions of Emperor Claudius landed in Britain in AD43, and within forty years most of the country was in Roman hands. They established Corinium (now Cirencester) as the largest town outside Londinium, and the fortified settlement of Glevum, fourteen-and-a-half leagues north-west along one of the two Ermine Streets, as the guardian of the routes to Wales that converged at the lowest crossing-point of the River Severn. By the sixth century the Saxons had crossed the North Sea from their North German homeland to sack the remains of this segment of the Roman Empire; subsequently the county of Gloucestershire materialized, with Glevum becoming the county capital, Gloucester. Whether gladiatorial activities took place in the area during Claudius's era is uncertain – that the word would be resurrected and associated with the county, centuries later, is well established.

While the bedrocks of British aviation, Frederick Handley Page, T.O.M. Sopwith, Edwin Alliott Verdon Roe, together with Eustace and Oswald Short, were founding their individual companies, one George Holt Thomas was following their progress with interest. His father was the founder of the *Daily Graphic* newspaper and so he appreciated the news value of these new enterprises; moreover as a press representative he associated with Henry and Maurice Farman, as well as one of the originators of international air mail, Gustav Hamel. Holt Thomas was far-sighted enough to appreciate transportation by air, and this resulted in his establishing Aircraft Transport and Travel, on 5 October 1916. Prior to this, and resulting from the friendship with the Farman brothers, he received licences to market their aeroplanes, together with Gnome engines, in the United Kingdom – all of which indicated that the next logical step was to form his own company.

With three manufacturing sites in the London area – Hendon, Merton and Walthamstow – Holt Thomas established the Aircraft Manufacturing Company in 1912. The following year, Hugh Burroughes left the Balloon Factory at Farnborough to become the manager of the new company, and in June 1914 he persuaded Geoffrey de Havilland to become the Aircraft Manufacturing Company's chief designer.

De Havilland's first design, the D.H.1 two-seat reconnaissance biplane, was followed by a scaled-down single-seat version, the D.H.2 scout/fighter. The commencement of hostilities in 1914 presented the company with orders that obviously could not be fulfilled in their existing premises. In the course of his search for new production locations, in April 1915 Burroughes made the acquaintance of a company specializing in high quality woodwork, H.H. Martyn and Company Limited, operating from the Sunningend Works at Cheltenham, Gloucestershire – and observations made at Cheltenham convinced Burroughes that H.H. Martyn could meet his company's requirements. Following an initial supply of spares for Farman and D.H.2 aircraft, the Cheltenham company came to play a major part in the production of complete fuselages and assemblies, to meet later D.H.4 and D.H.6 contracts.

The Birth of Glosters

So successful was the collaboration that, during the third year of the war, A.W. Martyn, Managing Director of H.H. Martyn, and Hugh Burroughes drew up a new structure under which the Cheltenham woodwork engineering company would join with the Aircraft Manufacturing Company on a fifty/fifty holdings basis.

So it was that on 5 June 1917, the Gloucestershire Aircraft Company Limited was formed, with a registered capital of £10,000. A board of directors was appointed with George Holt Thomas as chairman, A.W. Martyn as managing director, and Hugh Burroughes, Guy Peck and David Longden as directors. The company acquired all aircraft business from H.H. Martyn and Co. Ltd., and received contracts to manufacture D.H.6 and D.H.9 components, as well as F.E.2b assembly, together with Bristol F.2Bs. By the cessation of the war on 11 November 1918, a shop-floor workforce of over 750 was producing close on fifty complete aircraft a week. An aircraft storage park, precursor of the Maintenance Unit (MU), had been set up in 1915, seven miles away at Hucclecote, outside Gloucester; aeroplanes were transported there in sections by road from Cheltenham, and after final assembly they were flown from the grass runway.

Inevitably the armistice brought the cancellation of military contracts, and the fledgling Gloucestershire Aircraft Company, having been initiated to mass-produce warplanes, had not got round to creating a design team, such as would be a part of the more established aircraft companies, which could embark on fulfilling the obvious market for civil aircraft. Both the Nieuport Nighthawk and the Farnborough Royal Aircraft factory's F.E.2b, continued in production into 1919, but at a greatly reduced rate. The company's position was further weakened by George Holt Thomas's retirement due to illness, and Hugh Burroughes' decision to leave in order to concentrate on an engineering company producing aircraft that he had previously purchased, but had not been associated with. (He was to return to the Gloucestershire Aircraft Company a couple of years later.) Holt Thomas sold his interests in the old Aircraft Manufacturing

Company to the Daimler/BSA consortium, who promptly closed down all the premises in the London area.

With the departure of Holt Thomas and Burroughes, another new company structure placed A.W. Martyn as chairman, with David Longden becoming managing director; it was their responsibility to redirect the manufacturing abilities of the Sunningend Works, to undertake other work. A system was instigated whereby companies could claim against the government for financial losses due to cancelled military contracts, and the Gloucestershire Aircraft Company received remunerations sufficient to purchase the large existing stock of Nighthawk fighter components. The shrewdness of this decision quickly bore fruit when in 1920 Japan ordered fifty Nighthawks for the proposed Imperial Japanese Navy Air Service. The order was fulfilled in record time due to the component stocks being in hand, and the resulting aircraft were renamed Sparrowhawks.

Also in 1920, the Nieuport and General Aircraft Company, based in the North London suberb of Cricklewood, elected to close down due to post-war contract cancellations from which they had not

emerged so well. The Gloucestershire Aircraft Company bought all Nighthawk design rights and, even more important, were in a position to give employment to the defunct company's Chief Designer, Henry Phillip Folland. Having established a reputation as an outstanding designer at Farnborough, with the S.E.4 and S.E.5 to his credit, Folland took over as Chief Designer at Nieuport in 1917, where his Nighthawk fighter was well into production under subcontract at the Sunningend Works. Then hostilities ceased, but Folland's joining Gloucestershire Aircraft gave the company a respected nucleus upon which a design team could be established.

He started by redesigning his Nighthawk into the Mars I/Bamel racer, the whole undertaking being completed in less than a month. After its first flight, from the former aircraft acceptance park at Hucclecote on 20 June 1921, he was officially confirmed as Chief Designer, and he was joined by former Nieuport colleague H.E. Preston. The company's rating had been improved to the extent that the Air Board appointed an official, AID-approved works inspector; furthermore the Bamel won the same year's Aerial Derby, and on 12 December was also responsible

His Majesty King George V talks with George Holt Thomas, outside the pioneer's Aircraft Manufacturing Company in 1917, watched by Her Majesty Queen Mary and Hugh Burroughes, who had been the original manager of the Aircraft Manufacturing Company. Derek N. James.

Henry P. Folland, with hat and cane, poses alongside L.R. Tait-Cox, in front of his Nieuport Goshawk G-EASK. Tait-Cox set a British speed record of 166.5mph (267.9km/h) in the aircraft on 17 June 1920, a year before Folland joined the Gloucestershire Aircraft Company. Author's collection.

for raising the British air speed record to 196.4mph (316km/h) – this started a new era of prosperity.

Refinement of the Bamel produced two further Aerial Derby victories. Folland also developed a new wing section which came to be known as the high lift biplane (HLB), an innovation which provided a reduced wingspan aircraft with hitherto unrealized manoeuvrability. Mars derivatives from the basic Nieuport Nighthawk continued to be designed and produced; for the Mars VI, which followed the Japanese Sparrowhawk, the Nighthawk name was revived and this aircraft served with two RAF squadrons and was exported to the *Elliniki Stratrotiki Aeroporia*/Greek Army Air Force. The final development from the original Nieuport fighter was the Mars X Nightjar, of which twenty-two were produced; these also saw limited service with the RAF.

The company's first aircraft to go into large-scale production for the Royal Air

Force was the Grebe, which had evolved from the Mars-developed Grouse. The Grebe was also responsible for the beginning of an association with another manufacturer established in the county of Gloucestershire, the Bristol Aeroplane Company: this company's Chief Engineer Roy (later Sir Roy) Fedden approached Harry Folland with a proposal to instal a Jupiter engine in a Grebe fuselage. The combination was successful, and it formed the basis of the Gamecock, which went into production following the delivery of the last of 133 Grebes built; the Gamecock saw service in six RAF squadrons.

The company's increasing success, both in the United Kingdom and, even more importantly, abroad brought with it an unusual problem of phonetics. The correct pronunciation of the work 'Gloucestershire' presented difficulties that were recognized by the Board, and therefore on 11 November 1926 the more intelligible Gloster Aircraft Company Limited superseded the Gloucestershire Aircraft Company.

With a view to diversifying the company's interests, in 1925 Hugh Burroughes' attentions turned to the activities of Dr. Hele-Shaw and T. Beacham, who were perfecting an hydraulically operated, variable-pitch propeller. By the end of 1926, examples test-flown on a Grebe and two Gamecock aircraft showed that the units operated satisfactorily; but the hoped-for large-scale interest did not materialize, although there were hints of Air Ministry development contracts. In order to recover some of the private-venture costs, a limited licence was given to the Japanese Okurs Company to manufacture variable-pitch propellers, purely for their own operational use.

Eventually, in January 1929, a contract for a dozen units was issued. Four were test-flown on a Rolls-Royce-engined Fairey Fox, four more on an Armstrong Whitworth Siskin and a further four were fitted on a Bristol Bulldog; the following year a Gloster Gamecock undertook a seventy-five-hour test programme. An example of the variable-pitch propeller was subsequently displayed on the Gloster Aircraft stand at the Olympia International Aero Exhibition, and it caught the attention of Tom Hamilton, the representative for the American Hamilton Airscrews Company. Hamilton returned to the United States and patented a two-

A 1950s view of the Hucclecote/Brockworth complex, the parish boundary taking a line approximating with the taxi strip. Gloster's original Hucclecote factory is visible on the far left, adjacent to the main road. Derek N. James

position propeller, which was later manufactured under licence by de Havilland. Gloster's variable-pitch propeller was eventually sold by its then parent company, Hawker Aircraft, in 1936, to a Rolls-Royce/Bristol consortium, Rotol Airscrews Limited, also based in Cheltenham. In the 1960s, the Dowty Group amalgamated with them, to form Dowty Rotol Limited.

Expansion

By the mid-1920s the Gloster Aircraft Company had outgrown its Cheltenham roots; it had rented hangar space at Hucclecote for nearly ten years, and so put in a bid of £15,000 to purchase the airfield, together with all its buildings. Contracts were finalized in 1928, and by 1930 the company owned the site. A boundary ran through the property, dividing Hucclecote from the parish of Brockworth, and over

the years the latter name became applied to the airfield as a whole, especially when the late-1930s expansion programme was implemented and buildings for a new assembly line were erected on the Brockworth side of the parish boundary. However, Hucclecote has always appeared on Gloster's letterheads, so will be maintained in this narrative.

The increased shop-floor area and the departure from the woodworking dominance of H.H. Martyn encouraged Harry Folland to investigate the conclusive experiments undertaken by the metal fabrication section of the RAE at Farnborough. Burroughes supported the proposal for a change of construction material, and placed at Gloster's disposal the 50 per cent interest in the Steel Wing Company that he held. This development resulted in W.G. Armstrong Whitworth Aircraft, at Baginton, placing a subcontract for a number of their Siskin IIIAs to be produced at Hucclecote;

moreover further work was undertaken on de Havilland designs, due to that company's limited experience in the use of metal construction: these included the three-engined D.H.72 night bomber, and the D.H.77 monoplane fighter. From this inter-company liaison came an association between the aircraft's designer, W.G. Carter, and H.P. Folland, which would have a later, far-reaching effect on the Gloster Aircraft Company.

A subsidiary development came about through the Swiss engineer, H. Stieger, who had designed a single-spar cantilever wing in which the torsional strength came from the combination of a series of compressed transverse struts, with wire braces from the spar to the struts. With a couple of associates he formed the Monospar Wing Company Limited, and they approached Gloster with a view to the Hucclecote company constructing an aeroplane that Stieger had designed. Known as the Gloster-Monospar S.S.1, the aircraft was completed and test-flown in the winter of 1930. Further development of the S.S.1 was taken over by General Aircraft Limited, who went on to produce several variants of the Monospar.

Several prototype-only designs emerged in the early 1930s; obviously these did not do much to improve Gloster's profitability, and so non-aviation manufacturing work had to be accepted in order to keep the workforce intact. At this time Hawker Aircraft Limited had a burgeoning order-book that could not be fulfilled by their own existing production facilities: recognizing the potential at Hucclecote, in 1934 they made a take-over offer for the Gloster Aircraft Company which was accepted. The company's name would be retained and Hugh Burroughes would remain on the Board, but Hawker's Frank Spriggs took over as Chairman and David Longden retired as Managing Director.

Within months Hawker Hardys were coming out of the Hucclecote factory, to be followed by Audaxes and Harts. This steady production gave Folland and his team the time to give their attention to perfecting the SS.18 design already submitted to meet Specification F.20/27: while not being completely rejected, it had not met with full approval. From their studies emerged an association with Bristol's engine company, and a Jupiter VII, already proven in Bristol's Bulldog fighter, was chosen to power the SS.18B. The definitive development, the SS.19B,

Two of Gloster's endeavours in the quest for the Schneider Trophy. N224, the first of three biplane Gloster IVs built in 1927, and N249, one of two monoplane Gloster Vs produced in 1929. Although both types performed well in tests, neither was successful in their respective attempts. N224 was sold in 1930 and disappeared, while N249 was withdrawn from the contest in 1929. It did hold a record of 336.3mph (541.2km/h) for a few hours in September 1929, until the Supermarine S.6 beat it on the same day. Author's collection.

was powered by a 536hp Bristol Mercury VIS radial engine; it was named 'Gauntlet', and the subsequent installing of a 640hp Mercury VIS2 engine gave Gloster Aircraft a much-needed large production order for an indigenous design. The first production aircraft, flown by the ex-Hawker test pilot P.E.G. 'Gerry' Sayer on 17 December 1934, received good reports from the Aircraft and Armament

Experimental Establishment (A&AEE), which was in those days based at Martlesham Heath in Suffolk.

The Gladiator

So began a golden era for the company, such that they built a private venture design to meet Specification F.7/30: their

The Gloster Aircraft Company

It is believed that, from its formation on 5 June 1917, the Gloucestershire Aircraft Company Limited, which endured the title metamorphosis to the Gloster Aircraft Company Limited on 11 November 1926, produced a total of 8,819 piston-engined aircraft. In addition to the above total, fifteen Gamecocks were produced in Finland by the Finnish National Aircraft Factory at Helsinki, 150 A1N Gambits in Japan by Nakajima Hikoki K.K. and seventeen Gauntlets in Denmark by Flyvertroppernes Vaerksteder at Copenhagen. The Gnatsnapper is the reason for the slight doubt concerning the total, because it has been questioned whether the Mark III was a new airframe or in fact a modification of the Mark II. Such evidence that is available points to the latter being true, and this is reflected in the total shown. The breakdown of production runs is as follows:

Subcontracted production, totalling 7,456 aircraft:

D.H.6 & D.H.9	150
F2B	461
FE2b	165
Hurricane	2,750
Typhoon	3,330
Albemarle	600

Production of indigenous designs, totalling 1,363 aircraft:

Mars/Bamel	1
Nighthawk	54
Sparrowhawk	51
Nightjar	22
Grouse	1
Gannet	1
Grebe	133
Gloster II	2
Gamecock	96
Gloster III	2
Gorcock	3
Guan	2
Goral	1
Goring	1
Goldfinch	1
Gloster IV	3
Gambet	1
Gnatsnapper	2
Gauntlet	229
Gloster VI	2
Gloster AS.31	2
Gloster TC.33	1
Gloster TSR.38	1
Gladiator	747
Gloster F.5/34	2
Gloster F.9/37	2

In giving the number of squadrons that operated a particular type, it is being taken that the aircraft were accepted on charge by the squadron and not just temporarily seconded.

Gloster-designed aircraft that served with front-line squadrons:

Nighthawk	2 squadrons
Nightjar	1 squadron, plus 2 Fleet Air Arm training flights
Grebe	6 squadrons, plus New Zealand Air Force
Gamecock	5 squadrons, plus 3 Finnish Air Force units
Gauntlet	22 squadrons, plus various Met Flights
Gladiator	33 squadrons, plus 12 training units, various Met Flights and 8 Fleet Air Arm squadrons.

The last production Gladiator MkI, L8032, was bought by Gloster Aircraft in 1940; following its purchase by Flightways in 1952, who bought it for £250 with just eighty hours on the airframe, it was registered G-AMRK. The following year it was repurchased by Gloster, whose apprentices restored it to military operational standard; the company was granted official permission for the aircraft to be given the serial of a second production batch Gladiator, K8032. Author's collection.

SS.37 was a further improvement on the basic Gauntlet, and with a cowled Mercury IV engine and a four-gun armament, it first flew on 12 September 1934. Martlesham Heath indicated that slight improvements would make it a first-rate aircraft, and having taken note of the establishment's suggestions, the result was an order to meet production Specification F.14/35. In naming it, the Glevum roots were retraced: it was called 'Gladiator'.

Before reaching squadron allocation, the further-developed Bristol Mercury IX, giving 830hp, was installed; when the RAF finally received their Gladiators, it was their first fighter to be equipped with a fully enclosed cockpit, with a sliding canopy. A total of 747 Gladiators was produced over the five-year period prior to the outbreak of World War II, and the emergence of the monoplane fighter gave the Gloster aircraft the distinction of being the Service's last biplane interceptor.

During the years of Gladiator production, Harry Folland decided to realize a long-held ambition to establish his own aircraft company: in May 1937 he therefore resigned from Glosters in order to re-organise the British Marine Aircraft Limited at Hamble, in Hampshire, into Folland Aircraft Limited. The company's products would prove to be as diversified as the gargantuan engine testbed airframe built to Specification 43/37, to the Midge/Gnat lightweight fighter, the brainchild of the company's chief engineer, W.E.E. Petter. Folland's final design at Hucclecote followed the prevailing vogue, being an eight-gun single-seat monoplane offered to the fighter Specification F.5/34. Although the two Mercury-powered examples built, K5604 and K8089, were well received, the Hurricane/Spitfire duo were in production and the Gloster aircraft did not produce any performance improvements over them. Furthermore, under the 1938 expansion programme, the new production facilities on the Brockworth side were to be responsible for supplying 2,750 Hurricanes. These were followed by the total production of operational Napier Sabre-engined Typhoons, all 3,330 of them. An additional separate company, although a part of Gloster Aircraft, was also set up, entitled A.W.

Hawkesley. The name was contracted from 'Armstrong Whitworth/Hawker Siddeley' and the company was to produce the Armstrong Whitworth Albemarle, a medium bomber design that did not serve in that role but performed well, dragging Horsa troop-carrying gliders around the skies for two years. Six hundred of the 602 Albemarles built came from the A.W. Hawkesley factory.

The private venture SS.37 evinced a good enough performance at Martlesham Heath for the Air Ministry to register it as K5200, to become the prototype Gladiator. It participated in the 1935 RAF display at Hendon as aircraft number '1' in the Experimental Aircraft Park, the system operating so that spectators could identify individual aircraft by numerical listing in their programme – not likely to be necessary nowadays. Author's collection.

A fine photograph of the ninetieth production Gladiator MkI K7968, on air-test prior to squadron allocation. The type was the RAF's first fighter with a sliding cockpit canopy, and in this shot, the port-side underwing Colt/Browning machine gun is very visible, as is the extensive wire bracing still employed as late as 1937. Author's collection.

CHAPTER TWO

The Turbojet's Gestation

While Gauntlets were being manufactured at Hucclecote, an epoch was dawning on both sides of the English Channel: in Germany, Hans Joachim Pabst von Ohain, a physics student at Gottingen University, considered a means of propulsion that would, in theory, enable an aeroplane to exceed the speed limitations created by the propeller. He had a scale-model built in early 1936 by Max Hahn, an auto-engineer, and although the combustion chamber failed, his tutor Professor Pohl recognized that the principle held promise. Amongst the tutor's friends was one Professor Ernst Heinkel, the aircraft designer who had founded the Ernst Heinkel Flugzeugwerke GmbH at Warnemünde on 1 December 1922, and Pohl arranged an introduction for von Ohain.

Heinkel was a visionary: he had been working on a rocket propulsion application for aeroplanes with another young engineer, Wernher von Braun of the German Army experimental rocket establishment at Peenemünde, and he appreciated the potential of von Ohain's engine. Not only did he take both von Ohain and Hahn onto the company's staff, but he also sponsored the engine's development as a private venture. The first engine runs, burning oxygen, began in the autumn of 1937, and Heinkel himself had already turned his attention to designing an airframe that would accept this new mode of propulsion. Two years later, on 24 August 1939, the labours of the two men bore fruit when the Heinkel He178, piloted by Flugkapitan Erich Warsitz, also from Peenemünde, commenced taxiing trials. Three days later, on 27 August, Warsitz made a successful maiden flight of the world's first jet-propelled aircraft from Rostock-Marienehe. A month earlier, Fuehrer Adolf Hitler, together with the head of the Luftwaffe, Reichsmarshal Hermann Goering, had attended a demonstration of Heinkel's first rocket-propelled He176 – but they were not impressed, and were much more interested in seeing large numbers of twin piston-engined Heinkel He111 bombers coming off the lines at Rostock-Marienehe to join the Kampfgeschwader of the Luftwaffe. There was also the question of getting the new He177 into production: that was going to drop really big bombs on the British Isles – these new-fangled aircraft without propellers could not.

In fact, history has shown that Ernst Heinkel was never really in favour with the top echelon of the German Air Ministry/*Reichs Luftfahrt Ministerium* (RLM). This is possibly because, in modern parlance, he was 'his own man', with a decidedly uncompromising nature and one who strongly believed in his own abilities. The RLM's bigotry was exemplified when in August 1940 Heinkel presented his He280, the world's first aircraft designed specifically as a twin jet-powered fighter: it had all the impact of a feather landing on a blancmange. His great rival, Professor Willy Messerschmitt, was already engaged in producing the rocket-powered Me163 fighter, and he was instructed to proceed with his own Me262 project; although this was designed as a jet-powered fighter-bomber, in fact it only operated in the latter months of World War II as a defensive interceptor against the combined might of RAF Bomber Command and the US Eighth AAF. It could be argued that the RLM was right, because the Me262, with its Junkers Jumo engines, was a far better operational aircraft than the He280, flown at various times with Heinkel/Hirth, Jumo and BMW engines, could possibly ever have been.

The Allied air forces encountered Willy Messerschmitt's two new aircraft in the summer of 1944. On 29 May, Flt Lt Geoffrey Crakanthorpe of 'B' Flight, No. 542 Squadron, flying photo-reconnaissance Spitfire MkXI MB791, landed at Coltishall for refuelling *en route* to his home base of RAF Benson and reported having seen what he believed was an Me163 below him, while flying at 41,000ft (12,500m) during his sortie over northern Germany. Eight weeks later on 28 July, Captain Arthur Jeffrey, flying a Lockheed P-38 Lightning of the Wattisham-based 479th Fighter Group, on US Eighth AAF Mission 501, unsuccessfully pitted his two Allison twelve-cylinder piston engines against an Me163's Walter bi-fuel liquid rocket unit. Diving with 500mph (805km/h) indicated while chasing the enemy aircraft, he levelled off and 'blacked-out'; however, later camera-gun film examinations showed his deflection shots had not affected the German interceptor. Three days earlier a de Havilland Mosquito, also on a photo-reconnaissance mission, had sighted an Me262, but no contact had been made. It was not until 29 August that Republic P-47 Thunderbolts, their black-and-white chequerboard engine cowls showing them to be members of the 78th Fighter Group from Duxford, encountered an Me262 while they were engaged on attacking rail targets at low altitude near Brussels. In fact the German pilot instigated his own demise, because he crash-landed while avoiding the US fighters and was killed in the subsequent strafing of his jet-powered aircraft; the 78th Group's leader Major Joe Myers jointly claimed the 'kill' with his wing-man Lt Manford Croy, and official records confirm this.

Messerschmitt's 'Propless' Duo

In the mid-1930s German rocket engineer Hellmuth Walter was contracted by the *Deutsche Versuchsanstalt fur Luftfahrt* (D.V.L.) to develop a small liquid-fuel rocket motor, producing a thrust in the

HEADQUARTERS
FREEMAN FIELD
Air Materiel Command
Seymour, Indiana.

Heinkel HE-178 with He 58 engine

FFEF2/BEA/mm/

9 April 1946

RECEIVED
JUL 9 — 1947

FOREIGN EQUIPMENT DESCRIPTIVE BRIEF
Serial No. 46-11

Photographs of Heinkel Fighter

A. Purpose:

1. The purpose of this brief is to publish information and photographs on a German aircraft for further identification. This aircraft is not at Freeman Field.

B. Description:

Al Heinkel He-178 (his des)

2. The photographs of a German aircraft were received at Freeman Field. This aircraft is believed to be of Heinkel design. The information contained in this brief was extracted from P/W interrogations and is not confirmed as to its accuracy. The Heinkel single seat experimental fighter is referred to as the HET. This aircraft is described as an all-metal mid-wing monoplane of 26.2 ft. span. The length of the fuselage is 19.6 ft. The wing was to have been fitted with a high lift device, possibly a Fowler flap, to increase the wing chord by approximately 2 ft. The aircraft was intended for high altitude operation and the cabin is pressurized. A turbine of the propulsion unit was stated by a P/W as having been located in the forward part of the fuselage. The compressor is said to be of the exhaust turbine type with a maximum speed of 25,000 to 30,000 rpm. The propulsive "tuyere" is in the tail of the fuselage. The design is generally similar to the Italian jet-powered Caproni-Campini aircraft. No information has been received as to the designer or manufacturer of the propulsion unit. The power ratings were said to be 110% thrust for 5 minutes and 90% thrust for 30 minutes. Performance figures as stated by P/W seem incredible. The maximum speed was said to be 750 mph at 52,000-53,000 ft. at 95% thrust. This fighter was reported to be able to reach 19,500 altitude in 1 1/2 minutes, probably at best climb angle of 30°. Maneuverability, as might be expected from lack of inherent leverage to the airplane, was said to be unsatisfactory especially in turning or in violent maneuvers, at high speeds. The aircraft was said to be equipped with under wing rocket fittings for assisted take-off. The airplane was intended to be launched by catapult rocket charge from a skid

FEDB 46-11 (Cont'd)

runway 130 ft. long. Landing speed was said to be of reasonable speed, probably about 135 mph. No indication as to what type of armament this aircraft was to employ has been found. No aircraft answering this plane's description has been located or observed by Allied pilots or by photo interpreters of aerial reconnaissance. The aircraft was believed to have been intended to be used tactically as an interceptor.

Concurred by:

C. H. Belvin Jr.
C. H. BELVIN, JR., Lt. Colonel, Air Corps
Director, Engineering Services Division

DISTRIBUTION:
Historical Officer (Thru Adj)
Display Branch
Liaison & Translation Branch (2)
TSICD (8)

Prepared by: *Buell E. Andrus*
BUELL E. ANDRUS, Capt., Air Corps
Project Officer, Evaluation Branch

Approved by: *Kenneth M. Hammer*
KENNETH M. HAMMER, Capt., Air Corps
Chief, Evaluation Branch

Approved by: *Charles E. Thompson*
C. E. THOMPSON, Capt., Air Corps
Asst. Chief, Foreign Aircraft & Equipment Section

Left and Above:
The American report *Foreign Equipment Descriptive Brief No. 46*, issued on 9 April 1946, concerns the Heinkel He178, which is interesting in the number of inaccuracies that it contains. It was based on prisoner-of-war (P/W) interrogations, and whether they deliberately imparted false information or just made it up as they went along is open to conjecture. Their statement that it had not been observed by Allied pilots is not surprising, as the only example to fly is reported to have been destroyed in storage during an RAF attack on Berlin. Author's collection.

The maiden flight of the Heinkel He 280 V2, with two HeS 8A engines, was made from Rostock-Marienehe on 2 April 1941 with the company's test pilot Fritz Schafer at the controls. As unburnt fuel had collected in the cowlings during ground-running, the possibility of fire during the flight was averted by removing the front nacelle units. Author's collection.

order of 90lb (40kg). The object of the exercise was to attach the motor to one wing-tip of an aircraft and monitor its roll characteristics after the rocket had been fired. Walter had been engaged in experiments with hydrogen-peroxide as a fuel, designated *T-Stoff*, and he foresaw the possibilities of a mixture with this fuel, producing power for a high-speed aeroplane.

Dr Baeumker of the D.V.L. was considering a high-speed research aircraft project and made contact, through his assistant Dr Lovenz, with Professor A.M. Lippisch of the *Deutsche Forschungsanstalt fur Segelflug* (D.F.S.) – the German Institute for Sailplanes – based at Griesheim near Darmstadt. Reports of the several advanced tail-less designs already proposed by the D.F.S. convinced Dr Baeumker that his ideas could be taken further, but the Institute did not have the necessary test facilities. Consequently, in January 1939 a team under the leadership of Professor Lippisch joined the Messerschmitt A.G. at Augsburg. The team evaluated their DFS194 project in the test complex at Augsburg, and the R.L.M. designation Me163 was applied to the programme. The association between Lippisch and the aircraft manufacturer was rather acrimonious, however, to the extent that the professor left, once his expertise had been assimilated by Messerschmitt, to become curator of the Aeronautical Research Institute of Vienna.

In flight trials the DFS194 was piloted by Flugkapitan Heini Dittmar at Peenemünde-Karlshagen, and the aerodynamics of the design exceeded all expectations; following these trials two Me163 prototypes, V1 and V2, were completed in the spring of 1941. Rocket-powered flights in the Augsburg area posed a security risk, so preliminary Me163V1 flight trials were undertaken with the airframe as a glider; a twin-engined Messerschmitt Bf110 acted as a tug, taking the prototype to about 13,000ft (3,960m) before cast-off. In the summer of 1941, Me163V1 was transported to Peenemünde where a 1,650lb (248kg) thrust Walter HWKz R.11 motor was installed; flight testing began in August, with Heini Dittmar at the controls.

Further development led to the *Reichs Luft Ministerium* (R.L.M.) considering that the design had potential as an interceptor:

This very grainy ground-to-air shot of the He 280 prototype, with nacelle cowlings in place during a later flight, was most likely taken with an early Leica I, as issued to Luftwaffe officers. The aircraft's clean lines did nothing to impress the RLM – but that could not detract from the fact that it was the world's first twin-jet aircraft to fly. Author's collection.

the fuselage was therefore redesigned to convert it from the original research aircraft concept to a glider prototype fighter, and this produced the Me163A. Ten of these aircraft were built for a pilot-training programme before the powered production Me163B reached service, and several well known German glider pilots flew the Me163A, including Wolfgang Spate and Hanna Reitsch; they all gave very good reports of the aircraft's handling. Unfortunately during one test flight a glider crashed, and Heini Dittmar was seriously injured; his place as the programme's test pilot was taken by Rudolf Opitz.

The first production Me163B interceptor, by now known as *Komet*, flew in August 1943, powered by a Walter HWK 109-509A-2 bi-fuel rocket motor, producing 3,750lb (1,700kg) thrust. The fuel was a combination of concentrated hydrogen peroxide (*T-Stoff*) and a solution of hydrazine-hydrate in methanol (*C-Stoff*), which gave the aircraft a maximum speed capacity of 550mph (886km/h) above 30,000ft (16,460m). With a service ceiling of 54,000ft (16,460m), the Komet had an endurance of approximately 2.5 minutes after the climb to altitude. Series production enabled *Jagdgruppe* J.G.400 to be formed from *Erprobungs-Kommando* 16, at Bad Zwischenahn, by midsummer 1944. Although the US Eighth AAF suffered some losses from the rocket-powered fighter's interceptions, the three *Staffels* that comprised the total Luftwaffe strength of Me163Bs lost a larger part of their

Photographed at Bad Zwischenahn, this **Me163B-1a** Komet of Jagdgruppe **400, stands on its jettisonable undercarriage. The** C-Stoff **and** T-Stoff **fuel tanks' locations are shown by their respective labels in the dorsal and ventral positions.** Philip Jarrett.

strength through take-off and landing accidents, rather than in combat.

Production of the Me163B ended in January 1945, after 364 aircraft had been built. The later, more advanced Me163C was just starting to go into production by the end of hostilities in May 1945.

Willy Messerschmitt's other fighter not powered by a reciprocating engine was a different aircraft altogether – it was not, in fact, originally designed purely as an interceptor. Towards the end of 1938, the

R.L.M. proposed that the company put its mind to designing an aircraft powered by an entirely new type of engine, the role of the production aircraft envisaged to be that of a fighter-bomber. Both BMW *Flugmotorenbau* GmbH and Junkers *Flugzeug und Motorenwerke A.G.* were engaged on the development of axial-flow turbojet engines, either of which would power the new Messerschmitt aircraft.

The resultant design was designated Me262; it was approved and a mock-up was presented, and on 1 March 1940 three prototypes of a superbly streamlined twin-engined aircraft were ordered. The two engine companies were having great difficulty with their respective products, the thrust outputs obtained being nowhere near their design figures. Messerschmitt proceeded in meeting its order for the prototypes and, in view of there being no chance of receiving engines for some time, decided to investigate the flight characteristics of the basic airframe by installing a 700hp Junkers Jumo 210G piston engine in the nose of the first completed airframe.

Designated Me262V1, with the identification letters PC+UA and a tail-wheel undercarriage, the prototype made its maiden flight on 4 April 1941, and Messerschmitt A.G. received an order for a further five prototypes three months later, on 25 July. In November, the first

Messerschmitt Me163B *Komet* specification	
Dimensions:	Span 30ft 7in (9.32m) Length 18ft 8in (5.70m) Height 9.0ft (2.74m) Wing area 211sq ft (19.60sq m)
Armament:	Two 30mm MK108 cannon, with 60 rounds for each
Powerplant:	One Walter HWK 109-509A-2 bi-fuel rocket-motor, producing 3,750lb (1,704kg) thrust Maximum fuel capacity, 226gal (1,028l) *T-Stoff* 119gal (500.5l) *C-Stoff*
Weights:	Empty 4,200lb (1,904kg); loaded 9,500lb (4,308kg)
Performance:	Maximum speed 595mph at 30,000ft (958km/h at 9,144m); 515mph (829km/h) at sea-level Initial rate of climb 16,000ft (4,877m) per minute Time to 30,000ft (9,144m) 2.6 minutes Time to 40,000ft (12,192m) 3.5 minutes

pair of turbojet engines were received, these being 1,000lb (453.5kg) thrust BMW P3302s, and they were fitted in PC+UA in their designed underwing position – but the nose-mounted Jumo 210G was retained as a failsafe measure for the first flight. The precaution was not unfounded, as the turbojet turbine blades broke off and both engines failed.

In view of BMW's engines not meeting their specification, Jumo 004 engines producing 1,850lb (839kg) thrust were delivered and fitted on the third prototype, Me262V3 PC+UC; this also had a tail-wheel undercarriage. The first flight was made on 18 July 1942, and was the first to be made by the type entirely on turbojet power. The second flight by PC+UC ended in disaster, however, when it crashed, killing the chief test pilot of the Luftwaffe's experimental establishment; this annulled all further interest in the design by the German Air Ministry.

Heavy lobbying on the part of Messerschmitt A.G. gained them a small pre-production order for fifteen aircraft; this was later increased to thirty, and in

Messerschmitt Me262A *Schwalbe* specification	
Dimensions:	Span 40ft 11.5in (12.49m)
	Length 34ft 9.75in (10.59m)
	Height 12ft 7in (3.83m)
	Wing area 234sq ft (21.73sq m)
Armament:	Four 30mm MK 108 cannon
Powerplant:	Two Junkers Jumo 109-004B-1 turbojet, each producing 1,980lb (898kg) static thrust
Weights:	Empty 9,741lb (4,417.5kg); loaded 14,101lb (6,395kg)
Performance:	Maximum speed 538mph at 29,560ft (866km/h at 9,009m); 500mph (805km/h) at sea-level
	Initial rate of climb 3,940ft (1,201m) per minute
	Service ceiling 37,565ft (11,450m)
	Range 652 miles at 29,560ft (1,049km at 9,009m)
	Range 298 miles (479.5km) at sea-level

May 1943 the aircraft caught the interest of General Adolf Galland, who flew the fourth pre-production aircraft on May 22. The fifth pre-production aircraft was the first to be fitted with a (non-retracting) nose-wheel undercarriage. But despite the increased interest by the Luftwaffe, mass production of the type was denied by the R.L.M.

Demonstrations in November 1943

This Messerschmitt Me262A-2a Sturmvogel **shows the centre-line bomb carriers under the centre section.**
Philip Jarrett.

A total of 1,433 Me262s was built, of which 865 were produced in the four months of 1945 before the armistice. However, it has been estimated that only about one hundred actually reached operational service, the aircraft's Achilles heel being the lack of reliability in the engines.

The *Salamander*

It is perhaps indicative of the R.L.M.'s desperation that on 8 September 1944 they laid aside their former intransigence and placed a *Volksjäger*/People's Fighter specification with Arado, Blohm und Voss, Dornier, Fieseler, Focke-Wulf, Messerschmitt, Junkers – and Heinkel! The imaginative Professor Ernst was already engaged on a certain project, namely P.1073, and on 11 September 1944, three days after receiving the specification, he placed before the R.L.M. his He162 design which was based on the P.1073 (history does not record his feelings, but they must have been satisfying!). The basic requirements of the specification were a single-seat turbojet-powered fighter, employing the most economical construction methods using metal and wood, capable of 466mph (750km/h) at sea-level, plus an endurance of at least thirty minutes. Just *nine days later*, on 20 September, the first prototype He162V1 was built, and nine days after that, Heinkel was given an order for mass production – three weeks from receiving the

Heinkel 162A-2 Salamander, Werk Nr. **120227, which employed wood in nearly fifty per cent of its construction. Captured at Leck in Schleswig-Holstein where it served with JG1, it was transported to the United States, where this photograph was taken.** Author's collection.

before Reichmarshal Göring and other heirarchy, and two weeks later before Hitler himself, moved the official stance to accept the Me262, but in a bomber role. In March 1944 approval was given for large-scale production, although the resources of Messerschmitt A.G. were then already rather stretched, meeting piston-engined fighter commitments. Designated Me262A, the aircraft were produced as the *Schwalbe* (Swallow) with fighter armament and modifications; the latter requirements delayed production by several months, however, having to be manufactured to meet the *Sturmvogel* (Stormbird) parameters laid down by the Führer. The flying characteristics were very good, but the temperamental Jumo engines required experienced handling and the resultant high accident rate led to the production of a two-seat trainer, designation Me262B. In early 1945 the single-seat aircraft enjoyed limited success in night fighting, and this encouraged plans to adapt the Me262B into a true night-fighter under the title Me262B-2 – but the war ended before production got under way.

There is no doubt that, had World War II continued for another six months, and as long as production could have been maintained, the Me262A fighter, which in April 1945 was being operated by the elite J.V.44 unit commanded by General Galland,

would have had a definite effect on the balance of air power over Germany. An additional external armament of twenty-four 5cm R4M missiles came into service at that time, and this made the Me262A a devastating interceptor against massed bomber formations, as it operated outside the range of their defensive armament. In the three or four weeks that the combination was used, it had considerable success.

Heinkel He162A *Salamander* specification	
Dimensions:	Span 23ft 7.75in (7.2m)
	Length 29ft 8.5in (9m)
	Height 8ft 6.5in (2.6m)
Armament:	Two 30mm MK 108 cannon, with 50 rounds for each or two 20mm MG151/20 cannon, with 120 rounds for each
Powerplant:	One BMW 003 or 004 turbojet, producing 1,750lb (794kg) thrust
Weights:	Empty loaded 4,800lb (2,176.8kg), maximum 5,940lb (2,694kg)
Performance:	Maximum speed 522mph at 20,000ft (835km/h at 6,096m); 490mph (788km/h) at sea level
	Service ceiling 39,400ft (12,009m)
	Initial rate of climb 4,200ft (1,280m) per minute
	Service ceiling 39,400ft (12,009m)
	Time to 19,680ft (5,998m) 6.6 minutes
	Time to 36,000ft (10,973m) 20 minutes
	Range 410 miles at 36,000ft (659km at 10,973m)
	Range 136 miles (219km) at sea level

specification! The first prototype He162V1, registered VI+IA, was produced by the 1,360 workers at Heinkel's Vienna works: they put in a ninety-hour week and worked to a system whereby small problems were solved by on-the-spot decisions. Piloted by Gotthold Peter, VI+IA had its maiden flight from the airfield at Schwechat, just outside the Austrian capital, on 6 December 1944.

By 11 April 1945 the first *Gruppe* (group) of sixteen He162A *Salamander* aircraft was operating with *Jagdgeschwader* JG1, and on 4 May an RAF Typhoon was shot down; by this time the *Gruppe* had forty aircraft, of which three-quarters were serviceable. On 6 May, British land forces occupied their base at Leck in Schleswig-Holstein, and the Volksjager was unable to prove whether Ernst Heinkel had at last given the Luftwaffe a successful jet-powered fighter. Production was scheduled for 1,000 aircraft a month to be built at Rostock, with subcontractual manufacture of another 1,000 a month by Junkers, and a further 2,000 a month by Mittelwerke GmbH. However, due to the rapid advances made by the Allied armies, less than 120 aircraft had been completed by the end of the war.

At least two examples of the He162A-2 (Werk Nrs 120072 and 120098) were flown by RAE Farnborough test pilots, the aircraft having been ferried from Germany aboard a captured Arado Ar232B four-engined transport, due to the jet fighter's lack of range. They were found to be quite pleasant to fly, but required careful handling, and one did crash, due to the tail unit breaking away, during a display at Farnborough on 9 November 1945, killing the pilot, Flt Lt R.A.Marks. The Establishment considered that the He162 would have proved a very successful interceptor had the war continued long enough for its potential to be developed. So maybe Professor Heinkel was getting there!

On the 'Sceptred Isle'

On the other side of the Channel, Britain – eulogized by William Shakespeare as 'this sceptred isle...set in a silver sea' considerably earlier than the events already described – was engaged on independent but parallel developments. While the turbine as a means of driving a propeller had been considered for some time in Britain, the original thinking had been along the lines of using a gas-turbine alone as the means of propulsion for an aeroplane; this was the theme of a report written by Dr. A.A. Griffiths of the Royal Aircraft Establishment (RAE) at Farnborough.

As you drive across the county border into Warwickshire, most of the main routes announce the fact that you are entering 'Shakespeare's county'. However, those with an aeronautical bent, like myself, might sometimes mentally add the rider 'and Whittle's county', because about twenty miles from the bard's birthplace lies the Earlsdon district of Coventry, where Frank Whittle was born. Furthermore, between Stratford-upon-Avon and Coventry is the once elegantly Regent town of Leamington Spa, now the cosmopolitan centre of disc-brake and clutch-plate production. It was at Leamington College that Whittle, one of the engineering pioneers of the twentieth century, finished his education before joining the RAF.

The Rover Company, brought into the new world of the turbojet, quickly appreciated that there were aspects of the work in which they had no expertise, especially when it came to resolving problems of which there was no previous experience. Whittle himself had recognized errors in his original W2 design calculations and knew that certain elements would have to be reconsidered. Once this was in hand, the designation W2B was applied to the forthcoming modified engine.

Rover decided that they would manufacture the compressor/turbine assembly themselves, while subcontracting the combustion and fuel sections to specialist companies; after which they, Rover, would handle assembly of the complete engine. Joseph Lucas was chosen as the main subcontractor in view of the fact that their subsidiary company, C.A.Vandervell (CAV), was experienced in the field of fuel injection systems, while Lucas itself had been engaged on sheet metalwork for many years. As air-raids on the British Isles increased, pressure was mounting on Rover to find new premises for the very secret gas-turbine engine side of their business, in a comparatively safer area than the heart of the industrial Midlands. An advertisement placed in the *Manchester Guardian* on 12 September 1940 turned up a former weaving shed with an area of 165,000sq ft (15,328.5sq m) at Barnoldswick, owned and recently redecorated by Messrs British Celanese Limited; this was requisitioned by the Ministry of Aircraft Production (MAP) on 25 September. Known as Bankfield Shed, the premises were officially referred to as 'Number 6 Shadow Factory' and were earmarked for the production of all Whittle turbojet engines. The move to Barnoldswick was none too soon: on the night of 14 November 1940 Coventry endured the notorious *Blitzkrieg,* an eleven-hour air-raid which caused widespread devastation and in which the Rover factory was severely damaged. From Banbury, over twenty-five miles away, I well remember seeing the bright orange glow in the sky as Coventry burned that night.

An interesting coincidence resulting from that air-raid was the relocation of Rover's management, administration and engineering staff to the Chesford Grange Hotel, the pre-war conversion of a large country house situated just outside Leamington Spa, where Whittle went to college. The assembling of the first Rover-built W2 engine was completed in these sumptuous surroundings, prior to delivery to Power Jets for testing. Today one can enjoy top-of-the-bill variety acts, live, in the imposing banqueting hall, while consuming the offerings of an excellent kitchen.

In the early winter of 1940 further investigations were made to find additional production facilities and on 26 November 1940 a disused weaving mill in Clitheroe, Lancashire, known as Waterloo Mill, was officially requisitioned. Whittle engine development work was to be transferred to Clitheroe from Chesford Grange, and the MAP considered that by February 1941 the Rover Company, under the management of Maurice Wilks, would be capable of producing twenty W2B engines per week. Time would prove this to be a vastly over-optimistic figure for a new, untried engine, in a new working environment. The company records of Lucas state that Waterloo Mill was ready for production in May 1941, although no figures are given for the number of engines completed. When the first W2B engines were handed to Power Jets, as a kit of parts for assembly and testing, many sheet-metal components failed, thereby causing hold-ups in the programme.

In addition to these delays, progress towards an engine that would prove reli-

One of the early W1 engines, outside Power Jets Limited's facility at Lutterworth, in 1944, a much more viable flight engine than the original WU. *Aeroplane Monthly.*

able enough for flight trials was being thwarted by the failure of the materials used to manufacture the turbine blades. It had been hoped that the required strength at high temperatures would have been achieved by the American-developed Hastelloy. Blades made from this material in one W2B engine at Waterloo Mill completed a thirty-five-hour running test, but looked doubtful for any longer periods. In Britain, the Birmingham laboratories of the Mond Nickel Company were contracted by the MAP to investigate these problems, and they produced an alloy based on 20 per cent chromium with 80 per cent nickel. This was brought up to production status by the factory of subsidiary Henry Wiggins and Company Limited. Registered with the trademark 'Nimonic', the National Physics Laboratory tested and passed Nimonic 80, and blades manufactured in this material

would be used for many years, not only by Rover but subsequently by Rolls-Royce.

By July 1941 Rover had completed the production drawings for the W2B, based on the original drawings made by Power Jets, and the manufacture of six development engines was commenced at Rover's Birmingham factory, as the company felt that the Lancashire factory was still not ready for this work. Rover also complained that drawings of revised components were slow in being delivered by Power Jets and they proceeded to redesign parts of the W2B themselves. The areas involved were the compressor casing, the auxiliary-drive gearbox and bearings, together with parts of the fuel system. Obviously Whittle was made aware of these events, and this created unrest between the two companies, such that the MAP called a meeting in December 1941 to redefine the positions of Power Jets and Rover. The motor

company was given permission to redesign elements where they felt it necessary – and it can be fairly stated that relations between the companies went downhill from that moment.

The basic design of the W1 and W2 engines featured a reverse-flow air supply, in which the air reversed direction twice, from the double-sided impeller to the turbine. One serious problem revealed as a result of the company's engine testing was that of the compressor stalling due to pressure loss, which caused surging as the engine's speed was increased. However, the removal of restrictions on redesign given to Rover at the December meeting encouraged Maurice Wilks' team to follow the design path taken by de Havilland's engineering consultant, Major Frank Halford, who had incorporated a straight-through airflow system in his H1 gas-turbine engine. Whittle had already

Sir Frank Whittle (1907 – 1996), 'the Midlands' Mastermind'

In September 1923 No. 4 Apprentices Wing, RAF Cranwell, accepted 364365 Boy Whittle, F., to commence training as a fitter. Three years later he passed out as a leading aircraftsman (LAC) – and was promptly discharged from the Royal Air Force, thereby following the traditional route of rejoining the RAF College at Cranwell as a civilian in order to become a flight cadet: this Whittle did in September 1926. After only eight hours dual in the Avro 504K, he went solo, and on 27 August 1928 he passed out as a pilot officer, to be posted to No. 111 Squadron at Hornchurch. The following year he joined the Central Flying School at Wittering, and later became an instructor at No. 2 Flying Training School, Digby; he was to become a very professional display pilot.

So commenced the service life of the officer with an 'exceptional, to above average' flying assessment, and the engineer who would transform the hardware of the RAF to an extent that could not possibly have been imagined at Kitty Hawk.

In the course of his training at Cranwell, Frank Whittle encountered the seemingly insurmountable limitations of a piston-engine driving a propeller, even before von Ohain. He also learned of the respiration problems suffered by a reciprocating engine as it climbed into the decreasing density of air at higher altitudes. During his fourth term, in 1928, he wrote a thesis entitled 'Future Developments in Aircraft Design' in which he considered the possibilities of powering an aeroplane by an engine that drew in air, heated it and discharged it through a nozzle at velocity. Convinced of the validity of the principle, on 16 January 1930 Whittle filed provisional specification No. 347206 for his turbojet.

In 1931 he was posted to the Marine Aircraft Experimental Establishment at Felixtowe, where he flew the Fairey IIIF floatplane and was engaged in catapult launching trials. A year later he commenced an officers' engineering course at Henlow, and having proved his exceptional engineering ability by achieving a 98 per cent pass mark, was selected in July 1934 to read the mechanical sciences tripos at Peterhouse, the oldest Cambridge University college. He graduated with first class honours.

The patent he had taken out in January 1930 became due for renewal, but he could not afford the £5.00 fee; he therefore approached the Air Ministry for financial assistance, but was refused. It was at this juncture that two fellow ex-RAF officers, Rolf (later Sir Rolf) Dudley Williams and J.C.B. Tinling, suggested that they approach the merchant banker, Falk and Partners, with the idea of forming a company in order to develop Whittle's ideas of a gas-

Air Commodore Frank Whittle in 'civvies', before leaving the RAF and being knighted. *Aeroplane Monthly.*

drawn up a similar arrangement in his W2X and W2Y designs, but the financial limitations being experienced by Power Jets precluded any changes being made to the existing combustion arrangements.

This was the first major project to be undertaken by Rover's jet-engine team, and it was tackled with great enthusiasm; it was known by them as the 'ST' (denoting the 'straight-through' airflow). The official designation applied by the Ministry was W2B/26, indicating that it was a modification to the existing W2B, but Rover's internal reference was usually given as the ST or – in deference to officialdom – the B26.

Prior to the B26 redesign, W2B devel-

turbine being used to propel an aeroplane, to the point of producing a practical engine. The sum of £2,000 was made available, with the promise of an additional £18,000 in eighteen months time subject to the engine reaching trials stage.

The Air Ministry, cognizant of Whittle's inventiveness, allowed him to form Power Jets Limited in March 1936 and to work up to six hours a day on his project. The granting of this sort of licence to a serving officer was really most unusual, and one which was quite contrary to their normal policy. The new company did not have the facilities to fabricate the components necessary for building an engine, and so was obliged to approach other companies with a view to their undertaking contractual work. One of these was the British Thomson-Houston Company (BTH) of Rugby, which went so far as to allow Power Jets to use a section of their premises, where the first of the experimental jet engines could be tested.

Despite continuing financial difficulties and minimal assembly facilities, a single-combustion chambered experimental engine – known as the WU engine (an abbreviation for 'Whittle Unit') – had its first test run on 12 April 1937; this was a couple of weeks after von Ohain's first test, but it was a much more viable turbojet. Whittle started the engine himself, but on his own admission he had never been so frightened because the engine, running at 8,000rpm and screaming like a siren, was literally out of control during that test: while he personally became rooted to the spot, BTH staff in the vicinity fled for cover! But on the basis of the engine looking to have potential, BTH's chief engineer allowed Power Jets to rent alternative premises in a part of the disused BTH Ladywood Works at Lutterworth, about seven miles from Rugby. Due to the relocation, testing of the WU engine did not resume for nearly twelve months; shortly after this, on 6 May 1938, the turbine failed at 13,000rpm, wrecking the whole engine.

This involved major reconstruction, and it was decided to incorporate ten smaller combustion chambers set around the turbine casing, in place of the former single chamber. Test runnings were resumed nearly six months later, at the end of October 1938, and as a result of these, Power Jets was awarded a contract by the Air Ministry to produce a flight engine, designated the W1, to be followed by another, more powerful engine, the W2. These engines pass into Gloster's history.

Relations between Whittle and BTH deteriorated to the extent that other firms were sought to which W2 engine components could be subcontracted. The wife of a fellow Power Jets employee, J.C. Tinling, was a friend of the wife of Maurice Wilks, chief engineer at the Rover Motor Company; through this association, Whittle met Wilks in January 1940 and suggested that Power Jets place orders with Rover. Maurice Wilks' brother Spencer was Managing Director of the Rover Motor Company: he was brought into a subsequent meeting, when Whittle suggested that the proposed subcontracting should be discussed with the Air Ministry. From these initial contacts emerged the ludicrous outcome whereby the Air Ministry would deal direct with the Rover Company, together with BTH, in the issuing of contracts for production engines, and Power Jets would continue under Whittle, but purely as a research and development organization; following which in 1944 the company – having now been nationalized – was prohibited from making jet engines altogether.

Whittle was invalided out of the Royal Air Force at the beginning of 1948 with the rank of Honorary Air Commodore, and was subsequently knighted. In May 1948, in recognition of both his idea and his technical ability, he was awarded £100,000 by the Royal Commission on Awards to Inventors. Sir Frank Whittle went on to be honoured all over the world and and – belatedly – received his own country's highest civil award, the Order of Merit, from the Queen. While he found it hard to forgive the British political system and civil service, he always generously recognized the Royal Air Force, together with the achievements made by Power Jets. The latter years of his life were spent in retirement in America, where he instantly received the acclaim so grudgingly bestowed in his own country.

On 9 August 1996, shortly after his eighty-ninth birthday, Sir Frank Whittle died. He left behind a legacy from which the entire world has benefited, and one which is a true manifestation of British engineering at its best.

The original WU (Whittle Unit), first run on 12 April 1937, at British Thomson-Houston's Rugby works. Author's collection.

opment had reached a stage at the beginning of 1942 where it was obviously necessary to organize a more prolonged flight test. No endurance test runs had been made and it was clear that the planned delivery schedule laid down by the MAP for engines to be supplied to the Gloster Aircraft Company in March/April was not going to be met. Consequently, it was decided that an existing multi-engined aircraft would be employed as a flying testbed, the type selected being capable of modification to accept the installation of a W2B, together with the required engine test personnel. On 8 May 1942, representatives of Vickers-Armstrong Aircraft Limited were invited to join a committee which was to be set up for the further development of the turbojet engine *per se*.

Rover-built W2B No. SR105 was transported from Waterloo Mill to the Vickers-Armstrong complex at Weybridge in Surrey on 16 July 1942; there, one of the 401 Rolls-Royce Merlin X-engined Wellington MkIIs built, Z8570, was being converted to accept the new engine. The Weybridge drawing office had designed a modification where the rear Frazer-Nash two-gun turret was removed and a neat extension of the rear fuselage had a faired-in lateral air-intake positioned on either side, aft of the tail-plane. When the conversion was completed, about twenty-five minutes of ground running time was recorded, following which the aircraft was transferred, on 1 August 1942, to the Rolls-Royce test facility at Hucknall. Subsequent flight trials were conducted by Rolls-Royce flight crews, with Rover

personnel being responsible for the W2B during in-flight test programmes. Over ten hours of test-flying the W2B was achieved during August and September 1942, at various altitudes up to 20,000ft (6,096m), following which the engine was removed and returned to Waterloo Mill. A strip-down inspection revealed that the flame tubes were in good condition, and such buckling of the stub pipes that had occurred was easily rectified.

The aircraft's two Merlin Xs were later replaced by Merlin XX-series engines, and two further Wellingtons were modified in order to join the test flight: these were W5389 and W5518, which were basic MkII fuselages, fitted with MkVI wings which carried Merlin series 60 engines. These two aircraft were capable of providing turbojet-testing at a more representative operational altitude than Z8570.

Their history has been difficult to trace: the conversions were done by Vickers-Armstrong at Weybridge, and it is known that W5389 arrived at Hucknall on 23 November 1943, where some 125 hours of testing was carried out before it went to Power Jets at Bruntingthorpe in April 1946. Some sources have stated that a total of 512 hours, amassed in 366 flights, was achieved by the Wellington turbojet test-beds, with over a dozen different engines being evaluated. I recall seeing one of the trio near Chipping Warden airfield in Northamptonshire. It was quite some distance away, in side elevation and flying at low altitude with a faint smoke trail emitting from its rear. Knowing nothing of the true nature of things, my friends and I came to the conclusion that it was on fire, with some part of the aircraft hanging off the back end. When it disappeared behind

A Rover-built W2B installed in the rear fuselage of Vickers Wellington MkII, Z8570, with the custom-built cowlings removed for engine servicing. Author's collection.

Sir Wilfred Freeman, Chief Executive of the MAP, wrote a letter of appreciation to Spencer Wilks on 24 January 1943, recognizing the efforts that Rover had put into the turbojet's early development. At the completion of its involvement with jet-engines, the company's contribution was listed as follows:

On W2B engines:
Thirty-two W2B engines were produced, plus various additional components.

Nearly two dozen additional W2B engines were employed as development units.

100-hour Type Approval tests, with the W2B producing 1,450lb (657.5kg) thrust, had been passed.

25-hour Special Category Type testing, with the W2B producing 1,500lb (680kg) thrust, had been passed.

Two flight-standard W2B engines had been supplied to Gloster Aircraft in February, for installation in their F.9/40 aircraft. One W2B engine rated at 1,250lb (567kg) thrust was flying in Gloster Aircraft's E.28/39.

Successful flight trials in three Wellington testbed aircraft had been accomplished.

On ST/B26 engines:
Four B26 engines had been produced, with over 360 hours testing undertaken.

One B26 engine, giving 1,600lb (725.5kg) thrust, had successfully completed three 50-hour endurance tests.

A total of nearly 1,930 hours running time, by all the various types of turbojet engines produced by the Rover Company, had been achieved.

a wooded area about a mile away we thought it was possibly going to crash, but with no subsequent noise indicating disaster, the whole episode was dismissed as one of the many unknowns experienced in those days. Anyway, within half-an-hour we had our first sighting of a parked Avro Manchester which was visiting Chipping Warden's No. 12 Operational Training Unit (OTU), and the mystery *Wimpy* was put out of our minds.

In conjunction with flight trials in Z8570, a successful twenty-five-hour Special Category test was passed, with the W2B producing 1,250lb (567kg) static thrust; this was superseded by a further test at the end of 1942. Then in January 1943 a third test was passed, with the engine giving 1,400lb (635kg) thrust, following which a 100-hour Type Approval Test at a 1,250lb (567kg) thrust rating was completed. A few days later, on 26 January 1943, a similar type-tested engine was passed over to Gloster Aircraft, followed in February by two more.

While Rover-built engines were at last being delivered, behind-the-scenes negotiations had been taking place which would lay the foundations for the whole of

British jet-engine design and manufacture as we know it today. Maurice Wilks' brother Spencer had a long-standing friendship with Ernest Hives (later Lord Hives of Duffield), then a director and General Manager of Rolls-Royce. Fully aware of the technical difficulties Rover was experiencing in the jet-engine field and aware that these would most certainly increase, Wilks enquired about the possibilities of there being co-operation between the two companies. The concept was not seen by Hives as holding much promise, but he did arrange for Dr. (later Sir) Stanley Hooker, chief assistant to the Chief Experimental Engineer, to peruse the alterations that Rover had made to the basic Whittle engine. Through this contact Hooker became aware of the deteriorating relationship between Rover and Whittle, and also the fact that the car manufacturer's proposals to further redesign the engine in order to increase the thrust into the 3,500–4,000lb (1,600–1,800kg) range, implied a project beyond their capabilities.

Frank Whittle's determination to sever relations with Rover led him to suggest to the MAP an amalgamation between Power

Jets and Rolls-Royce, in order to get his current W2/500 engine design into production. Furthermore, Rover were making no secret of their desire to get away from turbojet development. So when a committee formed by the Tank Board started investigating the possibilities of the company being included in the manufacture of a new tank engine, Rover grasped the opportunity with alacrity. The Waterloo Mill factory at Clitheroe, together with Bankfield Shed in Barnoldswick, passed over to Rolls-Royce, and several other Rover factories that were coming to the end of the subcontractural manufacture of Armstrong-Siddeley Cheetah aero-engines transferred to the production of the tank engine. The exchange was finalized in a letter issued by the Rover Company Limited, with effect from 1 April 1943. It was purely coincidental that the tank engine's name was Meteor!

The changeover was comparatively straightforward, and Rolls-Royce decided that, while the reverse-flow W2B/23 engine – called the B23 by its new owners – was developed enough to warrant limited production, the W2B/26 (Rover's B26) had more potential. They incorporated changes in the airflow system which produced nearly 2,000lb (907kg) more thrust, and in this form the engine was designated the B37.

Rolls-Royce has a tradition of giving its engines names. The flowing of air in a turbojet could well be associated with the flowing of water, i.e. rivers. Therefore a new system was started whereby jet-engines would be named after rivers, with the B23 being named 'Welland', after the river which flows under seven bridges in the Lincolnshire market town of Spalding, on its way to The Wash. The B37 was named 'Derwent', after the river that goes through the Rolls-Royce heartland city of Derby – or was it after the one that flows into the River Ouse near Goole; or the river that meets the Irish Sea at Workington; or even the river joining the reservoir with the same name, to the River Tyne at Newcastle? You can take your pick!

CHAPTER THREE

Gloster's Farewell to the Airscrew

As they positioned the three-bladed airscrews down the Rolls-Royce Peregrine's drive-shaft splines on L8002, the second F.9/37, in February 1940, I wonder whether anyone in Gloster's experimental department at Hucclecote thought 'That's the last time we'll be doing that!' The twin-engined single-seat day and night fighter built to Specification F.9/37 was the first Gloster aircraft to come from the company's new chief designer, W.G. Carter, although its true derivation lay among various moribund projects conceived by his predecessor, Harry Folland. The last Gloster aircraft for which Folland was responsible, albeit in collaboration with H.E. Preston, was the single-seat monoplane fighter designed to meet the interim Specification F.5/34, from which both the Hurricane and Spitfire evolved. Although no production orders were forthcoming, the two aircraft built, K5604 and K8089, were used for flying at several experimental establishments, before becoming ground instructional airframes with the respective numbers 2232M and 2231M. Elements of the F.5/34 were to feature in the next Carter design to be built.

One of Frank Whittle's contemporaries at the RAF College was J.H.McC. Reynolds, and on 23 July 1931 the two men had filed a joint patent on the supercharging of piston engines. As a wing commander in 1939, Reynolds was the Air Ministry's overseer at the Gloster Aircraft Company. The two men had corresponded over the intervening years since Cranwell, and the Hucclecote-based officer was aware of Whittle's enterprise; he also knew of the availability of Gloster's design office, which was mainly occupied with projects. Consequently, Reynolds arranged a meeting between Whittle and George Carter at Hucclecote on 28 April 1939; he also introduced Gloster's chief test pilot Flight Lieutenant P.E.G. 'Gerry' Sayer,

plus his deputy Michael Daunt, to the turbojet designer.

Carter felt a certain empathy with Whittle's ambitions; in particular among the aircraft designs shown was his twin-boom layout to Specification F.18/37 for a Napier Sabre-powered fighter, with the engine driving a pusher airscrew. Frank Whittle saw his turbojet replacing the Sabre in such a layout, although no official interest in such an aircraft was forthcoming. Two months later, on 30 June 1939, Dr. D.R. Pye, the Director of Scientific Research, visited Power Jets at Lutterworth with a natural inclination to disbelieve all he had heard about the WU. The company pulled out all the public relations stops, and with the engine running successfully at nearly 16,000rpm, Dr. Pye's opinion was reversed: scepticism was replaced by conviction, and he returned to his department to compile an encouraging report for the Air Ministry.

The E.28/39

On the strength of Dr. Pye's detailed account of his visit to Lutterworth, an order was placed for a flight engine, and the first official considerations were given to the designing of an aircraft to carry it. The relationship fostered between Whittle and Carter was instrumental in the Gloucestershire manufacturer being considered for the project, particularly as Whittle considered Carter's earlier twin-boom layout would lend itself to adaptation. The Air Ministry was not so enthusiastic about the design, but in view of the Gloster design office's almost immediate availability, on 3 February 1940 Contract SB/3229 was issued, for the company to construct an indigenous aeroplane, meeting Specification E.28/39.

Frank Whittle co-operated strongly with George Carter in the configuration that the aircraft would take. In fact, when

K5604, the first prototype Gloster F.5/34, taxiing out for a demonstration flight at the 1938 Hendon Air Display, showing its number '7' for the benefit of spectators with programmes. This was the company's last single piston-engined type and H.P. Folland's final design for Gloster Aircraft. *Aeroplane Monthly.*

One of the very few photographs taken of the first E.28/39, following its transportation from Cheltenham to Hucclecote. The short-stroke nose-wheel leg is fitted, this only remaining during first taxi trials, as did the W1X non-flight engine installed at this time. Heat-sensitive paint-strips can be seen on the rear fuselage, before the aircraft went into the paint shop and received its W4041/G serial. *Aeroplane Monthly.*

the accounts were drawn up, Gloster Aircraft received an invoice for £500.00 from Power Jets, to cover the costs incurred by them in designing the 'Gloster-Whittle' aeroplane. As might have been expected, the Air Ministry wanted the E.28/39 to be a fighter and went so far as to stipulate in the specification that, while the prime object was the flight-testing of the new engine, the design was to be able to satisfy a subsequent fighter requirement. Thus in the layout, provision was made for the future installation of a four-Browning .303in (7.7mm) machine-gun armament, with 2,000 rounds of ammunition. However, when it is considered that the specification called for a maximum speed of 380mph (612km/h), one has to wonder at the thinking behind a new-generation fighter with a performance advantage of only 16mph (26km/h) over the Spitfire already in squadron service – and with only half the armament!

Both Carter and Whittle knew the existing Power Jets W1 did not produce enough thrust to power a fighter, but the aircraft had to be built in order to flight-test the engine, and the Air Ministry's attitude gradually came round to accepting the E.28/39 as being purely experimental. The maximum speed requirement of the specification was based on an engine

producing 1,200lb (5,442kg) thrust, but it was not until March 1943 that an engine in this category was ready, this being the Rover-built W2B rated at 1,250lb (567kg) thrust, which was installed in the second airframe, the contract covering the construction of two prototypes. The serial numbers W4041 and W4046 were allocated to the two aircraft, although by the time the two were completed, the numbers had become W4041/G and W4046/G, the suffix system having been introduced by the Ministry to indicate that the aircraft required guarding whenever they were landed away from the home base. This system was applied to nearly all experimental and prototype aircraft throughout World War II.

Once serious design work was under way, the F.18/37 twin-boom layout was discarded, due to the unknown factors of the engine's jet-flow effects on the tail-plane joining the rear end of the booms. Therefore the Gloster Type G.40 was drawn up as a simple, low-wing monoplane with a raised cockpit set between the ducting from a circular nose air-intake, and the engine, situated just aft of the c.g. behind the cockpit, exhausting at the fuselage rear end via a straight-through jet pipe. Both the wing planform and the fin/rudder assembly were very reminiscent

of Folland's F.5/34, as was the fuselage construction of all-metal monocoque with light alloy stressed skin. The two-spar mainplanes, together with the tail unit, also employed a stressed-skin covering, while the elevators, rudder and ailerons were fabric-covered. The rudder and elevators were both comparatively large in order to compensate for the loss of airscrew slip-stream at low speeds. The split trailing-edge flaps were hydraulically oper-ated and all-metal constructed, and the ailerons were fitted with automatic balance tabs. An 81-gallon (368ltr) fuel tank was situated between the cockpit and the engine.

The British designers were bolder than their German counterparts when it came to the undercarriage, although the posi-tioning of the engine did not really give them much alternative, as Whittle felt there was not enough power to lift the rear end of a tail-wheeled design on take-off. Both Heinkel and Messerschmitt used a tail-wheel configuration for their first turbojet prototypes, but Gloster had Dowty Equipment Limited 'just down the road' in Cheltenham and the two compa-nies co-operated in designing a retractable tricycle landing gear, with an oleo nose-wheel steerable from the rudder pedals. All three legs of the undercarriage were kept as short as possible, and retraction was hydraulically operated by an accumulater, pre-charged to 1,500lb (680kg) per sq in before each flight, with a bottle of compressed air fitted internally and so available for an emergency lowering of the landing gear. The nose-wheel retracted rearwards, while the main wheels retracted inwards, into the wings, their thickness requiring enlargement of the wheel-well depth which, being greater than the wing thickness, produced protrusions above and below the wing outer skin surface. Two sets of wing design were drawn up, one having an NACA 23012 section, the other employing an EC1240 section and known as the 'high-speed' wing.

Construction of W4041 started at the Hucclecote experimental department in February 1940, with W4046 following shortly afterwards. In view of the highly secret nature of the project and also the vulnerability of Gloster's factory complex as a Luftwaffe target, it was decided that work on W4041 would be continued in the premises of Regent Motors, situated at the centre of Cheltenham's commercial sector. The experimental department's superintendent, Jack Johnstone, went with the aircraft, and construction proceeded through 1940 and into early 1941. Power Jets built a special engine, the W1X, producing only 750lb (340kg) thrust, for installing in the aircraft for taxiing only. This engine was the original WU rebuilt for this purpose, and as it was considered that the heat generated by the rear bearings when the engine was running at its maximum power would require dispersing, a radiator was fitted internally on each side of the intake ducts leading to the engine.

With the construction and assembly of the first E.28/39 completed, on the morning of 7 April 1941 it was transported from the Regent garage to Hucclecote, the NACA23012-section wing being fitted at this stage. Later in the afternoon 'Gerry' Sayer took up his position in the cockpit and started the engine. The ground at that time of year at Hucclecote was very muddy, and the W1X needed running up to 12,000rpm before the aircraft would even move. Whittle himself also did some taxiing, and while some observers were a little disappointed at the tardy performance, both the designers and the pilot realized that the soft conditions were against them; it was therefore decided to postpone further activity until the following day in the hope of conditions improving, although a set of official photographs was exposed onto 10 x 8in (26 x 20cm) glass negatives.

Tuesday 8 April was certainly a better day, and the throttle stop was adjusted to cater for the engine being run at its 15,000rpm maximum. Frank Whittle undertook the first taxi runs and reached a speed of about 60mph (97km/h); satisfied with this performance, he passed the controls over to Sayer, who made several trial taxi runs with the engine speed set to 16,000rpm – during one of these the aircraft made a few hops off the ground, so the undercarriage was locked down at this stage. Both the engine designer and the chief test pilot conducted further taxiing trials over the following three weeks, and then W4041 was put aboard the road transporter once more to be taken to another of Gloster's requisitioned sites in Cheltenham, Crabtree's Garage. A new, longer-travel nose-wheel was fitted at Crabtree's and retraction tests of the whole undercarriage were completed without problems. It is also believed that the 'dark earth'/dark green camouflage

Flt Lt Philip E.G. 'Gerry' Sayer tested Gloster-built aircraft from 1934 until 1942; as the company's chief test pilot he took the E.28/39 on its first flight on 15 May 1941. He was killed flying a Hawker Typhoon – ironically built under licence at Hucclecote – on 21 October 1942. Derek N. James.

paint scheme, with yellow underside and A-type roundels, was applied here. The E.28/39 was – and in fact sometimes still is – referred to by the unofficial name 'Pioneer'. Just when this first came into use is difficult to determine and extensive research through contemporary files has not helped. Although it is entirely appropriate, the fact that at no time was it officially allocated has led me to conclude

that it was entirely colloquial and I, personally, have always stuck to the specification's reference, E.28/39.

First Flight

Following completion of all system tests at Crabtree's Garage, W4041/G – as the serial now appeared – was dismantled

A GLOSTER AIRCRAFT CO. LTD. SECRET

TEST FLIGHT REPORT No.: 1

PILOT P.E.G.Sayer.

Type of Test : 1st Flight. General experience of the type.

Date and Time of Start 15.5.41. 1940 hrs. Duration 17 mins.

AIRCRAFT : Type and No. E.28/39. W.4041.

Type of Undercarriage Dowty nose wheel type. All retractable.

Other Features Main wheel lever suspension type. Nose wheel strut type.

AIRSCREW : Type and No. No airscrew fitted with this method of propulsion.

Dia. :

Pitch Setting Fine   Coarse

Ground Clearance Flying Position   Tail on Ground

ENGINE : Type and No. Whittle Supercharger Type W.1.

Reduction Gear

R.P.M. O.G. Fine Pitch 16500 Take-off.   Coarse Pitch

Boost O.G.   ..   ..

Type of Air Intake

Radiator Stbd radiator blanked off, Port radiator in circuit.

Other Features

WEIGHTS CARRIED : Petrol Paraffin 50 galls.   Oil 1 gall.

Cooling Liquid 3.5 galls water.

Total Weight 3441 lb. estimated from Tare C.G.

C.G. Position .284 A.M.C. U/C Down. .297 A.M.C. U/C Up calculated from (Tare C.G.

Loading Sht. No. 142   Date 7.5.41.

REMARKS :

Exhaust System

Cooling System

Oil System

Guns and Mountings

Bombs and Racks

Sights

Nav. and Ident. Lamps

Aerial

Fairing

Type of Cockpit Heating

Pilot Position & Type

Nose wheel leg total travel 12" as against 10" on original nose wheel leg fitted for taxying trials at Brockworth. Static travel 6" instead of 7" on the first leg. Nose wheel strut pressure reduced from 140 lbsq.in. to 115 lbsq.in. Tyre pressure reduced from 35 lbsq.in. to 20 lbsq.in. Steering on nose wheel 11° either side of the centre line Brakes on all three wheels.

TEST INSTRUMENTS :

Ican. Altimeter No. :   Calibrated

A.S.I. Instrument No. :   ..

R P.M.   ..   ..   ..

Boost Gauge ..   ..   ..

Air Temp.   ..   ..   ..

Signature of Pilot   335

A reproduction of a very historic document in the annals of aviation: the first flight report of an Allied turbojet-powered aeroplane, when 'Gerry' Sayer flew E.28/39 W4041/G for its seventeen-minute maiden flight. The W1 engine was still referred to as a 'Whittle Supercharger' at that time. Author's collection.

early in May for transportation to the airfield designated for flight testing. Hucclecote's concrete runway had yet to be constructed – it was completed later, in August/September – so flight trials could not be conducted from Gloster's own airfield; and secrecy was essential, so it was decided that the unpopulated, open spaces of Lincolnshire would be preferable, and Cranwell had a 3,300ft (1,006m) asphalt runway. (It is purely coincidence that Cranwell was where Whittle first put his theories down on paper; besides, the word 'sentimentality' does not appear in Ministry publications!) On arrival at Cranwell, the 860lb (390kg) thrust W1 flight engine was installed, and on 14 May 1941, preparations were made for the maiden flight.

Poor weather conditions determined that the day's activities had to be confined to taxi runs, and as at Hucclecote in April, hopes were pinned on an improvement the following day. Initially it looked as if the 15th would be no better, but by the early evening conditions had improved: Sayer therefore lined up Britain's first turbojet-powered aeroplane on the runway at 19.45 hours and, after a run of only 1,800ft (549m), it lifted into the air for its maiden flight. Seventeen minutes later he landed, and reported that the engine ran well and that the aircraft, with 240mph (386km/h) indicated, behaved normally – he had found the elevators to be very sensitive, but they could be adjusted. Whittle had never doubted the outcome once the E.28/39 had become fact, and was understandably elated – and when some unthinking onlooker exclaimed 'It flies!', he retorted curtly: 'Well, that was what it was bloody well designed to do, wasn't it?' In typical ministerial fashion, no official photographer was present, and the only visual record of this milestone of aviation was an unauthorized, hand-held cine-film with grain like gravel. How very different from today's laser-lit razzmatazz!

Over the next two weeks the flight time increased, so that by the fourteenth flight the engine's ten-hour clearance had been achieved. In the course of these tests, 300mph (483km/h) was exceeded several times, an altitude of 25,000ft (7,620m) was reached, and a maximum endurance of fifty-six minutes was provided by the internal fuel load. W4041/G was then transported back to Hucclecote for inspection, and for the installation, at a later date, of a W1A engine which would give 1,160lb (526kg) thrust. This 'later' proved to be several months, during which time – to be specific, on 15 August 1941 – the Air Ministry changed the service camouflage on day fighters from dark earth/dark green to dark earth/medium sea grey with B-type roundels; so the opportunity was taken to have the aircraft resprayed to bring it into line with the new scheme, even though it was not a fighter. In fact it was not until the beginning of 1942 that W4041/G was again ready for flying, and this was to be from a different base.

Problems

On 23 October 1642, the first major encounter of the Civil War between King Charles 1's Royalists and the Roundheads under the Earl of Essex took place at Edge Hill in Oxfordshire. Nearly three hundred years later, in October 1941, an airfield was completed on the plateau overlooking the former battlefield, the satellite for No. 12 OTU based at Chipping Warden. The airfield at Hucclecote – henceforth referred to as Brockworth – had never been suitable for test flying and Cranwell was too far away from Gloucester, so it had been decided that a new site should be selected, preferably within easy reach of the aircraft company and Power Jets' centre at Lutterworth. Edge Hill was more or less equidistant between the two and was therefore ideal. So it was to this new airfield that W4041/G was transported at the end of January 1942.

When I lived in Banbury during the early 1940s, the airfield, nine miles away to the north-west, was always known as Shenington, after the village that nestled in its south-east corner, but for some unknown reason the official name became Edge Hill. The unit was not very keen to give ATC cadets 'air experience', certainly by comparison with the others in the area, so it did not become a regular venue for us; but rumours of the new arrival at the beginning of 1942 did generate a certain amount of cycling effort, and while it was never seen on the ground, we did catch the odd glimpse of the small, fast newcomer.

At Hucclecote a W1A engine developing 1,160lb (526kg) of thrust had been installed, and once taxiing trials were under way at Edge Hill on 4 February 1942, Sayer was eager to get airborne. This time the aircraft carried a barostat, which would automatically reduce the fuel flow in order to allow for the decrease in atmospheric pressure at altitude; it was scheduled for the forthcoming W2B engine and was incorporated in the W1A in W4041/G for testing. The pilot reported that the new engine was smoother than its predecessor, but following the sixth flight and after less than 150 minutes flying, it had to be removed from the airframe: this was because wrinkling of the exhaust cone due to the heat was discovered, and the clearance between the shroud ring and the turbine blades had become reduced to

Such was the secrecy surrounding Britain's turbojet aircraft experiments that it was not until 7 January 1944 that the Press was allowed to reveal anything about the activities. By this time, both E.28/39s and five F.9/40s had flown, while the first production Meteor F.1 was being prepared for its maiden flight in five days' time. Author's collection.

below safety limits. The problem was rectified by Power Jets within ten days, however, and flight trials were resumed.

Further trouble occurred two flights later, when Sayer experienced vibration during a climb to 30,000ft (9,144m); this prompted him to slow down the engine to 10,000rpm and return to base, where

inspection of the W1A showed that a turbine blade had failed. Trials were therefore postponed until repairs had been completed. On 2 June the 30,000ft (9,144m) test was restarted, only to be aborted once more, this time because the barostat's relay piston was sticking, causing a reduction of power. Four days later, during a level speed run at 30,000ft

As can be seen in this later photograph of W4041/G, the longer-stroke nose-wheel leg is installed and the Type C.1 fuselage roundel would indicate that it was taken after 21 May 1942. The aircraft is fitted with the EC1240-section wing which in this view obscures the serial, but the lettering on the nose reveals that this is the first prototype as displayed in the Science Museum, London. Author's collection.

(9,144m), the engine again vibrated, but this time it flamed out completely and Sayer had to execute a good dead-stick landing at Edge Hill; it was revealed that a bearing had failed because oil in the feed pipe had congealed, thereby reducing the flow to both bearings, and the gearbox. It was not a happy time.

Three and a half months elapsed before a replacement W1A, incorporating a modified oil system, was delivered and installed in the aircraft. It was just unfortunate that the 'Law according to Mr. Murphy' decided to accompany the delegation of United States dignitaries who visited on 27 September 1942 to observe W4041/G's first flight with the modified engine. As soon as the aircraft lifted off

Edge Hill's operational runway, the high oil pressure dropped, although the low pressure registered as satisfactory; but Sayer elected to return to base immediately. He put the aircraft down safely, but the port wing-tip touched the ground, damaging the bottom skin.

That was 'Gerry' Sayers last flight in the E.28/39. Twenty-four days later he was flying a Hawker Typhoon in formation with another of the same type during a visit to RAF Acklington with Gloster's Service Manager, Fitzgibbon Carse, and the two aircraft collided in mid-air; they crashed into the sea off the Northumberland coast, killing both pilots. Indicative of Sayer's professionalism was the fact that he had kept his deputy, Michael Daunt, fully

informed on every aspect of his work on W4041/G; so having stepped into Sayer's shoes as Gloster's Chief Test Pilot, Daunt was quite prepared and equipped to undertake three preliminary handling flights on 6 November 1942, the damaged wing having been repaired. The problem with the oil system had finally been cured by increasing the bore of the plumbing and lagging it all against the high-altitude temperatures.

Testing Continues

The MAP was now fully convinced that the turbojet was here to stay, and in fact already had operational fighters on order;

Just where this photograph was taken cannot be confirmed, but W4041/G has been fitted with small stabilizing fins on the tail-plane, in order to cure slight instability at the higher speeds that the more powerful W1A was able to propel it. The shape of these fins is slightly different from the ones fitted at Farnborough in 1944, and the Type A.1 roundel suggests this is earlier, so it could be a temporary installation made during trials. Author's collection.

they also considered that service pilots should become acquainted with the new type of propulsion, and therefore directed that W4041/G should be transferred to RAE Farnborough, where it stayed for several months operating under the security codename 'Weaver'. Meanwhile back at Hucclecote the second aircraft, W4046/G, fitted from the start with the EC1240 wing, had been completed for some time, and Gloster were awaiting the delivery of the Rover-built W2B. Producing 1,200lb (544kg) thrust, the new engine arrived in February 1943 and was duly installed; W4046/G was then transported to Edge Hill for flight trials. Michael

Daunt was fully occupied with the preparations to give Gloster's first real fighter prototype, the Meteor-precursor F.9/40, its maiden flight. Responsibility for flight-testing the second E.28/39 was handed to John Grierson who, having joined the company in 1941 as a production test pilot on subcontract-produced Hurricanes and Typhoons, was now a member of the experimental test pilots team. Initially some brake-overheating occurred, due to the higher idling thrust of the engine, but on 1 March 1943 Grierson twice treated Britain to the sight of a turbojet-powered aircraft in airborne condition, and over the subsequent two weeks he made twelve

further flights. The date of the first cross-country flight was 17 April, when he took W4046/G from Edge Hill to de Havillands' airfield at Hatfield: here the aircraft was demonstrated to the Prime Minister Mr. (later Sir) Winston Churchill – I bet his cigar quivered with excitement!

Sixteen days later, on 3 May, this aircraft was also transferred to Farnborough for engine development, which was to entail over fifty hours flying. The delivery was made by another Gloster experimental test pilot, John Crosby-Warren, who at 6ft 8in (2.057m) tall was well over half the height of the aircraft! He came onto the staff of Gloster Aircraft in

1940 as a production test pilot – this being before John Grierson – and had flown many of the 200 Hawker Henleys built in the Brockworth shadow factory. Once there, the aircraft was fitted with a new Rover-built W2B engine delivering 1,526lb (692kg) of thrust, which made it the most powerful turbojet flown in an E.28/39 to date; it was to be engaged in a series of tests on performance measurement, under the direction of Alec Baxter, who later became a professor at Cranfield and president of the Royal Aeronautical Society (RAeS). At Farnborough a new Turbine Flight had been started, commanded by Squadron Leader Douglas 'Dougie' Davie, but the commanding officer, Group Captain Allen Wheeler, flew the first of the series, followed by Wing Commanders H.J. 'Willie' Wilson and C.G.B. McClure, plus Alan Macracken, with tests made at 35,000ft (10,668m) for durations up to fifty-five minutes. (Wilson

appears again later in this history, when as a group captain he broke the world's air speed record.) Frank Whittle had lobbied the MAP himself for some time, in order to get permission to fly the E.28/39 – he had taxied it, but had never actually taken it aloft. This permission was eventually granted – but as he was about to get into the cockpit on the appointed day, he was informed that the aircraft was unserviceable for an indefinite period!

The RAE's trials continued for over two months, and the first incident of any note occurred on 27 July when Wg Cdr McClure was flying W4046/G at 6,000ft (1,829m) and had a flame-out. The E.28/39 was now fitted with a relight switch and to the pilot's delight it worked, the engine bursting into life to register the first aerial relight. Then just two days later, on 30 July 1943, as Sqn Ldr Davie climbed to 35,000ft (10,668m) and applied full aileron, the aircraft yawed and pitched

down so violently that he was thrown through the cockpit canopy, his oxygen mask being torn off in the process. He became slightly unconscious and thinks he had fallen about 10,000ft (3,000m) before his parachute opened. Oxygen sucked from the emergency bottle kept him awake for the long descent, and the only damage he sustained was slight frostbite in one hand; in fact 'Dougie' Davie considered he was fortunate to survive the first British bale-out from a turbojet aircraft. The E.28/39 crashed and was destroyed, subsequent investigation drawing the conclusion that the aileron probably jammed through differential thermal contraction at altitude. Britain was back to one E.28/39 – although Michael Daunt had an F.9/40 in the air by this time. Later, on 1 April 1944, one of these was to cost Davie his life.

W4041/G had returned from Farnborough to Gloster's experimental

The first E.28/39 carried the 1,760lb (796kg) static thrust Power Jets W2/500 in its engine bay; the heat-shroud fitted on this higher-output engine is quite evident in this photograph (believed to have been taken at Farnborough in 1944). Author's collection.

Gloster G.40 E.28/39 specification

Dimensions:	Span 29ft 0in (8.8m)
	Length 25ft 3.75in (7.6m)
	Height 9ft 3in (2.7m)
	Wing area 146.5sq ft (13.5sq m)
	Fin and rudder area 12.8sq ft (1.19sq m)
Armament:	Specification called for four .303in (.76cm) machine guns and space was allocated in the design, but the guns were never fitted
Powerplant: (W4041/G)	One Power Jets W1X turbojet, producing 750lb (340kg) (for taxiing only)
	One Power Jets W1 turbojet, producing 860lb (390kg)
	One Power Jets W1A turbojet, producing 1,160lb (526kg)
	One Power Jets W2/500 turbojet, producing 1,700lb (771kg), this later being increased to 1,760lb (798kg).
(W4046/G)	One Rover-built W2B turbojet, producing 1,200lb (544kg)
	One Rover-built W2B turbojet, producing 1,526lb (692kg)
Weights:	Empty, approximately 2,890lb (1,311kg) as weight changed with different engines;
	Loaded, approximately 3,750lb (1,701kg) as weight changed with different engines
Performance:	Maximum speed (W1 engine) 310mph (499km/h)
	Maximum speed (W1A engine) 388mph (624km/h)
	Maximum speed (W2/500 engine) 460mph (740km/h)
	Maximum speed (W2B engine) 476mph (766km/h)
	Normal service ceiling 32,000ft (9,753m)
	Maximum altitude reached 41,600ft (12,679m).

In 1944, a limited number of W2/700 engines were produced, which followed the final Whittle reverse-flow design. This engine was rated at up to 2,700lb (1,224kg) thrust, and photographic evidence exists in John Golley and Bill Gunston's book *Whittle: The True Story* that unit number 15 was in W4041/G during March 1945.

department in the early spring of 1943, where a Power Jets W2/500 engine was installed; initially providing 1,700lb (771kg) thrust, this engine was ultimately giving 1,760lb (798kg). Michael Daunt took the aircraft for its first trial flight with the new engine before handing it over to John Grierson to continue the programme. On 12 June 1943 Gloster had taken up temporary residence in half a hangar at Barford St John, Oxfordshire – which will feature later in this narrative – and Grierson's programme was conducted from here, with nearly two dozen flights being made over a two-week period. On 30 June, an EC1240-section wing was delivered

and W4041/G first flew with it fitted on 6 July; Grierson was surprised to find that it increased the stall speed by 4mph (6km/h).

The W2/500 engine was removed in the late summer and returned to Glosters, who installed it in an F.9/40. The pressure was off E.28/39 flying, and W4041/G's replacement engine did not arrive for many weeks, by which time it had been decided that all its future flying would be conducted by RAE Farnborough; moreover it was not until April 1944 that this flying was resumed. There were other changes: modifications had been incorporated in the cockpit canopy to make it jettisonable;

small stabilizing fins had been fitted on the tail-plane, to cure the certain amount of inherent directional instability that had always been acceptable during the earlier engine trials programmes; and a cine camera was housed on the upper port wing-tip, to record the results of tufting installed at the wing's root.

Just when the last flight of W4041/G took place is a bit of a mystery, but it had fully achieved the original requirements, and due to its unique standing in British aviational history had already been chosen for preservation. It was handed to the Science Museum in Kensington on 28 April 1946, where it has been on permanent display for over fifty years.

Just as a little aside, it is interesting to contemplate the different attitudes of mind that are separated by the Atlantic Ocean. When General Henry 'Hap' Arnold, Chief of Staff of the United States Army Air Corps, came to Britain on a fact-finding mission in March 1941, the first E.28/39 was nearly ready to fly – and to say that the general was surprised is putting it mildly. America was nine months away from becoming one of the Allies, yet on 1 October we cheerfully answered his request and sent a Whittle W1X engine across the Atlantic, packed in the bomb-bay of a B-24. General Electric (GE) were selected to build fifteen engines, which they called the I-A, under licence and the Bell Aircraft Corporation received a contract on 5 September 1941 to build three aircraft powered by the GE-built engine. In true American style they worked flat out and, on 2 October 1942, the first Bell XP-59A made its first flight from Muroc, California, propelled by two GE I-16 engines. The original order for three aircraft was increased to twelve, built as YP-59A trainers and one was received at Moreton Valence in September 1943 for evaluation against the F.9/40. The aircraft was given the full British experimental aircraft camouflage upper surface/yellow underside treatment, including a yellow prototype 'P' in a circle and a '/G' serial (RJ362/G). A limited production was put in hand by Bell for evaluation by the USAAF, and as such the aircraft was designated P-59A Airacomet.

CHAPTER FOUR

Archetypes of a Fighter

Once the G.40 design to meet E.28/39 had been established at the start of 1940, and Gloster's drawing office was supplying dye-lines to the experimental department for construction, George Carter focused his attention on producing a jet-powered fighter, firm in the knowledge that existing engines could not supply enough thrust for a single-engine layout. Turbojet engine development was a lengthy process, so if full advantage was to be taken of Whittle's design and an operational aircraft put into service in the shortest possible time, then a twin-engined configuration was essential.

A preliminary brochure was tendered in August 1940, and three months later the Air Ministry issued Specification F.9/40, written around the Gloster G.41 draft, for a single-seat fighter with two Whittle-type engines. By December the design arrange-

ments had been completed, so a fuselage mock-up was constructed the following month at the experimental design and construction facility established at Bentham, three miles from the main factory. On 7 February 1941 the Gloster Aircraft Company received Contract SB21179/C23(a), covering the manufacture of twelve 'Gloster-Whittle aeroplanes' to meet the requirements of Specification F.9/40 (see above). The contract also ordered the company to set up jig and tooling for the construction of eighty aircraft a month, while intimations were received from the Ministry that plans for long-term production on a larger scale would follow. Serial numbers DG202 to DG213 inclusive were allocated to the twelve prototypes.

The positioning of the two engines required a solution at a very early stage of

design: installation could be either under the wing or within the fuselage, and both had merits. From an operational perspective, with fitters needing to provide a quick turn-around of an aircraft in squadron service, good accessibility was considered of paramount importance in Carter's mind, so the mounting of the engines in a more orthodox manner, within nacelles on the wing, was favoured. From this, fresh problems arose, as the engines would have to be situated between the front and rear spars in order to retain the wing's strength. Ducting intake air past the front spar was comparatively easy, but getting the hot jet efflux around the rear spar was another matter altogether. Following several different proposals, all of which presented weight penalties, it was decided to route the jet pipe straight through the rear spar and a design was formulated, whereby the

The first of over 3,500. DG202/G shows the original metal rear canopy fairing, fluted to allow vision through a pair of small windows set behind the hinged hood. Author's collection.

spar split into a 'banjo'-shaped structure, with local reinforcement around the circular aperture through which the jet pipe passed. Wind-tunnel testing of the proposal was carried out at RAE Farnborough, where it was found that the unit posed no adverse drag factors; moreover the good accessibility of the engine, plus ancillaries, received favourable comments. Carter was aware that several engines were in various stages of development by manufacturers other than Rover/Whittle, and the wing-mounting on his design would enable different engines to be fitted if necessary – he could not have known just how far this would go!

With a Dowty tricycle undercarriage already featured on the E.28/39, the positioning of the engines in the F.9/40 design dictated that the c.g. would be farther aft than on twin piston-engined aircraft, and consequently the Cheltenham-based company was approached to design a nose-wheel type undercarriage for Gloster's fighter, too. They produced units embodying their levered suspension principle, which featured oleo-pneumatic shock absorbers, actuated by a lever action on the trailing wheel forks, the non-steerable nose-wheel castoring through 180 degrees, with spring-operated centring. Gloster also designed a gravity lock, whereby the undercarriage could not retract while the aircraft's weight was on the wheels. Besides this, a duplicated emergency lowering system was designed, so that if there was an hydraulic failure and the hand-operated pump became inoperative, a single-shot compressed air system could be activated. The latter was entirely independent from the aircraft's Dunlop-designed and manufactured braking system.

One of several stipulations made by the Air Staff in the specification was that the fighter should have a six-cannon armament, with a minimum of 120 rounds per gun. This had been stimulated by one of Gloster's original design proposals, which showed a pair of cannon under the fuselage and two on either side of the nose. However, when it came to working out the details, there were obvious disadvantages in having an under-fuselage installation: first, the absence of propellers meant that the undercarriage legs could be kept short, and it could be foreseen that the servicing and removal of such an installation in an operational environment would present

problems. There was also the weight factor, bearing in mind that the precise power available from the selected engines was something of an unknown quantity. It was therefore proposed that the underside installation be abandoned in favour of a four-cannon armament sited in pairs on either side of the nose, with 150 rounds per gun. This was approved by the Ministry and incorporated in the mock-up, which was inspected by their Armaments, Research and Development representative and passed for operational use. The pilot's seat was situated within a strong pressure cabin structure, behind which the four 150-round magazine cans were carried in an ammunition bay. Behind this was located the 300-gallon (1,365ltr) fuel tank, divided into two separate compartments of equal capacity; various units of the radio were collectively mounted aft of this. As it was considered that early F.9/40 test-flying would be undertaken with the aircraft unarmed, provision was made for carrying ballast weight in lieu of the cannon and ammunition.

With effects of a jet engine's efflux on the normal airflow around an aeroplane was unknown, it was decided to position the tail-plane high enough on the fin to clear the two exhaust streams. It was appreciated that this might present problems in terms of the strength of the structure required and the airflow around such a configuration; however, it was

considered that there was no real alternative, and that it would be in the hands of the test pilots to confirm whether it was acceptable or not.

Another specification stipulation was that the fighter would have the capacity for operating at high altitude, which was why the design incorporated a pressure cabin – in fact the original thinking was for the pilot to use a pressure suit, but this was put aside on the understanding that it would be given further consideration at a later date. The designer wanted to keep the overall weight as low as possible to start with, again because of the uncertainty concerning the thrust available from the early flight engines. The MAP advised George Carter that W.E. Petter, who was Chief Designer at Westland Aircraft in Yeovil, had considerable experience of designing pressure cabins, together with their ancillary equipment, and it was felt that his knowledge would be helpful to the Gloster team. Carter took the Ministry's advice, and with several members of his team, went and met Petter, who was pleased to impart much information that assisted them with their cabin design. The specification's requirement for the fighter to operate above 40,000ft (12,200m), with a cockpit condition equivalent to 25,000ft (7,620m), meant that a pressure differential of 3.5lb/sq in (1.6kg/sq cm) was demanded.

Gloster's General Manager, Frank

DG202/G has been well restored, after many years in the open. It occasionally sees the light of day: here it was displayed at a mid-1960s 'Battle of Britain' day at RAF Gaydon; it can be seen that the original metal rear canopy fairing has not been retained, and that a bullet fairing has been added at the tail-plane/fin intersection. Philip Jarrett.

The third F.9/40, DG204/G, photographed at Bentham prior to the running of its Metropolitan Vickers F.2 engines. Philip Jarrett.

McKenna, was in constant touch with the MAP concerning the production of jigs and tools, which would have to be sub-contracted due to his company's preoccupation with Hawker aircraft. To the MAP's credit was the fact that they arranged for nearly a dozen engineering companies, both within and outside the aircraft industry, to manufacture the necessary components. Another subject of much communication between McKenna and the Ministry was choosing a name for the forthcoming production fighter, a process which took a lot longer than finding the jig and tool subcontractors.

The MAP proposed quite a large number which, in retrospect, sound rather ridiculous: Cyclone, Scourge (a squadron of Scourges?!), Terrific, Terrifier, Tempest, Thunderbolt and Wildfire were all suggested. The American Wright Engine Company's radial engine reduced the number by one, but the Ministry produced a further, even longer list a few weeks later, which included Avenger, Dauntless, Tyrant, Violent, Wildfire and Vortex. Gloster rather liked Avenger, but put up a few suggestions of their own such as Ace, Annihilator and Reaper. By

August 1941 the company had been informed that the Ministry considered Avenger could be confused with Vengeance, the RAF name given to the American Vultee 72 dive bomber supplied under Lend/Lease, and that the name 'Thunderbolt' had been chosen. Gloster's general manager tersely advised the mandarins that Republic were already turning out a five ton (5,079kg) fighter with the USAAF designation P-47D, which the RAF was going to operate as the Thunderbolt. So it was back to the drawing board, and although the company favoured either Ace or Reaper, in February 1942 the MAP instructed Gloster that their production twin-jet fighter would be called 'Meteor'. End of story!

Back in March 1941, arrangements had been made for Boulton Paul Aircraft Limited in Wolverhampton to make the F.9/40's mainplanes and control surfaces, while Parnall Aircraft Limited, situated at Yate in Gloucestershire, would produce the complete tail unit. The latter's participation in the F.9/40 ended when an air-raid destroyed their drawing office, and Gloster had to absorb the additional work. The MAP had decreed that the prototypes

would be pretty well hand-built, but Gloster considered this be too labour-intensive and preferred a larger part of the workforce be occupied in setting up the production line. As far as the Ministry was concerned, completion of the twelve prototypes was of paramount importance, and a schedule was drawn up for the first aircraft to be finished by February 1942, with another two the following month and three in April; the balance was to be produced as three more in May and the final three in June. All this was based on the premise that the subcontractors would meet their respective delivery dates, about which McKenna was rather sceptical; but the onus was firmly on Gloster's, and ministerial instructions were for the subcontractors' unfinished work to be taken, together with their workers, for completion at Bentham.

Engine Troubles

This could not be applied to the engine companies, however, and it was here that the problems centred. Even at the time of the E.28/39's first flight, Frank Whittle's main concerns were getting W2B engines to Gloster's for their prototypes; but the first units that were delivered, on 20 May and 9 June, were far from flight standard. The break-up of turbine blades at Rover's was putting their schedules back to an unacceptable limit, and the problem was not overcome until Nimonic 80 was used in their construction. DG202/G, the first prototype F.9/40, received these engines, although it was only cleared for preliminary taxiing with them – but at least a pair of engines had arrived, and this reinvigorated the rather jaded atmosphere that had developed at Gloster's.

Once again East Anglia was selected for the early trials of a Gloster turbojet-powered prototype. The all-grass airfield at Newmarket Heath had been used as a landing ground as far back as 1935, when the Prince of Wales flew in to join a motor cavalcade for reviewing the Jubilee Review

at Mildenhall. On 1 September 1939, No. 99 Squadron took up residence with their Wellington ICs, but by July 1942 it was No. 75 Squadron with Short Stirlings. This was when DG202/G arrived by road transporter, and after re-assembly, began serious taxi trials with Gerry Sayer at the controls. It soon became obvious that the original plans to conduct flight trials from the airfield would have to be abandoned, the chief test pilot being adamant that the uneven grass surface was quite unsuitable. But he did get the feel of the aircraft, and made recommendations for adjustments to the brakes, and to the nose-wheel shock absorbers which he considered were too soft.

Because of the delay in receiving flight engines from Rover, the MAP gave increasing support to both Metropolitan-Vickers and de Havilland's individual endeavours to develop jet engines. Metro-

Vick had taken the axial-flow path right from the start, in the firm belief that the smaller overall diameter would give aircraft designers more flexibility in determining the size of their projects. Their F2 was bench-run in 1941, passed a Special Category Test for flight clearance in 1942, and was scheduled for its maiden flight in the rear fuselage of the modified Lancaster prototype BT308 in the summer of 1943.

The de Havilland Aircraft Company, on the other hand, went the centrifugal-flow way, in keeping with Whittle. This was principally because Major Frank Bernard Halford, their independent engine consultant – who occupied a suite of offices provided by de Havilland at Stag Lane – had been responsible for developments in the design of the Napier Sabre engine, together with its single-sided supercharger impeller. Talks between Major Halford and Sir Henry Tizard, the Technical

The Halford H-1-powered DG206/G, the fifth F.9/40 and the first to fly. The configuration of the H-1 turbojets required the nacelles to be much fatter than those housing Whittle engines. *Philip Jarrett.*

The seventh prototype F.9/40, DG208/G, was extensively used in attempts to cure the directional instability problems. Several trial solutions were tried, including a flat-sided rudder, an increased fin area which gave a straight-line leading edge, and – the only one to become permanent – a bullet-shaped fairing at the fin/tail-plane intersection. The braking parachute housing aft of the intersection was purely a test-flying precaution. Philip Jarrett.

Adviser to the MAP, resulted in de Havilland being invited to design a new jet fighter, powered by a new jet engine designed by Halford.

It was decided that an engine developing 3,000lb (1,360kg) thrust would be required and, because there was no rig available to test a single annular combustion chamber, Halford chose a layout consisting of sixteen straight-through combustion chambers, rather than Whittle's reverse-flow. Design commenced in April 1941, drawings of the Halford H-1 (originally referred to as the 'H-1 Supercharger') were issued on 8 August, and the first engine started test-runs eight months later, on 13 April 1942. By the beginning of September, 200 hours of bench-testing had been completed with two engines, and on 26 September 1942, one of them finished a twenty-five-hour flight approval test.

As far as the MAP was concerned, both the Metro-Vick F2 and Halford's H-1 were developed and produced as an insurance against failure of the W2B, although de Havilland's priority lay in their DH100 aircraft, for which they had received an Air Ministry contract for the manufacture of three airframes to Specification E.6/41. These emerged as prototypes for the Vampire, which shared Fighter Command service with the Meteor for many years, powered by the Goblin derivative of the H-1. The H-1, designed as a 3,000lb (1,360kg) thrust engine, was inherently larger than that of Power Jets/Rover and

could meet the flight requirements of the F.9/40. Because of Rover's failure to deliver, the Air Ministry arranged for the second most advanced airframe, this being the fifth prototype, DG206/G, to be modified to accept Halford's engine. At the same time, Gloster Aircraft was instructed to prepare an airframe for the F2, which they decided would be DG204/G, the third prototype, as more airframe modifications were required to take the axial-flow engine.

The taxiing trials with DG202/G were completed in August 1942 and the aircraft returned to Bentham, where the limited-clearance engines were removed, ready for two new flight W2Bs promised by Rover. A new set of wheels was also fitted, since the original tyres had been worn out by excessive brake-heating while the aircraft was at Newmarket Heath. In keeping with other delivery assurances by Rover, DG202/G's engines did not arrive, due partly to the protracted blade-cracking problem and partly to the MAP's insistence that the flight-cleared standard engine must be flown in an E.28/39 before it was installed in an F.9/40. At the start of September, the modifications necessary for DG206/G to accept the Halford engines were nearing completion. Because the H-1 engines were larger in diameter than the Rover units, the rear spar 'banjos' required enlargement and the centre section had to be modified, which gave this airframe a 15in (38cm) greater wingspan. The designation F.9/40H was applied to the aircraft,

which was the first to be fitted with clear glazing of the rear canopy, the restricted rearwards vision on DG202/G having been criticized by Sayer during the Newmarket Heath trials. A mock-up of the engine arrived in the first week of the same month, and on 30 September 1942, Frank McKenna received confirmation from de Havilland that the first two engines were ready. Major Halford was aware that the aircraft was not yet in a suitable condition to receive them, so came to an arrangement with McKenna that they could be retained by de Havilland to assist in further development work, with the proviso that Gloster's gave two weeks' notice of the date the engines were needed.

A mock-up of the Metropolitan-Vickers engine arrived on 9 September, five days after the Halford mock-up. The F2 had an axial-flow compressor and was longer than Power Jets' engines, so it would not fit between the main spars. Considerable modifications therefore had to be undertaken on the designated airframe, DG204/G, in particular to the engines which had to be situated in an underslung position, similar to the Messerschmitt Me262 (which was unheard of at Bentham). The title F.9/40M was applied to this aircraft, which was also fitted with a glazed rear canopy, and a rear-view mirror in a clear blister above the windscreen framing.

The month of December 1942 was a somewhat emotional seesaw for Gloster's. The situation with Rover was causing

George Carter's Second String

At one point the MAP seriously considered cancelling the mass-production plans, mainly because the W2B engine with flight clearance was still conspicuous by its absence at Bentham. Gloster then approached the Ministry for consideration of a new single-engined design that had been drawn up in their project office (records do not state the engine: perhaps the Halford H-1?); this aircraft was proposed as a contingency design against Rover's further lapse in supplying F.9/40 power plants. The MAP was in general agreement with the proposal, and Specification E.5/42 was drawn up. In fact the F.9/40 engine crisis was resolved in time; Gloster's E.5/42 project, while not being entirely abandoned, was allowed to be refined without any urgency – two years later a revised contract was drawn up, for the aircraft to be built to meet a new E.1/44 specification. The company resurrected the name 'Ace' – previously included in their list of proposed names for the F.9/40 – for the E.1/44; besides which the aircraft was the first

Gloster design to come under an SBAC standardized type-numbering system introduced in 1944, and so was also called GA.1. In fact the name Ace did not gain much use. Following the cancellation of two of the three airframes originally ordered, a new contract was issued for three GA.2 prototypes to be built. This was followed by two pre-production contracts covering forty aircraft, to be called GA.4s, for which the serial batches VP601 to VD620 and VR164 to VR183 were allocated. Then a week or so after receiving the second contract, the company was informed that it was cancelled!

The three prototypes were allowed to proceed, but with a very low priority due to Meteor production, and it was July 1947 before the first, SM809, was completed. By now, Rolls-Royce was firmly in charge of Whittle-derived turbojet production, and the final centrifugal-flow designed engine, the Nene, giving 5,000lb (2,268kg) thrust, sat in SM809. It was being conveyed on a 'Queen Mary' to the A&AEE at Boscombe Down, from where the first flight was to be made, when the transporter

was involved in a road accident: the aircraft was a 'write-off'. (As a point of interest, the police forces of three counties have no records whatsoever of this accident, which seems rather remiss, considering that quite a sizeable amount of public money was involved!) The prototype's loss meant that the construction of the second airframe now became a priority, and it was completed, with the serial TX145, for a maiden flight from Boscombe Down on 9 March 1948. During flight-testing, a handling problem arose, from turbulence affecting the low-positioned tail-plane. However, a newly designed tail unit was given wind-tunnel tests at RAE Farnborough and cured the problem; the new tail was incorporated in the construction of TX148, the third airframe. Subsequent flight trials improved the type's handling so significantly that consideration was given to fitting the unit on a Meteor – but this comes later in that aircraft's chronology.

The first prototype Gloster GA.1, SM809, built to specification E.1/44, which evolved from the E.5/42 project drawn up as an insurance against late deliveries of Rover-built engines for the F.9/40s. This aircraft was damaged beyond repair while being transported by road to Boscombe Down for its maiden flight. Author's collection.

considerable despondency amongst the workforce when Frank McKenna was notified that the first Halford H-1 flight engine had passed its final test on 22 November and was ready for delivery to Bentham, with the second promised for arrival on 5 December. But on 26 November the MAP instructed Gloster to stop all manufacture of the Rover-engined production Meteor

F.1, and this was followed by the original contract SB21179/C23(a) being reduced to six aircraft – this figure was increased to eight after the F.9/40H had flown. On the positive side, plans had also already been drawn up for the production of H-1 powered aircraft as the Meteor F.2, with a provisional total of fifty aircraft having been agreed, but the Ministry would not

allow any further work on these either, until DG206/G – the prototype F.9/40H – had flown. It seemed that the whole Meteor programme was resting on the maiden flight.

The air of despondency lifted a little with the arrival of the first H-1 flight-standard engine on 28 November. But then the second, due on 5 December,

Gloster GA.2 TX148, the second E.1/44, photographed with the new tail assembly which proved so successful that it was introduced into Meteor production, starting with VT150, the F.8 prototype. Philip Jarret.

suffered shaft damage and could not be delivered on time – whilst all Gloster's could do was hope that another Rover saga was not beginning to evolve, as they went off to put presents under their Christmas trees. De Havilland's delivery of the second engine on 12 January 1943 meant that the aircraft was able to have its first ground-running trials on 26 January, although they had to be curtailed due to equipment malfunction. The following

day, Michael Daunt nearly became involved in an unexpected engine inspection, which again interrupted the ground-running schedule.

February 1943 started with the whole F.9/40 programme revitalized, and progress on the six prototypes was accelerated to the point where four of the airframes were seventy-five per cent finished, with the remaining two confidently expected to be completed before the end of the year. The

ground-running of DG206/G's engines finished during the first week, and its dismantling began in preparation for road transportation to Cranwell, which had been selected for the first flight (Sayer having considered Newmarket Heath unsuitable). The fuselage plus centre-section were loaded on one Commer 'Queen Mary', and the engines and wings were installed in cradles on another, the whole operation being ready for the journey to start on 12 February. Because the Halford engines had made the overall width of the centre-section span so much greater, it was quite impractical to move it by night (nowadays it is almost impossible to imagine what driving in a blacked-out Britain was like – try going along a country lane on just your parking lights, and it was not as good as that!); therefore military and civil police provided escorts, and the route was cleared all the way from Bentham, including the temporary removal of lamp-posts. On arrival at Cranwell the elements were unloaded from their respective transporters and reassembly was completed within a week.

A picture that encompasses the British turbojet fighter programme in July 1943. Taken at Barford St John, it shows the fourth F.9/40 prototype, DG205/G. Ranged in front of it are, from left to right, John Crosby-Warren, an experimental test pilot sharing Gloster's turbojet development test-flying; Michael Daunt, Gloster's chief test pilot at the time; Frank McKenna, the company's production manager; Wing Commander Frank Whittle, and George Carter. The aircraft's rear-view mirror and clear-view canopy fairing are noticeable, as is the fact that the bullet fairing at the fin/tail-plane intersection had yet to be introduced. This aircraft put in eighty hours test-flying before it crashed at Moreton Valence on 27 April 1944, killing Crosby-Warren. Derek N. James.

System checks occupied the next ten days, but by the end of the month, DG206/G was ready.

F.9/40 Takes to the Air

Michael Daunt started taxiing trials on 3 March and could feel almost immediately that this aircraft, on tarmac, moved a lot more quickly than DG202/G, when he had done some taxiing at Newmarket Heath. The H-1 engines each produced 2,300lb (1,043kg) thrust, which was considerably greater than the 1,400lb (635kg) thrust of each W2B in the first prototype, although that aircraft had been 231lb (105kg) lighter. The increased weight and speed meant that braking was less effective, as were the nose-wheel shock absorbers, but Daunt found that he was soon able to compensate for the difference. Two days of taxi trials gave him all the answers he required, and so, later in the day, the F.9/40H, Britain's first twin-jet, was prepared for its maiden flight.

It was felt advisable to minimize the all-up weight and to restrict the engine power output for the first flight, and so just 150 gallons (682l) of fuel were taken aboard, a little over half the total capacity, and the H-1 engines were derated to give 1,500lb (680kg) thrust at 8,000rpm. To save fuel, the aircraft was ground-handled onto the runway. On Friday 5 March 1943, with 25 degrees of flap selected and after a take-off run of approximately 1,200 yards (1,097m), Michael Daunt lifted DG206/G into the air. At about 200mph (322km/h) a directional control problem arose which increased with airspeed, so that at 230mph (370km/h) yawing from side-to-side became too much to contain and the rudder bar could not be held steady. The engines were throttled back to see if the instability came from engine efflux, but this was soon found not to be the case, and the aircraft had to be put into a gentle climb in order to reduce airspeed. At 160mph (257km/h) a reduction of the oscillations made the controls more manageable.

Flaps and undercarriage were lowered at 140mph (225km/h), and on touch-down the engines were opened up to see if the instability reoccurred. It did not, and the landing run was completed within 1,500 yards (1,370m), the whole flight having lasted only twelve minutes. Details of the yawing were forwarded to RAE

The 'Undaunted' Test Pilot

Born in 1909, Neill 'Michael' Daunt was to become only the second British test pilot to fly a turbojet-powered aeroplane, one of the few who was instrumental in translating Gloster's first twin-jet design into an operational aircraft. He joined the Royal Air Force on a short service commission, and qualified from No. 5 Flying Training School (FTS) at Sealand in Flintshire with a grade that earned him a posting to the elite No. 25 Squadron, operating Hawker Furies at Hawkinge in Kent. The squadron supplied the RAF's display team, specializing in aerobatics with their aircraft linked at the wing-tips by ribbons – they performed the world's first formation roll like this.

In 1935 Daunt left the RAF to join the de Havilland School of Flying as an instructor, but his flying ability had been recognized by Gp Capt Paul Ward Spencer 'George' Bullman, who with P.E.G. 'Gerry' Sayer and Philip Gadesden Lucas at Hawker Aircraft had formed one of the most famous test-flying partnerships of all time. Bullman had been appointed chief test pilot and a director of the company in June 1935, and he asked Daunt to join his company's test team at Hucclecote/Brockworth, under 'Gerry' Sayer. From early production test-flying of Gauntlets and Gladiators, Michael started prototype testing with the single-engined Gloster F.5/34, followed by both of the twin-engined F.9/37s.

Subcontracted production Henleys and Hurricanes were followed by the first Gloster-built Typhoon, powered by the completely under-developed and unreliable Napier Sabre twenty-four cylinder, sleeve-valve engine. Michael Daunt is on record as adjudging the Typhoon to be 'the bloodiest aircraft ever', after flying early versions of the type. A catalogue of problems included exhaust gas ingress to the cockpit, vibration, failure of the oil cooling system and rear fuselage structural failure. One of his more memorable flights involved the loss of oil, such that the engine seized and the

resulting belly-landing bent the 14ft (4.26m) propeller back, so that the aircraft skidded along on the blades, going between a pair of trees that removed the wings, before it ground to a halt.

Harry Folland's company, that he formed after leaving Glosters, had built a dozen engine testbed airframes to specification 43/37. The single-engined aircraft had fixed, spatted undercarriages and an enormous wing area; it carried a crew of one pilot, plus two observers in a roomy cabin, with all the necessary instrumentation for monitoring complete engine performance details in flight. In construction it was a mix of a semi-monocoque light alloy fuselage, and plywood-covered wings which featured automatic wing-tip slats, together with generous landing flaps. At least four 43/37s were engaged on various Sabre test programmes, so that both Sayer and Daunt became involved with the aircraft, known to them as the 'Frightful'. During diving trials on one aircraft, the tail became separated from the rest of the airframe and Daunt was hurled through the canopy, as his harness failed under an 8g stress. His parachute opened – although he was not too sure how – and from his subsequent very heavy landing, he sustained a badly torn mouth, among other injuries.

Michael Daunt was hospitalized for several months, and his licence was only re-issued after his convalescence; this was just a few days after 'Gerry' Sayer was killed. So he was back in harness at the deep end, and dependent on the regular progress reports that Sayer had given him. He was appointed Gloster's chief test pilot, and continued E.28/39 testing until the aircraft was ready for delivery to Boscombe Down. F.9/40 trials followed, starting with DG206/G at Bentham where on 13 January 1943, he again nearly lost his life: he was standing in front of the port nacelle when the engine was opened up, and as he bent down to verify an oil leak, a flap on his flying jacket was sucked into the nacelle, closely followed by Daunt himself, head first. Members of the ground crew tried in vain to pull him out, and it was only

Farnborough, who suggested the installing of trimmer cords on the rudder trailing edge as a possible cure. The fitting of the cords was put in hand, but before they could be flight-tested a group of Turkish Air Force officers arrived at Cranwell, and for security reasons, flight testing was abandoned. DG206/G was again dismantled and loaded back onto its 'Queen Mary' transporters, the decision

having been taken to use Newmarket Heath once more, until arrangements could be made at a more suitable airfield.

Within two weeks, DG206/G was ready to fly again. Vibrations that occurred during take-off on the maiden flight had been traced to the nose-wheel, and all three wheels, together with their brake units, were changed. On 17 April the F.9/40H was flown for the second time,

when the engine had been shut down that he came free. While not actually physically injured, he was so badly bruised and psychologically shaken that it was another two days before he returned to work. As a result of this misadventure steel grills were made to fit over air intakes when the engines were running, and these became variously known as 'Daunt stoppers' and 'anti-Daunt grills'.

The maiden flight which took place on 5 March 1943, when the yawing occurred, was followed by many more, some of which were certainly hazardous, to say the least. Once a compressor disintegrated, causing damage that required a prompt belly-landing in a potato field; and on another occasion, centre-section rivets were shed after a hard pull-out manoeuvre. This particular event prompted him to pen the following piece of prose to the chief designer:

Sing a song of shock stall,
Words by Ernst Mach,
Four and twenty slide rules
are shuffling in the dark.
Begone, oh doubting fancies,
Our George will fill the bill,
But George, please make the Meteor
A wee bit meatier still!!

Turbine disintegration still occurred, however. The loss of fellow test pilot John Crosby Warren in 1944 seriously affected Michael Daunt's health, so that later in that same year he retired. He was awarded the Order of the British Empire (OBE) for his services to test flying. He was succeeded as CTP by John Grierson, and enjoyed his retirement together with his wife Monica until her death in 1989, a loss from which he never really recovered. Two years later he fell over in his garden, fracturing a femur, an accident which led to his death on 26 July 1991; he was eighty-one. Thus British test-flying had lost another colourful character.

Photographed at Cosford's Aerospace Museum, decades after their first union, Michael Daunt stands between a W2B Welland engine and the first F.9/40, DG202/G. The aircraft as preserved, differs from its original configuration in having the clear-view rear canopy and a fin/tail-plane intersection bullet fairing. Derek N. James.

and during the short flight 230mph (370km/h) was attained without any loss of stability: Daunt brought the aircraft down after seven minutes, satisfied that the RAE's suggested trimmer cord appeared to have worked. It was nearly three weeks before the next flights, these being two made on 7 May, but Daunt was still not happy operating from Newmarket Heath. Because of the poor surface, the fuel loads had to be kept low, which not only placed an extra obligation on the pilot in that he had to monitor the fuel gauges very carefully, but inevitably it reduced the sortie durations. The airfield's distance from the factory at Hucclecote also proved problematic, and the consequence was that it was unlikely the test trials would achieve the expected time schedule.

Just after the start of World War II a landing ground was opened at Haresfield, six miles south-east of Gloucester; it served as a satellite for the Staverton-based No. 6 Air Observer and Navigator School (AONS), whose Ansons used it regularly. In anticipation of an increase in flying training requirements, the site was developed into a full three-runway station during 1941, and in September of that year it was renamed Moreton Valence, the extending of the base now placing it nearer to that Gloucestershire village than its neighbour, Haresfield. The following year the unit was renamed No. 6 Air Observer School (AOS), with courses taking navigators up to OTU level, and a pilot refresher training unit (PRTU) was also opened for a short time, before going to Scotland.

The MAP was aware that Gloster Aircraft needed a purpose-built flight-test facility, and early in 1943 it was suggested that Moreton Valence could be adapted to meet the company's requirements. New assembly buildings were erected and the main runway was extended, not only to cater for all Meteor testing, but for projected future prototype flying. While this construction work was in hand, an alternative to Newmarket Heath was urgently sought. Consideration was given to Peplow, near the village of Childs Ercall in Shropshire. This was a very large airfield, with work under way to construct a 2,000 yard (1,830m) main runway, which both Daunt and Grierson considered would be ideal for their purposes. However, the Irish labour-force employed on the building was viewed as a potential security risk, with Eire being neutral and therefore open to communications with Germany, and bearing in mind the great secrecy surrounding the development of a jet-powered fighter.

With reasonable proximity to Hucclecote a necessity, the operational training airfield at Barford St John, where a 2,000 yard (1,829m) main runway already existed, was eventually selected and Gloster was granted a half-hangar facility, to share with the Wellington IIIs of No.16 OTU. The ground services arrived in the second week of May 1943, and DG202/G was the first aircraft to arrive from Bentham on 22 May, conveyed aboard a transporter. It was still fitted with W2B/23 engines, as was DG205/G, which arrived the next day, also in a 'Queen Mary' convoy. During the time that these two prototypes were being taken by road to

Barford St John, DG206/G made five more flights from Newmarket Heath, all with a restricted fuel load; in the course of one of these, one of its engines suffered a flame-out, and it was found that the aircraft handled perfectly satisfactorily on one engine. Then on Sunday 23 May 1943, with a maximum fuel load which necessitated gentle taxiing and a very long take-off run, the F.9/40H made its first cross-country flight, leaving behind the undulations of Newmarket Heath.

The 80-mile (129km) flight to Barford St John, set on a plateau five miles south-west of Banbury, took under half-an-hour, the lofty sandstone spire of Our Lady of Bloxham church, which would become a good landmark over the next five months, passing under the starboard wing as Daunt turned into the approach of his new, temporary test centre. With Hucclecote only 40 miles (64km) away to the south-west, Barford St John was ideally situated, and the company's hack Gladiators would become quite a common sight in the circuit. Security was strictly observed in both RT and land-line telephones, Barford St John always being referred to as Position X and never by name.

The brake problems encountered during taxiing trials at Cranwell and Newmarket Heath required a redesigning of the wheel/brake assembly, to facilitate better brake cooling. New units were delivered to Barford St John, and had been fitted on all three of the prototypes by the end of May. DG206/G was the first to have a bullet-fairing installed on the leading edge of the tail-plane/fin intersection to assist airflow in the region. The aircraft also showed a bulge on the top port side of the fuselage, which was a fairing over the early siting of the cabin pressurizing pump. On 12 June, Michael Daunt gave the W2B-engined DG205/G its first flight and reported that he felt it was underpowered compared with the F.9/40H; but he did say that he felt the type, when developed, had good potential as a low-level fighter. The maiden flight lasted nearly thirteen minutes, and again brake overheating caused trouble, on this occasion bursting the inner tube of the port mainwheel while taxiing back to Gloster's facility. The aircraft then had to await delivery of two brand-new W2/500 engines, which were to give 1,650lb (748kg) thrust, as well as replacement mainwheels. The first prototype, DG202/G, stood in the hangar for several weeks awaiting various items, and was

---

Oxfordshire Observations, 1940 to 1944

Pre-war aerial activity over Westcliff-on-Sea featured a fair percentage of Short Brothers' products, and this was hardly surprising since their works were at Rochester, just on the other side of the Thames estuary. 'C' class flying boats involved with Alan Cobham's early flight-refuelling trials vied for attention with the Short-Mayo composite. Then in 1939 their place was taken by Blenheim Is and Hurricanes from Rochford aerodrome (now swallowed into Southend municipal airport), following which Junkers Ju87s attacked convoys forming up off Southend pier. Heinkel He115s on mine-laying sorties in the estuary were vaguely followed by the puffs of anti-aircraft fire, and one misdirected load rearranged the architecture of our house, resulting in a family retreat to Banbury in Oxfordshire.

During the next four years it can truthfully be said that the skies were seldom without aircraft – and considering that there were at least ten airfields within easy cycling distance, this is quite understandable. Our Grammar School formed No25F Squadron of the Air Training Corps, and Barford St John's No. 16 Operational Training Unit (OTU) became our 'parent' unit. We scrounged 'air experience' flights nearly every weekend, and became quite blasé about Ansons, Blenheims, Harvards, Oxfords and Wellingtons, as well as Whitleys – unless we were in them, or they were lower than usual. Then the formations started: twenty or thirty Hectors or Masters tugging Hotspur gliders from Weston-on-the-Green or Croughton presented quite a sight, as did formations of Whitleys pulling Horsas from Brize Norton, while Finmere's Bostons flew in tree-top gaggles. Ninety-four very low-level Lancasters, flying to rendezvous over Upper Heyford prior to raiding the Schneider armament works at Le Creusot, constitutes a sight – and sound – not easily forgotten.

In 1943 the USAAF was getting into its stride so that previous formation-sightings paled into insignificance. That summer, clear blue early-morning skies might be almost obliterated by the silvery ribbons of condensation were dragged by B-17s and B-24s, droning high overhead in their hundreds. You just could not get blasé about those! Nearly every airfield that we visited at weekends or during the holidays seemed to receive Eighth Army Air Force representative aircraft at some time, many bearing evidence of enemy interception and the salvage crews were kept fully occupied. On Monday 24 January 1944 I was watching as a mass of B-17s went over, when one dropped out of formation, with Very-flares arcing all over the place; as it lost height its trajectory said 'Barford St John'. Through the grapevine we heard that its undercarriage had collapsed on landing, and having a full bomb-load, it caused something of a stir. We fervently hoped it would still be there on Saturday, and when the day arrived, we pedalled like mad over the five miles to the airfield. There we came across *two* damaged B-17s from the 92nd Bomb Group's base at Podington, with white triangles on their fins and carrying the group's 'B' identity letter. Two days previously, a crew of eighteen had arrived in B-17 42-30716 to handle repairs to the aircraft that I had seen going down on Monday, and this aircraft's undercarriage had also failed on landing! We were allowed full access to this second Flying Fortress, and I remember being surprised to see that combat holes in the nose-cone had been repaired by stitching in patches of perspex with wire strands. A touch of irony was the fact that 42-3461, the aircraft that had crash-landed on 24 January, was repaired and returned to base to become an element of Project *Aphrodite* – war-weary B-17s which were stripped of all unnecessary fitments, packed with 20,000lb (9,070kg) of explosive and special radio equipment, to be used as guided flying bombs – while the second aircraft, with the repair crew, had to be scrapped!

The freedom given to us with the B-17s had certainly been lacking the previous year, when Gloster Aircraft was given the use of half the T2 hangar alongside Milton Lane, situated away from the main buildings – officially we were not allowed anywhere near this site. Between May and October 1943 the company based its F.9/40 test-flying here, while the main runway at Moreton Valence was being lengthened in preparation for a

---

occasionally cannibalized to keep DG205/G flying. During this time, W4041/G, the first E.28/39, spent a couple of weeks at the base, and after being fitted with an EC1240-section wing, nearly two dozen flights were made before it departed

to RAE Farnborough once again.

On 28 June 1943 Daunt flew DG205/G, and reported that the ailerons were unstable at high altitude, and that engine surge had been encountered at 25,000ft (7,620m). Although only the port engine

forthcoming nineteen-year tenure. During this six months, the first E.28/39, W4041/G, as well as F.9/40s DG202/G, DG204/G, DG205/G and DG206/G were all present at some time, although the F2-powered DG204/G did not stay long, nor did it fly. All test-flying had to be undertaken at times when it did not impede No. 16 OTU's training schedules, and only when the weather was calm, all of which usually meant late afternoon or early evening. It was this restriction that prompted our hedgerow vigils, which started as mentioned in the Preface.

I recall that F.9/40 flights seemed to be of a short duration, and whenever one returned to the hangar there was much removing of panels and suchlike. Before each flight a red Very cartridge was fired into the air, and 16 OTU aircraft kept their distance until after take-off; it was a similar proce-dure each time an F.9/40 returned. It is interesting that although RAF police patrolled the road to Bloxham and stopped trucks and cars, they never stopped us – it must have been our innocent expressions! There was nearly always a lot of conversation going on with the pilot and groups of civilians, while the small band of overalled techni-cians were constantly on the go. W4041/G, which was there for nearly three weeks, eluded us on the ground, but DG205/G and DG206/G were very often active. One of the F.9/40s spent a lot of time in the hangar, sometimes with parts missing, and although we could not see its serial number, history has revealed this to have been the first prototype, DG202/G. While there were subtle changes in nacelle outlines between them (though I never saw DG204/G), one of the most noticable differences was the bullet-fairing at the fin/tail-plane joint on DG206/G. This aircraft also had an anti-spin parachute housing behind the bullet-fairing, but we did not know at the time what this extension was for.

Milton Lane then was just a footpath beaten through long grass, at the start of which was an inoffensive weather-beaten notice board saying PRIVATE; but as there was no explanation or other restriction, I am afraid it was ignored – in fact, school cross-country runs were routed down this path. We made frequent visits to the viewing-hole in the hedge alongside the T2, and sketches were made so that a model could be constructed. The owner of the model shop in Banbury was an enter-prising business man: he knew that Hotspur training gliders contained a lot of balsa wood and that crashes occurred fairly regularly, and he came to agreements with certain persons at both Croughton and Weston-on-the-Green, whereby he purchased large chunks of written-off gliders in order to keep his customers happy – and we were!

My friend Bob, who shared that wonderful hour quoted in the Preface, was an excellent model-maker and a very creditable F.9/40 – which by then we had heard called Thunderbolt, but doubted, because of the P-47 – was made. Our ATC squadron had open evenings at the end of the school year where our individual talents were displayed; our commanding officer was our headmaster during the day, and in 1943 he had invited Barford St John's C.O. as guest of honour. On the platform the F.9/40 model glistened with fresh paintwork – and the reaction to it quite surprised us: it was removed from its promi-nent position a lot quicker than the aircraft itself got off the runway, and we were summonded before our C.O. – who suddenly became our headmaster! We had to explain exactly how we came to be so accurate in our interpretation, and stern reprimands were given; the next time we went to Barford St John, Milton Lane was closed by a forest of barbed wire, which I was told remained long after the war ended.

By October 1943 Moreton Valence was ready and operations at Barford St John were terminated. As the F2 engines were still with Metropolitan-Vickers, the F.9/40M was loaded onto a transporter for the move, while the remaining three aircraft were flown out in the same week. No. 16 OTU reclaimed their half-hangar space from Gloster's and the airfield's period in British jet aviation history was over, with the Wellingtons being replaced at the end of 1944 by Mosquitos. Today the runways and perimeter track still remain. A criptic board states that the plethora of radio-masts and single-story buildings in the middle of the site are 'RAF Barford St John, 422 Air Base Squadron Operating Location Alpha', whatever that means.

tional instability occurred, and various counter-measures were subsequently employed in an attempt to rectify the problem: wing tufting; attention to the metal coverings; ailerons skinned with metal and trim-tabbed; mass-balance weights within the wing; even lengths of cord hung off each aileron trailing edge – but none of these enabled the ailerons to be light and constant at all altitudes.

Development flying progressed through the month of July, and on 12 July the first prototype, DG202/G, having been taxied at both Bentham and Newmarket Heath, made its maiden flight with Michael Daunt at the controls. Also during the month, DG204/G arrived by 'Queen Mary'. This was the airframe selected to be fitted with Metropolitan-Vickers F2 engines, rated at 1,900lb (861kg) thrust; as such it was designated F.9/40M. Apart from replacing the ailerons for the modified type flown on DG205/G and many hours of ground-running the engines, not a lot happened to the aircraft until 3 August, when Michael Daunt commenced taxiing trials. The engines' high idling speed presented more brake overheating and, although Metro-Vick had a team of engineers at Barford St John, they were unable to rectify the problem. It was therefore decided to return the F2s to their manufacturer – and that was the end of the F.9/40M's activities in Oxfordshire. On 16 August, DG205/G flown by Daunt, and DG206/G with John Grierson at the controls, took off for a test in which they would compare speeds, a flight which lasted just over half-an-hour. Subsequent comparison of results showed that the two aircraft had similar perfor-mances, although the H-1 engines were more powerful. The higher drag factor around their nacelles was considered to be a possible reason. Rippling of the top centre-section and nacelle skin on DG205/G was reported to the factory, and heavier gauge metal in this area was incor-porated into production Meteors.

Testing at the RAE

By the time DG204/G's engines arrived at Moreton Valence, the MAP had decreed that the majority of F.9/40 flight-testing would be handled by the RAE; so once the engines were back on the airframe, DG204/G was again transported by road, arriving at Farnborough in October 1943. Following reassembly and taxiing trials, the

had been affected, both were throttled back and the pilot brought the aircraft down to 20,000ft (6,096m). During the shallow dive he reached 330mph (531km/h) and found the aileron control very over-balanced. Attempts to repeat the effect in level speeds up to 360mph (579.3km/h) were unsuccessful, but Daunt considered that the inspection panels hinged to the aileron leading edges stood too proud and that the gap should be faired in. It was in the shallow dives that direc-

aircraft's first flight, lasting fifteen minutes, was made in the hands of Wg Cdr Wilson on 13 November, and six further flights, totalling 3hr 20min flying time, were made over the next six weeks; but then on 4 January 1944 the aircraft was fifteen minutes into its eighth flight when it crashed, killing the pilot, Sqn Ldr Davie. An axial-flow engine was not flown again in the Gloster aircraft until the Metro-Vick Beryl, in the 1948 Meteor F.4 engine testbed. It is a fine testimonial to Gloster's test pilots that they conducted an enormous flight-testing programme, mastering entirely new circumstances such as engine flame-outs and compressor surge, without any loss.

The first F.9/40 flown by the A&AEE at Boscombe Down was DG205/G, tested on 24 and 25 February 1944. Their impressions of the aircraft were summarized as follows:

1. The aircraft is easy to fly and from the point of view of quietness, absence of vibration and fumes, etc. is very pleasant.
2. The controls are very badly harmonized, as the rudder is immovable at ordinary level and at diving speeds after the first few degrees of movement; the elevator is too heavy; whilst the ailerons are too light at low to moderate speeds. A directional oscillation of small amplitude is present in bumpy conditions, and this must be eliminated before accurate aiming is possible. The elevator trimmer is much too sensitive and has an excessive amount of backlash.
3. The seat should be tilted back a few degrees, whilst repositioning of the throttles, the fuel shut-off controls, and some engine instruments is desirable.
4. An emergency braking system is essential and continuous reading fuel contents gauges are required.
5. The minimum time restriction of ten seconds on throttle movement from idling to maximum rpm should be eliminated, as should the five-degree maximum aileron movement at high speed.
6. The aircraft appears to be statically stable stick fixed, and also gives the impression of being dynamically stable.
7. The stick force per g in recovery from trimmed dives at 300–400mph ASI is about six, and in sustained turns at 300mph ASI is about eight.
8. The rate of roll compares favourably with Spitfire performance.

The sixth F.9/40 airframe, DG207/G, was designated to be the prototype Meteor F.2, for which Gloster had made provisional plans to build fifty examples until the embargo placed by the MAP at the end of 1942. De Havilland received a contract to put their DH100 Vampire fighter into production. (The DH100 was originally to be named 'Spider Crab', which

Eric Greenwood, who became Gloster's Chief Test Pilot on Michael Daunt's retirement in 1944 and is credited with being the first pilot to exceed, in turn, 400, 500 and 600mph (643.7, 804.6 and 965.5km/h). In 1945 he joined Gp Capt Hugh J. Wilson, as the RAF High Speed Flight. Derek N. James.

hardly trips off the tongue – there must have been some strange characters at the MAP in those days.) In view of this aircraft being designed around Major Halford's engine, which also went into production as the Goblin, it was felt that de Havilland's engine production facilities could not cope with supplying engines for the Meteor as well as the Vampire. Consequently, just a pair of engines was supplied for DG207/G, and the aircraft was flown by John Grierson from Moreton Valence for its maiden flight on 24 July 1945. By now the H-1 Goblin engine was giving 2,700lb (1,224.5kg) thrust, and Grierson remarked on this aircraft having the best performance of all the F.9/40s that he had flown. It was the first to be fitted with the sliding canopy that became standard on production Meteor F.3s. Because of the cancellation of the Meteor F.2, DG207/G was flown in September to de Havilland's airfield at Hatfield for their use as a Goblin development test aircraft, and Gloster had no further dealings with it.

DG208/G, powered by W2B/23 engines, was first flown on 20 January 1944, eighteen months before DG207/G took to the air; it was used as a test aircraft to try and cure the directional instability that was plaguing the design. During these trials an enlarged fin and rudder was fitted, the upper fin area above the tail-plane intersection having the straight leading-edge line continuation of the lower fin; later, however, the fin/rudder profile reverted to standard. The aircraft was also the first on which airbrakes were installed and later it received flat-sided rudders. A&AEE pilots test-flew the aircraft at Moreton Valence on 16 March 1944 without the aileron tab balance and made two observations:

1. The ailerons are heavy at speeds above 300mph [483km/h] ASI but are reasonably effective; at 350mph [563km/h] ASI and up to 400mph [644km/h] ASI a vibration or snatch is felt on the control column in the lateral plane and though silent, the snatch is most noticeable and is particularly unpleasant.
2. In bumpy conditions the directional oscillation is accompanied by a rolling motion and the aircraft tends to fly in a series of left- and right-hand bank turns.

Obviously the A&AEE felt there was quite a bit to do in the directional stability field. After Gloster had finished its testing programmes, in 1945 the aircraft went on the strength of the de Havilland Engine Company at Hatfield. On 18 April 1944, the eighth F.9/40 DG209/G had its maiden flight. This, the final prototype, was powered by two 1,600lb (725kg) thrust Rolls-Royce W2B/23 Welland engines, and on 10 June was delivered to Rolls-Royce's test airfield at Hucknall. Here it was operated for eighteen months on W2B/37 Derwent I engine development, until 24 January 1945; it was then taken to RAE Farnborough, and finally scrapped on 13 July.

Following a port engine explosion when taking off from Church Broughton on 13 December 1944, DG202/G was returned to Moreton Valence for repairs, which were completed on 14 May 1945. Later in the year, on 11 August, Eric Greenwood, who had taken over as Chief Test Pilot following Michael Daunt's retirement, flew the aircraft to the Royal Naval Air Station at Abbotsinch, in Renfrewshire (now Glasgow Airport). From there, DG202/G was taken aboard a lighter to join up with the carrier HMS *Pretoria Castle*, anchored in the Firth of Clyde, to undergo two weeks of deck-handling trials.

With these completed, the aircraft returned to Moreton Valence, from where on 25 April 1946 it was taken from here to No. 5 School of Technical Training at RAF Locking, where it stayed for five years. In January 1951, assigned the instructional airframe number 5758M, the first prototype F.9/40 went to RAF Yatesbury to stand as a gate guardian, minus its camouflage/yellow paint scheme. Today, restored to its 1943 appearance, the aircraft is on permanent display at the Aerospace Museum, Cosford.

Reports exist of serial DG210 being allocated to an additional airframe, which was to be built to test a later Metro-Vick F2 derivative; but by June 1944 they had decided against using an F.9/40 for this engine's development, and so the number remained void.

CHAPTER FIVE

The Meteor Enlists

At Hucclecote, production started as soon as Gloster received its contract, no. 6/ACFT/1490/41, dated 8 August 1941; this covered the manufacture of twenty aircraft which were given the designation G.41A Meteor F.Mark 1. (During the war, aircraft mark numbers were indicated in roman numerals, a system which carried on for a short time after hostilities ceased, when arabic numerals were introduced. The change took place during Meteor Mk 3 production, the first few off the line being referred to as Mk IIIs. To avoid confusion, arabic numerals will be used throughout this account of the Meteor's history.) The serial batch numbers EE210 to EE219 inclusive were allocated to the aircraft, and the first airframes were laid down in the summer of 1943. Just before Christmas, the prototype F.1, EE210/G (still secret and needing guarding when away from home) was taken onto the Moreton Valence tarmac for taxi trials. In essence it was an F.9/40 fitted with full provision for the four 20mm cannon armament, a 5-degree dihedral at the wing-tips and a glazed canopy situated aft of the side-ways-hinging cockpit hood. Power was supplied by two Rolls-Royce W2B/23

A poor quality but rare photograph of the third production Meteor F.1 EE212/G, flying without a ventral fin during the early trials which were aimed at improving lateral stability. The aircraft was later used as the aerodynamic prototype airframe for the Meteor F.3, before going to RAF Cosford as Instructional Airframe 5927M. Derek N. James.

Wilfred George Carter, CBE

In 1916 George Carter was Chief Draughtsman at the Sopwith Aircraft Company, under the Chief Designer Captain B. Thomson; later, Thomson became chief designer at H.G. Hawker Engineering Company, and he took Carter with him; when he left the company in 1923, Carter took over the post of Chief Designer of Hawker Aircraft. His initial work was a revision of Thomson's last design, the Hawker Woodcock, in which he replaced the original Armstrong-Siddeley Jaguar engine with a Bristol Jupiter, and incorporated a single-bay wing. In this configuration the aircraft became the Woodcock MkII and was

Hawker's first design to enter service with the RAF. In 1923 Sydney Camm joined Hawker, initially working under Carter, who went on to design the Hedgehog, followed by the Hornbill to Specification 4/24, using a mixture of wood and metal. The master welder Fred Sigrist had encouraged Carter to incorporate metal in the Hornbill design, and the Horsley that followed was designed by Camm under Carter's direction. Because he had worked on earlier de Havilland aircraft which employed metal in their construction, in 1925 the Gloucestershire Aircraft Company offered him a position in their design team under Harry Folland and Carter took up the offer, leaving

Camm to take over as Hawker's chief designer.

Folland left to form his own company in 1937, and George Carter took over as Chief Designer. His first project was the single radial-engined fighter designed to specification F.9/37, which stemmed from Folland's earlier F.5/33 and F.34/35 proposals. To meet Specification F.18/37, in March 1938 Carter designed a twin-boom twelve-gun fighter with a pusher Napier Sabre engine; this project was rejected in favour of Hawker's design, the Typhoon, but during a meeting with Frank Whittle in 1939, it was seen as being a possible application for the turbojet engine. This initial association between the two engineers culminated in the F.9/40, and once it was established as a design, changes were made at Gloster. In order to keep George Carter free to concentrate on new projects, the F.9/40 development programme was placed in the hands of Mr F. Sanders, who was to monitor each prototype's progress from the moment it left Bentham's assembly buildings to its finished trials programme. Furthermore, on 19 July 1943 Richard Walker – who had joined the company as assistant chief designer in 1937 – was made responsible for all Meteor development design, with instructions to bring the aircraft up to operational standard as quickly as possible.

During 1947 Carter's design office prepared several projects to meet Specifications F.3/48 and F.4/48. Richard Walker took over as Chief Designer in 1948, and his development of Carter's original project became the GA.5 Javelin. George Carter became Technical Director when he handed over to Walker, and he remained on the company's board of directors. In 1954 he decided to semi-retire and assumed the role of technical consultant, a position which he held until 1958.

Wilfred George Carter, who originally worked for Gloster Aircraft in 1928 and joined the company in 1931. His association over nearly thirty years progressed from being simply a designer, to Chief Designer and Technical Director, up to his semi-retirement as a technical consultant. Derek N. James.

Welland engines, giving 1,770lb (771kg) thrust. On 12 January 1944 Michael Daunt lifted the aircraft off the extended runway: Britain's first production turbojet fighter, three-and-a-half years after George Carter submitted his initial design.

The aircraft stayed at Moreton Valence for the rest of the month, undergoing preliminary flight trials; it was then dismantled in February, for shipment to the Muroc Air Force Base (now a part of the vast Edwards Air Force Base in the

Mojave Desert of California) as the exchange aircraft for the Bell YP-59A. Meteor production ran a little behind schedule to start with, the second aircraft, EE211/G, due for completion in January, not getting airborne until 16 April 1944. It was delivered to RAE Farnborough a few days later – and there it remained, dormant for the next eleven months. The original W2B/23C Welland engines were replaced by a pair of W2/700s, and the first flight with them installed was made in March

1945, this being only the second flight by the airframe. In flight-testing at RAE Farnborough it had been found that the airflow around the engine nacelles deteriorated at about Mach 0.75, and this caused strong buffeting due to the increased drag of the turbulent air. Several remedies were tried, the most successful being the lengthening of the nacelles ahead of and aft of the wing chord. RAE test pilot Flt Lt Philip Stanbury found that their installation increased the maximum sea-level speed by

EE223/G, the fourteenth production F.1, was the first aircraft fitted with two Rolls-Royce Derwent 1 engines, which were installed in short-cord nacelles. It was the first Meteor to have a pressure cabin, and spent nearly all its life at Hucknall and Boscombe Down, before being scrapped in June 1946. Mike Hooks.

Meteor F.1 EE227, having served with No. 616 Squadron as YQ-Y, went to RAE Farnborough to assist in the stability trials. It was converted by having the top fin and rudder areas removed, as is shown in this rather poor quality photograph, the 'give-away' being the tail national marking positioned under the tail-plane. The trials were of comparatively short duration, following which EE227 went to Rolls-Royce, to be fitted with two Trent engines and become the world's first turboprop powered aircraft. Author's collection.

1 Starboard detachable wingtip
2 Starboard navigation light
3 Starboard recognition light
4 Starboard aileron
5 Aileron balance tab
6 Aileron mass balance weights
7 Aileron control coupling
8 Aileron torque shaft
9 Chain sprocket
10 Cross-over control runs
11 Front spar
12 Rear spar
13 Aileron (inboard) mass balance
14 Nacelle detachable tail section
15 Jet pipe exhaust
16 Internal stabilising struts
17 Rear spar "spectacle" frame
18 Fire extinguishing spray ring
19 Main engine mounting frame
20 Engine access panel(s)
21 Nacelle nose structure
22 Intake internal leading-edge shroud
23 Starboard engine intake
24 Windscreen de-icing spray pipe
25 Reflector gunsight
26 Cellular glass bullet-proof windscreen
27 Aft-sliding cockpit canopy

28 Demolition incendiary (cockpit starboard wall)
29 RPM indicators (left and right of gunsight)
30 Pilot's seat
31 Forward fuselage top deflector skin
32 Gun wobble button
33 Control column grip
34 Main instrument panel

35 Nosewheel armoured bulkhead
36 Nose release catches (10)
37 Nosewheel jack bulkhead housing/attachment

38 Nose ballast weight location
39 Nosewheel mounting frames
40 Radius rod (link and jack omitted)
41 Nosewheel pivot bearings
42 Shimmy-damper/self-centering strut
43 Gun camera
44 Camera access
45 Aperture
46 Nose cone
47 Cabin cold-air intake
48 Nosewheel leg door
49 Picketing rings
50 Tension shock absorber
51 Pivot bracket
52 Mudguard
53 Torque strut
54 Door hoop
55 Wheel fork
56 Retractable nosewheel
57 Nosewheel doors
58 Port cannon trough fairings
59 Nosewheel cover
60 Intermediate diaphragm
61 Blast tubes
62 Gun front mounting rails
63 Pilot's seat pan
64 Emergency crowbar
65 Canopy de-misting silica gel cylinder
66 Bullet-proof glass rear-view cut-outs
67 Canopy track
68 Seat bulkhead
69 Entry step
70 Link ejection chutes
71 Case ejection chutes
72 20-mm Hispano Mk III cannon
73 Belt fed mechanism
74 Ammunition feed necks
75 Ammunition tanks
76 Aft glazing (magazine bay top door)
77 Loading ramp
78 Front spar bulkhead
79 Oxygen bottles (2)

80 Front spar carry-through
81 Tank bearer frames
82 Rear spar carry-through
83 Self-sealing (twin compartment) main fuel tank, capacity 165 Imp gal (750 l) in each half
84 Fuel connector pipe
85 Return pipe
86 Drain pipes
87 Fuel filler caps
88 Tank doors (2)

89 T.R. 1143 serial mast
90 Rear spar bulkhead (plywood face)
91 Aerial support frame
92 R.3121 (or B.C.966A) IFF installation
93 Tab control cables
94 Amplifier
95 Fire extinguisher bottles (2)
96 Elevator torque shaft
97 T.R.1143 transmitter/receiver radio installation
98 Pneumatic system filter
99 Pneumatic system (compressed) air cylinders
100 Tab cable fairlead

101 Elevator control cable
102 Top longeron
103 Fuselage frame
104 IFF aerial
105 DR compass master unit
106 Rudder cables
107 Starboard lower longeron
108 Cable access panels (port and starboard)
109 Tail section joint
110 Rudder linkage
111 Tail ballast weight location
112 Fin spar/fuselage frame
113 Rudder tab control
114 Fin structure
115 Torpedo fairing

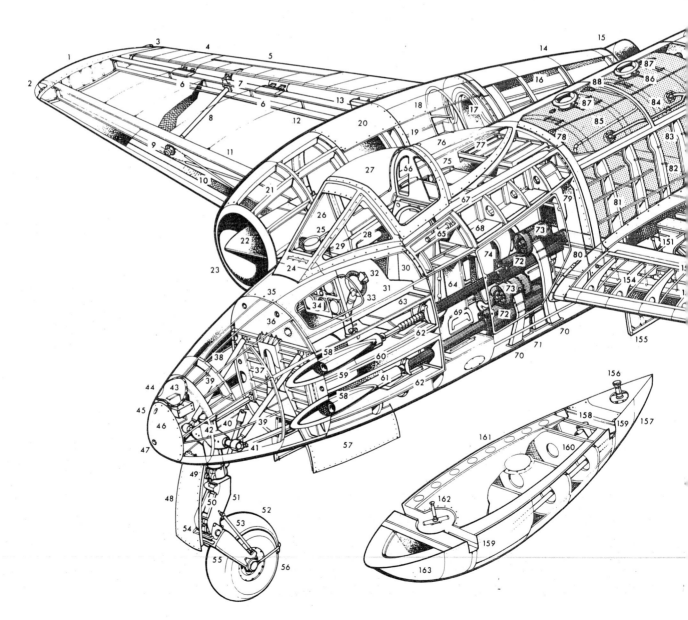

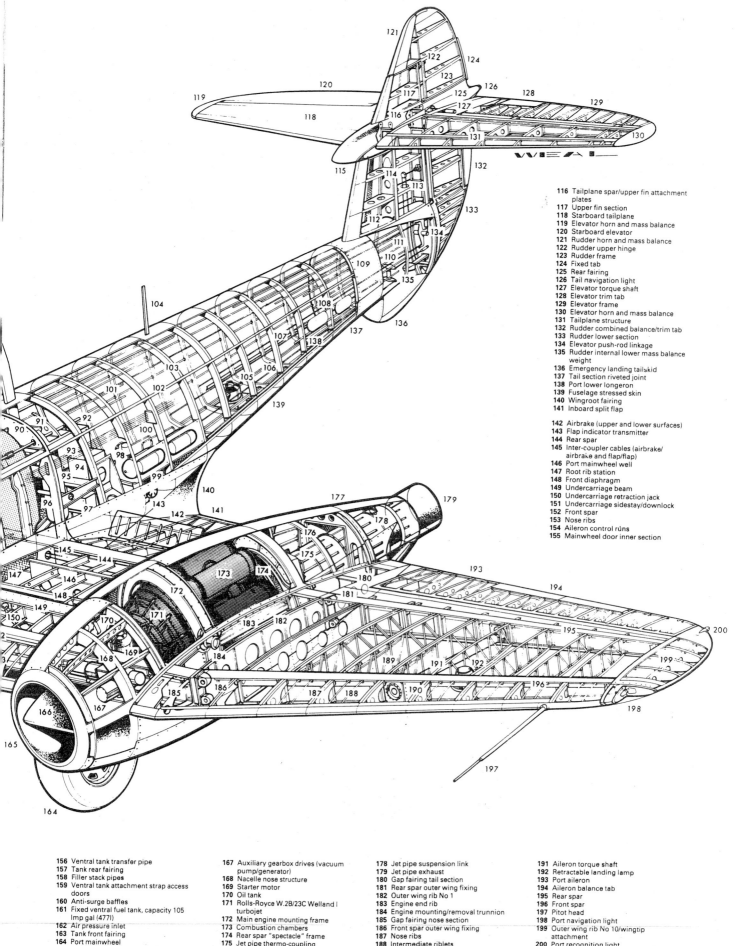

116 Tailplane spar/upper fin attachment plates
117 Upper fin section
118 Starboard tailplane
119 Elevator horn and mass balance
120 Starboard elevator
121 Rudder horn and mass balance
122 Rudder upper hinge
123 Rudder frame
124 Fixed tab
125 Rear fairing
126 Tail navigation light
127 Elevator torque shaft
128 Elevator trim tab
129 Elevator frame
130 Elevator horn and mass balance
131 Tailplane structure
132 Rudder combined balance/trim tab
133 Rudder lower section
134 Elevator push-rod linkage
135 Rudder internal lower mass balance weight
136 Emergency landing tailskid
137 Tail section riveted joint
138 Port lower longeron
139 Fuselage stressed skin
140 Wingroot fairing
141 Inboard split flap

142 Airbrake (upper and lower surfaces)
143 Flap indicator transmitter
144 Rear spar
145 Inter-coupler cables (airbrake/airbrake and flap/flap)
146 Port mainwheel well
147 Root rib station
148 Front diaphragm
149 Undercarriage beam
150 Undercarriage retraction jack
151 Undercarriage sidestay/downlock
152 Front spar
153 Nose ribs
154 Aileron control runs
155 Mainwheel door inner section

156 Ventral tank transfer pipe
157 Tank rear fairing
158 Filler stack pipes
159 Ventral tank attachment strap access doors
160 Anti-surge baffles
161 Fixed ventral fuel tank, capacity 105 Imp gal (477l)
162 Air pressure inlet
163 Tank front fairing
164 Port mainwheel
165 Starboard engine intake
166 Intake internal leading-edge shroud

167 Auxiliary gearbox drives (vacuum pump/generator)
168 Nacelle nose structure
169 Starter motor
170 Oil tank
171 Rolls-Royce W.2B/23C Welland I turbojet
172 Main engine mounting frame
173 Combustion chambers
174 Rear spar "spectacle" frame
175 Jet pipe thermo-coupling
176 Nacelle aft frames
177 Nacelle detachable tail section

178 Jet pipe suspension link
179 Jet pipe exhaust
180 Gap fairing tail section
181 Rear spar outer wing fixing
182 Outer wing rib No 1
183 Engine end rib
184 Engine mounting/removal trunnion
185 Gap fairing nose section
186 Front spar outer wing fixing
187 Nose ribs
188 Intermediate riblets
189 Wing ribs
190 Aileron drive chain sprocket

191 Aileron torque shaft
192 Retractable landing lamp
193 Port aileron
194 Aileron balance tab
195 Rear spar
196 Front spar
197 Pitot head
198 Port navigation light
199 Outer wing rib No 10/wingtip attachment
200 Port recognition light

No. 616 Squadron aircraft on their steel-mesh hardstanding. The foreground aircraft, with its sideways-hinging cockpit hood, is an F.1, and two F.3s with sliding hoods are behind it. Three more F.1s are parked behind them, while an F.3 brings up the rear of this line-up. Derek N. James.

nearly 60mph (96.5km/h), with the aircraft's handling being good at up to Mach 0.84. The longer nacelles would become standard on the Meteor, and were introduced during F. Mark 3 production. These RAE trials were made in conjunction with A&AEE Boscombe Down, as were a later series of cockpit-hood jettison tests. The Establishment still

considered that a thorough investigation of the handling qualities of a representative aircraft should be made as soon as possible, as there were several features present on the Meteor which merited fuller exploration.

When all its various trials programmes had been completed, EE211/G was allocated the instructional airframe

number 5927M; the aircraft is believed to have been broken up in the 1950s.

EE212/G, the third production F.1, was completed early in 1944 and was first flown on 15 April, a day before EE211/G. This aircraft was retained by Gloster Aircraft, to become extensively involved with directional stability and handling trials: during these the ventral fin was deleted, together

The temporary white coat of paint applied to No. 616 Squadron aircraft during the winter of 1944/45 is shown here, on EE239, the tenth production F.1 which went to No.1 School of Technical Training, Halton, as 5787M in January 1946. Author's collection.

with its adjacent rudder area, which terminated on a line with the top rear fuselage. A small bumper was installed under the rear fuselage, as protection during abnormal take-offs. The aircraft was later restored to standard and used as the aerodynamic testbed for the next production model, the Mark 3. The first flight of EE214 – the first Meteor to have a serial number without the '/G' suffix – took place on 9 May 1944, and it was used to test a fixed ventral 100-gallon (450-litre) additional fuel tank, as part of the trials to increase the Meteor's operational range. The aerodynamic affects on the aircraft were found to be negligible, and later a series of trials involving a jettisonable tank was conducted on several Meteor F.3s. EE214 later went to RAE Farnborough, to help familiarize RAF pilots with the flying of turbojet aircraft.

The First RAF Jet Squadron

Back in 1926, on 5 October, No. 503 Squadron had been formed at Waddington as a special reserve squadron; twelve years later it was operating Hawker Hinds at Doncaster. Then on 1 November 1938 it was disbanded, but renumbered the same day as No. 616 (South Yorkshire) Squadron of the Royal Auxiliary Air Force. The Hinds were followed by Gloster Gauntlets, then early in 1939 with Fairey Battles for six months, and finally the squadron became a Spitfire operator, from October 1939 to July 1944, by which time it was based at Culmhead in Somerset. The commanding officer then was Sqn Ldr Andrew McDowell, DFM: as a sergeant pilot, McDowell was involved in the first RAF action of World War II, when on Sunday 3 September 1939 he had engaged enemy aircraft making an air attack on the Forth Bridge; later he became a top scorer in the Battle of Britain. In the first week of July 1944, together with five fellow pilots and Wg Cdr H.J. Wilson, McDowell was transferred on attachment to RAE Farnborough, where the party was introduced to production Meteor F.1s EE213 and EE214. They were subjected to a short intensive conversion course, then returned to Culmhead as the RAF's first qualified jet pilots; and on 12 July they received the squadron's first aircraft, EE219.

The next four weeks were hectic, to say the least. No. 616 was an operational

Gloster G.41 Meteor F.1 and F.3	
Dimensions:	Span 43ft 0in (13.1m) Length 41ft 3in (12.5m) Height 13ft 0in (3.9m) Wing area 374sq ft (34.7sq m)
Armament:	Four 20mm Hispano cannon with total of 780 rounds
Powerplant:	Two Rolls-Royce W2B/23C Welland turbojets each producing 1,700lb (771kg) thrust (Mark F.1); or Two Rolls-Royce W2B/37 Derwent I turbojets each producing 2,000lb (907kg) thrust (Mark F.3).
Weights:	Empty 8,140lb (3,737kg); loaded 13,795lb (6,258kg)
Performance:	Maximum speed 415mph at 10,000ft (674km/h at 3,048m) Service ceiling 40,000ft (12,192m)

Photographed when acting as a 'gate guard' at Coltishall in 1962, minus a serial, this F.3 was EE419: it saw service with No. 245 Squadron and the CFS, before going to Coltishall as Instructional Airframe 7247M. The aircraft was scrapped and burnt in 1969. Mike Hooks.

squadron, flying Spitfire Mk VIIs on sweeps in support of the Allied land offensive in northern France, and on convoy patrols over the English Channel; it had moved to Manston, in Kent, in order to carry out its role. When not flying operational sorties, the pilots had to convert to Meteor flying – and this farcical state of affairs existed until the last week in August, when the last Spitfire departed. The squadron had their C.O., plus Wg Cdr Wilson, Sq Ldr Watts, Fg Offs Clerk, Dean McKenzie and Roger, plus W/O Wilkes, type qualified, and another twenty-four pilots were converted by 27 July when No.

616 flew its first mission. Changing to turbojet aircraft did not prove to be as difficult as the crews had originally anticipated, and the faster, smoother performance was quickly mastered. It was the tricycle undercarriage that took longer to get acquainted with, especially on landing; but not having to weave in order to see ahead when taxiing, as they did on the Spitfire, was much appreciated.

The squadron received a total of seventeen F.1s, of which at least two were replacements for accident-damaged aircraft, and their prime role was the interception of the Fiesler-designed FZG

De Havilland DH100 Vampire F.1

Dimensions:	Span 40ft 0in (12.19m)
	Length 30ft 9in (9.37m)
	Height 8ft 10in (2.68m)
	Wing area 261sq ft (24.24sq m)
Armament:	Four 20mm Hispano cannon with total of 624 rounds
Powerplant:	One de Havilland H-1 Goblin 1 turbojet producing 2,700lb (1,224kg) thrust
Weights:	Empty 6,372lb (2,889.7kg); loaded 10,480lb (4,752.6kg)
Performance:	Maximum speed 540mph (869km/h)
	Service ceiling 40,000ft (12,192m)

The fifth production de Havilland Vampire F.1 TG278, on a maker's test with John Derry at the controls. For some reason, early Vampire F.1 serials had an oblique line between the letters and numerals, a fact that has never been successfully explained. In May 1947, TG278 was modified to be the testbed for de Havilland's Ghost turbojet engine, and it established a world altitude record of 59,446ft (18,119m) on 23 March 1948. *Aeroplane Monthly*.

76 flying bomb, colloquially known as the V-1, from the German *Vergeltungswaffe* (reprisal weapon). The first of these had devastated Grove Road, Bethnall Green in London's East End on 12 June 1944, killing six people. With a speed of around 400mph (644km/h) at 10,000ft (305m), they were proving difficult to catch, with only the RAF's top-performance operational piston-engined fighter, the Hawker Tempest Mk V, being successful. These anti-V-1 sorties were code-named *Divers* by the RAF, and No. 616's first mission, on 27 July, was flown by Fg Offs Dean and McKenzie, with W/O Watts, in a three-aircraft flight. Only Watts saw a V-1, and although he caught up with the flying bomb quite easily over Ashford, armament malfunction prevented a successful conclusion to the interception. It was not until 4 August that the squadron's account was opened when Fg Off 'Dixie' Dean, flying EE216, easily caught up with a V-1 over Tunbridge Wells – but he suffered cannon jamming, too. However, determined to get his 'kill', Dean pulled alongside the flying bomb and, placing a wing-tip under the FZG 76's wing, made a quick banking manoeuvre, in so doing tipping the V-1 sideways into an uncontrolled dive, into forestry land near Tonbridge. On the same 'Diver', Fg Off Roger had more success with his armament and sent another V-1 down before it could reach its intended London target.

A succession of pairs of aircraft was airborne throughout the daylight hours, one lot being relieved every forty-five minutes by two other Meteors held in readiness at Manston; thus an effective patrol system was established, and a total of thirteen flying bombs was destroyed by the squadron before Allied land forces had captured all the launching sites in the Pas de Calais area of France.

The deployment of Willy Messerschmitt's Me 163 and Me 262 against USAAF formations in August 1944 was quickly seen as a serious threat, which influenced the American hierarchy in its palatial Daws Hill Lodge headquarters to ask the Air Ministry to assist them in drawing up new tactics to employ against these new German fighters. At the end of September it was decided that, in order for the B-17 and B-24 crews, as well as their escorting fighters, to gain some experience of operating against jet fighters, a series of tactical trials would be conducted during the following month. The former RAF airfield at Debden in Essex had been 'semi-Americanized' when it was the home base of No. 71 'Eagle' Squadron, and in September 1942 it had received the other two RAF 'Eagle' squadrons, Nos. 121 and 133. On 29 September of that year, the base was officially transferred to the USAAF as Station 356, headquarters of No. 65 Fighter Wing, with the three former 'Eagle' squadrons being renumbered 334, 335 and 336 Fighter Squadrons, thereby forming No. 4 Fighter Group.

Early in October 1944, Wg Cdr Andrew McDowall flew to Debden to meet the commanding officer of No. 4 F.G., Col Donald J.M. Blakeslee, for a preliminary discussion, and on 9 October, four Meteor F.1s were flown into the US fighter base, followed by transport aircraft carrying their groundcrews, and also spares. A week-long tactical exercise started the next day, with four box-formations of B-17s and B-24s assembled with their No. 4 F.G. P-51 escorts, accompanied by some P-47 fighter squadrons, over Cambridgeshire. Flying on south-easterly, then north-westerly legs, the bomber formations were attacked by the Meteors which employed hit-and-run tactics to which the American forces had

Bell P-59A Airacomet

Dimension:	Span 45ft 6in (13.87m)
	Length 38ft 1in (11.6m)
	Height 12ft 0in (3.66m)
	Wing area 385.8sq ft (35.84sq m)
Armament:	One 37mm M4 cannon and three 0.50in (12.7mm) machine guns
Powerplant:	Two General Electric J31-GE-3 turbojets each producing 2,000lb (907kg) thrust
Weights:	Empty 8,165lb (3,704kg); loaded 13,700lb (6,214kg)
Performance:	Maximum speed 409mph at 35,000ft (658km/h at 10,670m)
	Service ceiling 46,200ft (14,080m)

The P-59A was evaluated by 412th Fighter Group, USAAF, in 1944, who found that it had an inadequate performance, and was an indifferent gun platform. The aircraft was put into limited production for training purposes.

422609, one of the twenty Bell P-59A Airacomets produced, flying in formation with a P-63A 'Kingcobra', Bell's last production piston-engined fighter. The P-59 was the company's last fixed-wing production aircraft, after which they started turning out helicopters, by the thousand. *Aeroplane Monthly.*

no answer. The escort leader was quoted as remarking that, although he saw the Meteors coming in across the top of the bombers, before he could turn into them, they were gone. But to every question there is an answer, and the piston-engined fighter crews found that the most effective procedure was for them to fly at least 5,000ft (1,524m) above the bombers, then to half-roll into a near-vertical dive in order to build up the speed necessary to catch the intercepting jets.

The ground personnel found the exercise beneficial because they had to maintain their aircraft under field conditions, a situation which would continue when the squadron started operating on the European mainland, early in 1945. Once the trials with the US Eighth AAF were finished, the detachment returned to Manston and in December started taking delivery of Meteor F.3s. As has already been stated, of the twenty F.1s built, seventeen were issued to No. 616 at one time or another; and one of them, EE227 – given the squadron letters YQ:Y – went to RAE Farnborough in December 1944, to contribute to the ongoing trials to cure the Meteor's tendency for directional instability. The fin and rudder area above the tail-plane was deleted, making the aircraft the only Meteor ever to have a T-tail configuration; however, the modification did nothing for the object of the trials. In February, EE227 left Farnborough and went to Rolls-Royce's Hucknall facility, to be modified into the Trent turboprop engine testbed (this will be covered in another chapter).

Reheat Trials

The sixth production F.1 EE215 was the first aircraft fitted with the four 20mm Hispano cannon armament, and it was used for gun-firing trials conducted by the A&AEE. Having completed these, the aircraft was passed to Farnborough where its W2B/23C Welland engines were converted for testing a Power Jets-developed reheat system. The installation consisted of a flame-tube fitted at the end of the engine's turbine fairing, with a spark-plug to give ignition to the pilot flame. A ring with twelve holes drilled in it was installed at the end of the engine's jet pipe and fuel was sprayed through the holes as a fine atomized mist; this was drawn into the flame-tube and ignited by the pilot flame, to burn in the jet pipe until either the system was turned off or it ran out of fuel.

With the reheat fitted on the starboard engine only, 11.5 hours of flying were accomplished; however, weld failures were encountered, due to vibration when the system was switched on. This problem was resolved by fitting a steel liner within the first 18in (45.7cm) of the jet pipe. Further flight-testing was started at the end of 1944, and by 2 February 1945, both engines were fitted with reheat units. It was felt that an observer would be necessary to monitor the flight trials fully, so the armament, plus the mechanism fitted in the ammunition bay, was taken out so that an additional seat could be installed. The observer was able to obtain data in the form of instrument readings, and to interpret certain reheat operating characteristics while in flight, so that the appropriate action could be taken at once. This kept the number of flights to a minimum, and out of a total of thirty sorties, only two failed to produce data – and one of these was because adverse weather conditions forced abandonment of the flight.

In a summary by the Principal Director of Scientific Research (Air) at the Ministry of Supply, dated April 1945, it was stated that effective operation of the reheat was obtained up to 13,000ft (3,962m), but that above that height, the reheat burning became unstable. It was estimated that in flight, as compared with aircraft fitted with standard engines, the reheat improved net thrust per engine by 23 per cent and increased the level speed performance of the aircraft by 46mph (74km/h). The rate of climb from ground level was increased by 40 per cent, for an increase in gross fuel consumption of 65 per cent. The system was very reliable in its operation and there was no evidence of deterioration of the engine when reheat was used.

Further trials and modifications were made at Bruntingthorpe throughout 1945, and W2/700 engines were modified to test the system, which was being progressively improved. However, by 15 January 1946 results were depreciating, and when an engine was removed on 21 January it was found to have deteriorated so badly that replacements had to be installed. Testing resumed on 14 May, and on 20 December the final series of trials was started, these being concluded on 7 May 1947. The net result of the whole series was a gain in airspeed of 50mph (80.4km/h) at 5,000ft (1,524m), and 68mph (109km/h) at 25,000ft (7,620m); also an increase of 46 per cent in rate of climb and 25 per cent in take-off performance was obtained. EE215 does not appear to have been used for any further testing after 7 May and it was struck off charge on 29 November 1947. Sadly, not one of the twenty Meteor F.1s built exists today.

Lockheed P-80A Shooting Star

Dimensions:	Span 39ft 11in (12.17m)
	Length 34ft 6in (10.52m)
	Height 11ft 4in (3.45m)
	Wing area 238sq ft (22.11sq m)
Armament:	Six 0.50in (12.7mm) machine guns
Powerplant:	One General Electric J33-A-11 turbojet producing 4,000lb (1,814kg) thrust
Weights:	Empty 7,920lb (3,592kg); loaded 14,500lb (6,577kg)
Performance:	Maximum speed 558mph (898km/h)
	Service ceiling 45,000ft (13,715m)

The production of 240 examples of this version was not started until 1946.

A Lockheed P-80A Shooting Star photographed after 18 September 1947 when, for the first time in its history, America had an independent Air Force. On 8 November 1950, an F-80C shot down a Chinese MiG-15 over Korea, in the first aerial combat between turbojet-powered fighters. *Aeroplane Monthly.*

Allied jet aircraft in production, August 1945

By the end of World War II, the Allies had four turbojet-powered aircraft in production, all of them for the fighter role, although the Meteor was the only one to see active service. The first production de Havilland Vampire F.1 made its maiden flight on 20 April 1945 and would join the Meteor in RAF service by March 1946.

The United States had benefited greatly from Britain's generous donations of engines and data, and the first production Bell P-59A Airacomet was accepted for evaluation by the USAAF in August 1944. The Lockheed Aircraft Corporation received a Halford H-1 engine in July 1943, and 143 days later had flown their prototype XP-80, which by August 1945 was in production as the P-80A Shooting Star.

CHAPTER SIX

Threes, Fours and Records

The F. Mk3

Gloster Aircraft received Contract No. 6/ACFT/1490/CB7(b) to manufacture 210 Meteor Mark 3 aircraft, as the F.3, in five sub-batches. Serial numbers EE230 to EE254, EE269 to EE318, EE331 to EE369, EE384 to EE429 and EE444 to EE493 inclusive were allocated to these, and the first, EE230, which acted as the Mark's prototype, made its first flight on 11 September 1944. This Mark, carrying the company Type G.41C designation, had several improvements over the previous F.1: the earlier sideways-hinging cockpit canopy was replaced by a sliding unit, with a shorter glazed portion aft; the internal fuel capacity had been increased from 300 gallons (1,365 litres) to 330 gallons (1,501 litres) by lengthening the tank; while slotted airbrakes were installed aft of the undercarriage mainwheel wells, on the upper and lower centre-section surfaces. The airframe had also been strengthened generally by about 20 per cent.

Rolls-Royce had only just got the W2B/37 Derwent 1 into production when the F.3 started coming off the Hucclecote line, so it was decided that the initial fifteen airframes, EE230 to EE244 inclusive from the first batch of twenty-five, would be fitted with W2B/23C Welland engines. Derwent-powered aircraft started with the sixteenth airframe, EE245, and as such they were known as G.41Ds; although a few of the Welland-powered aircraft were retro-fitted with Derwents, it is believed they retained their G.41C designation. Following makers' handling and proving flights, EE230 was used for ground cannon-firing trials at Boscombe Down, before being struck off charge on 31 May 1949. As a point of interest, when they were collecting aircraft from the manufacturer, Air Transport Auxiliary (ATA) pilots were warned to check in the aircraft's logbook as to which engines were fitted, because the power available from the Welland was about 25 per cent less than from the Derwent.

No. 616 Squadron received its first F.3, EE231, on 18 December 1944, and by 17 January 1945, when they moved from Manston to Colerne in Wiltshire, nearly all the F.1s had been replaced by the later Mark. The Air Ministry had selected Colerne as the first RAF Meteor station, and resident No. 504 Squadron AAF started to replace its Spitfire IXEs for F.3s on 10 April 1945, EE280 being the first. Four months later, in August 1945, the squadron lost its auxiliary status and was renumbered No. 245 Squadron. No. 74 Squadron returned from operating on the Continent and took its Spitfire LFXVIEs to Colerne on 16 May 1945, where they were promptly succeeded by Meteor F.3s. The Wiltshire base retained its association with the Meteor, either as an operator or Maintenance Unit (MU), for quite a few years.

By the beginning of 1945 the decision had been taken to operate the Meteor with the 2nd Tactical Air Force (2TAF) on the European mainland, as a form of 'throwing down the gauntlet' to the Me 262; it was hoped that the Luftwaffe would take up the challenge, and that a comparison could be made between the two jet fighters under combat conditions. In retrospect, the German aircraft was considerably faster and carried a heavier armament than the

No. 500 Squadron at West Malling with their F.3s, which started arriving in July 1948. EE339 had been used for test-flying by both Rolls-Royce and the NGTE, before starting squadron service. Author's collection

No. 124 Squadron, based at Molesworth, started receiving Meteor F.3s in August 1945; they put up a formation carrying their 'ON' squadron code, for this photograph taken from a Lancaster's rear entrance. On 1 April 1956, the squadron, having moved to Bentwaters, was disbanded and renumbered No. 56 Squadron; its US code, which had been carried since September 1939, was then applied to the F.3s. Author's collection.

Meteor, but its weakness lay in the unreliability of its Jumo turbojets. Junkers themselves considered the engine was forced into production by the RLM before it was really ready for operational service. In January, a flight of four No. 616 Meteors flew to Andrew's Field, five miles west of Braintree, in Essex, from where the 322nd Bomb Group of the US Ninth AAF operated four Martin B-26 Marauder squadrons. (One of their aircraft, B-26B 41-31773 *Flak Bait*, was the only aircraft of the Western Allies to complete over 200 bombing missions.) Following the short stay in Essex, the detachment flew to B 58 airfield at Melsbroek, to the north-west of Brussels, where they were flown over adjacent Allied airfields and gun positions in the hopes that their shape would come to be recognized. Aircraft recognition was never given enough priority by the Allied forces – I know, because I used to try to teach it – and I well remember a conversation with a B-24 gunner whose basic philosophy was 'If it's got four engines, it's one of ours. If it ain't, shoot!'

The winter of 1944/45 was particularly severe, and 616's aircraft were sprayed overall white as a camouflage for when they were on the snow-covered airfields, or engaged in low flying. All pilots operated under strict instructions not to fly over enemy territory, to obviate any chance of an aircraft falling into the wrong hands. On 31 March the rest of No. 616 Squadron joined the detachment at B 77/Gilze-Rijen in Holland, and the earlier embargo on over-flying German lines was discarded. The first offensive strike was made on 17 April against enemy convoys (by this time – on 13 April – the squadron had moved to B 91/Kluis, outside Nijmegen). On 20 April they went to B 109/Quackenbruck, thus landing on German soil for the first time, followed six days later by another move, much deeper into Germany, to B 152/Fassberg. There, Wg Cdr McDowell left the squadron, placing it in the competent hands of Wg Cdr W. Schrader DFC. On 3 May the squadron was on airfield B 158/Lubeck – and it was there five days later, on 8 May 1945, when the war in Europe ended and everyone was looking through the bottom of a beer glass, instead of a windscreen. The squadron remained at Lubeck (which had been captured by No. 2806 Squadron of the RAF Regiment on 5 May) as a component of the Allied occupation forces until it was disbanded on 30 August as an Auxiliary Air Force unit and immediately renumbered No. 263 Squadron of the Royal Air Force, following which it left Germany and went to Acklington. The other Meteor-operating auxiliary squadron, No. 504, joined 616 at Lubeck in July 1945, but as already stated, it too was disbanded and renumbered No. 245 Squadron.

Meteors were coming off the Gloster production lines at a steady rate, and the majority were flown to No. 39 MU at Colerne, before being allocated to particular squadrons. No. 124 at Molesworth in Huntingdonshire replaced its Spitfire HFIXEs with F.3s in August 1945, followed in October by No. 222 Squadron, also Molesworth-based. In February 1946, the third squadron at the Huntingdonshire airfield, No. 234, gave up its Spitfire IXs and received EE254, their first F.3. Five further squadrons received Meteor F.3s in 1946, the first being No. 56 at Bentwaters, Suffolk, in April; No. 56 had been operating Hawker Tempest Vs since June 1944. The Church Fenton airfield in Yorkshire was home to No. 257 Squadron, flying Hawker Typhoon IBs for over four years; it received F.3s in September, with No. 266 Squadron at Boxted in Essex also replacing the Typhoon IB in the same month. No. 1 Squadron, based at Tangmere airfield in Sussex – notable for its Battle of Britain associations – was flying Spitfire F.21s until

A fine and typical Charles E. Brown photograph taken in 1949, showing F.3 EE389 during the early flight-refuelling trials. Author's collection.

October, when they took delivery of their first Meteor. Also in October, Duxford in Cambridgeshire saw No. 91 Squadron give up its Griffon-engined Spitfire XXIs for Meteors, with one of the early ones being EE332, flown as DL:E. The next year, No. 91 was renumbered No. 92 Squadron and in 1950 its coding was changed from DL to 8L. No. 66 Squadron, also at Duxford, received F.3s in March 1947, replacing their Spitfire LF16Es, as did No. 63 Squadron at Thorney Island, Hampshire,

in April 1948. No. 500 Squadron, based at West Malling in Kent with Spitfire F.22s, was the last to receive F.3s, in July 1948.

Although the Meteor F.3 was in squadron service, it was appreciated that there were several areas requiring improvement, and lengthened nacelles, which had been proved by the RAE to reduce airflow turbulence in that area, were introduced on the last fifteen aircraft of the final production batch, starting with EE479. From the second batch, EE311 saw no RAF service, but went on charge to the Royal Canadian Air Force (RCAF) on 28 September 1945. Shipped to the Turbo Research Company, it was flown by the Test and Development Flight at Rockcliffe on a series of winterization trials. On 29 June 1946, the aircraft ran out of fuel during a flight and ditched in Helen Bay Lake, one of the thousands of inland stretches of water in the state of Ontario. Six weeks later it was salvaged, but consigned to the scrapyard.

Another Meteor F.3 to go abroad was EE395, from the fourth production batch. In November 1945 the aircraft was loaned to New Zealand for a demonstration tour, and under the tutorage of Sqn Ldr McKay of the Royal New Zealand Air Force

EE590, an early production F.4 used by the Central Gunnery School, photographed after flying to France in November 1946. Author's collection.

EE311, the production F.3 seen here during its winterization trials at Rockcliffe in Canada, at the end of 1945. In June 1946 it had to be fished out of an Ontario lake. Author's collection.

(RNZAF), fifty-six pilots converted to turbojet flying in a total of 240 flying hours. On 15 March 1950 the Meteor was sold to the RNZAF and renumbered NZ6001. A decade later, in 1961, it became a ground instructional airframe at Hobsonville, having been renumbered once more, to INST 147. The aircraft is the oldest production Meteor known to still exist, as it now preserved at the RNZAF Museum in Auckland.

Following the deck-handling trials with DG202/G on HMS *Pretoria Castle*, two production F.3s, EE337 and EE387 from the third production batch, were modified at Hucclecote to a Royal Navy (RN) operational standard. New Rolls-Royce Derwent 5 engines, giving 3,500lb (1,587kg) thrust, replaced the standard Derwent 1s, although the short nacelles were retained. Equipment not required for RN operations was removed and new, stronger undercarriages fitted, with the mainwheel doors being deleted in order to obviate their catching on the deck arrester wires; also an 'A'-frame arrester hook was

fitted on each aircraft, as were modified brake airbags. The two aircraft were resprayed Silver overall, and were used by the A&AEE for a programme of simulated deck landings: from Boscombe Down they began a series of preliminary carrier deck landings on HMS *Illustrious*, followed in the spring of 1948 by over thirty proper landings on HMS *Implacable*. The trials went well and the RN was satisfied with their results. Whilst with the Senior Service, the aircraft were resprayed in the then-current Dark Slate/ Grey/Sea Green naval markings, and photographic evidence exists of EE337 being operated by the Royal Naval Air Station (RNAS) at Ford in Sussex, with the station's 'FD' on the fin, coded 051.

Rolls-Royce had the first B41 engine, later named 'Nene', bench-running in November 1944, when it was producing well over 4,000lb (1,814kg) thrust and showed promise of developing 5,000lb (2,267kg). This sort of thrust interested Gloster Aircraft, but with an overall diameter 13.5in (34.3cm) greater than the

Derwent 1, there was no chance of it being used as a Meteor powerplant without a major redesign of the aircraft. Rolls-Royce's engineering management proposed that the company should produce a scaled-down version, and it is a tribute to their expertise that, within twenty-five weeks, they had the smaller engine passing a 100-hour Type Test at 3,000lb (1,360kg) thrust. By the middle of 1945 production commenced, with the engine designated the Derwent 5 and rated at 3,500lb (1,587kg).

The F. Mk4

From the third production batch, EE360 remained with Glosters and participated in the company's trials with longer nacelles, EE211 having been delivered to No. 2 School of Technical Training (2STT) at Cosford on 12 April 1946. Early in 1945, Eric Greenwood had succeeded John Grierson as Gloster's Chief Test Pilot, so it was he who first flew EE360, on 17 May,

Into the Record Books

Ever since 26 April 1939, the World's Absolute Air Speed Record had stood at the 469.22mph (754.97km/h) achieved by Fritz Wendel in a one-off Messerschmitt Bf209V1, over Augsburg.

Gloster's General Manager, Frank McKenna, contacted Air Marshall Sir Ralph Sorley, Controller of Research and Development within the MAP, to obtain official approval for such an attempt. The Ministry, Gloster Aircraft and Rolls-Royce together formed the High Speed Committee, who elected that the pilots should be Eric Greenwood and Gp Capt Hugh Wilson AFC, Commanding Officer of the Empire Test Pilots' School (ETPS) at Boscombe Down (Hugh Wilson had gone with Andrew McDowell and the first No. 616 pilots, for Meteor conversion at Farnborough in July 1944). Two airframes, EE454 and EE455, were taken from the final batch of the Mark 3 production line to be fitted with Derwent 5 engines. All armament, plus other military equipment including the wireless, was removed, and the cannon ports sealed off. EE360 was to be used as the back-up aircraft and the whole team would operate from Manston. A highly polished gloss finish was applied to the two participating aircraft: in the case of EE454, given the name 'Britannia', this was over the standard service camouflage; and EE455 was resprayed an overall yellow, and a large Union Jack flag painted near to the nose. On the forward fuselage the legend 'Gloster Meteor IV', with 'Rolls-Royce Derwent engines' underneath and smaller, was inscribed in a style with which no self-respecting first-year art student would ever wish to be associated – in my opinion it rated with the Ford Cortina's 'go-faster' stripes and must have been an embarrassment to the pilot, Eric Greenwood. Gp Capt Wilson was to fly EE454 Britannia, and a 1.86-mile (3km) course was selected over Herne Bay, off Whitstable on the North coast of Kent. With a 4-mile (6.5km) turning circle at each end of the speed course, the whole circuit was about 33 miles (53km) in length and the *Federation Aeronautique Internationale* (FAI) height of 246ft (75m) had to be maintained over the course, in order for the attempt to be credited for the record.

On Wednesday 7 November 1945, Wilson took off from Manston to set a new record of 606.675mph (975.675km/h) in EE454 *Britannia*, with Greenwood flying EE455 later in

the day, and achieving 603.125mph (970.609km/h). The new record was ratified by the FAI – but Britain was not alone in wanting to hold the record. As was to be expected, the United States was in the vanguard of ambitions to raise it further, with the Lockheed P-80 'Shooting Star' being its contender. Therefore the Air Ministry proposed that the pre-war RAF High Speed Flight

(HSF) should be officially resurrected with effect from 14 June 1946, operating from Tangmere. Gp Capt (later Air Cdre) E.M. Donaldson was named Commanding Officer of the Flight, together with two highly experienced RAF officers, Sqn Ldrs Neville Duke DSO, DFC and W.A. 'Bill' Waterton AFC; both would become respected elements of British aviation history.

Group Captain H.J. Wilson, AFC, who gained the world speed record on 7 November 1945, and the Royal Aero Club's certificate proclaiming the event; the record was obtained in an F.3 airframe fitted with Derwent 5 engines, so qualifying for the 'Meteor IV' entered on the certificate. Derek N. James and Author's collection.

EE454, the long-nacelled F.3 which was Gp Capt Wilson's record-breaking aircraft, shown before the name 'Britannia' had been painted on its nose. Derek N. James.

The two aircraft employed for the 1945 record attempt, with Eric Greenwood's gaudily finished EE455 in the foreground, taken at Manston. Author's collection.

THE ROYAL AERO CLUB
OF THE UNITED KINGDOM

CERTIFICATE OF PERFORMANCE
(UNDER THE COMPETITION RULES OF THE ROYAL AERO CLUB)

Type: Gloster "Meteor" IV
Constructor: Gloster Aircraft Co. Ltd.
Engines: 2 Rolls-Royce "Derwent" V

Pilot: Eric Greenwood

Place: Herne Bay, Kent
Date: 7th November, 1945.

Performance.
Speed: 603·125 m.p.h.

A reproduction of Eric Greenwood's certificate recording his endeavours in the yellow EE455 on 7 November 1945. Author's collection.

The RAF's High Speed Flight of true Meteor F.4s, set up for the 1946 record attempt, both being fitted with reinforced metal hoods. EE549, in which Gp Capt Donaldson attained the new record, receives some attention at Tangmere, while Bill Waterton taxies EE550 for his later attempt. Author's collection.

Six airframes fitted with Derwent 5 engines were allocated to the Flight, all from the newly established Meteor F Mark 4 production line, their serials being EE527, EE529, EE530, EE548, EE549 and EE550. The last two aircraft were selected for the actual record attempt and they would feature a reduced wingspan which later would be introduced to the production line and fitted on many later Marks. EE548 was to be held as a reserve, and the other three aircraft employed for preliminary flying, working up to the record attempt. As the flight was established at Tangmere, a new 1.86 mile (3km) record course adjacent to the airfield, was laid out off the Sussex coast, between the resorts of Angmering-on-Sea and Rustington-on-Sea. The preparation of the aircraft was similar to that for the earlier record flights, with all unnecessary military equipment being removed, and gun-ports and structural joints being sealed, prior to receiving an overall gloss finish. An additional 69 gallons (320 litres) of fuel was carried in three tanks fitted in the ammunition bay, while 1,000lb (453.5kg) of ballast was located in the front fuselage. The standard cockpit hood on both EE549 and EE550 were supplanted by reinforced metal hoods, with two port-holes on each side. Someone in authority had the good taste not to repeat the previous all-yellow finish and

The robust figure of Sqn Ldr W.A. 'Bill' Waterton prepares to enter his office. A development test pilot when he joined Gloster Aircraft in 1946, he became Chief Test Pilot following Eric Greenwood's retirement in 1947. Derek N. James.

attempt was ratified by the FAI as 615.78mph (990.97km/h). Then at 18.11 hours, Waterton took off in EE550, and his official average speed was recorded as 614mph (988km/h); so Gp Capt Donaldson was credited with a new Absolute World Air Speed Record, flown in EE549. Possibly because this record speed can be rounded off to 616mph (991.3km/h) and 616 was the number of the first established Meteor squadron, sentimentality seems to have taken over and the record is often quoted as 616mph (991.3km/h). But it is wrong!

Further flights were made by the HSF, but not under official conditions; besides, no higher figures were obtained, and on 26 September the High Speed Flight was officially disbanded. On 16 January 1947 Bill Waterton flew EE549 from Le Bourget outside Paris, to Croydon, south of London, taking 20min 11sec for the 208 miles (334.7km), giving him a new record speed of 618.4mph (995.19km/h) for the London–Paris flight. After spending a period with the Central Fighter Establishment (CFE) at West Raynham, Norfolk, the aircraft moved around: for a while in the mid-fifties it was at Cranwell, when it carried the instructional airframe number 7008M; six years were spent on display at Innsworth; and a further nine years, from 1971 to 1980, at the RAF Museum at Hendon, who are now the aircraft's owners. In September 1981 it went on display at St Athan where it remained until 1989; then it was transferred to the Aerospace Museum at Cosford. Finally on 19 September 1992, EE549 made one last move, this time to the airfield from where it made history: the Tangmere Military Aviation Museum Trust (TMAM) occupies a newly erected aircraft exhibition hangar on the historic airfield, and the Meteor stands beside the record-breaking Hunter 3 WB188. Sqn Ldr Neville Duke DSO, DFC is the president of the TMAM. Incidently, Duke's 727.6mph (1,170.9km/h) record in the Hunter was made on 7 September 1953, exactly seven years to the day after Donaldson's record flight in EE549. EE550 joined No. 615 Squadron at Biggin Hill in 1950 and was written off on 6 January 1951.

amateur lettering artists were kept well away from Sussex!

A period of two months was allowed for the Flight to work up, during which both Neville Duke and Bill Waterton exceeded 620mph (997km/h) on several occasions. On 8 August, the two aircraft prepared for the record attempt were officially issued to the RAF High Speed Flight and arrived at Tangmere. Saturday 7 September 1946 was chosen as the date for the record attempt, with

Donaldson electing to pilot EE549 and Waterton to fly EE550. Neville Duke had the consolation of demonstrating a Meteor to Czechoslovakian officials in Prague on that day, for which he received the Czech Military Cross. The weather off the Sussex coast was none too good for record-breaking, and it was not until 17.45 hours that Donaldson took off for his attempt. By 18.00 hours he was back at Tangmere, having flown five runs over the course, one of them at 624mph (1,004km/h). The average speed for his record

after the Derwent 5s had been installed. Enthusiasm was widespread within the company as a result of Greenwood's finding the new combination faster than had been anticipated. The RAF too, was keen to accept this as the next operational Meteor – and Gloster saw nothing but

good in the proposal to use the type for an attempt at the air speed record.

The new Derwent 5, together with the aerodynamic improvements made to the F.3 and the extensive airframe strengthening made to the record-breaking aircraft, demonstrated the

Meteor's true potential as a fighter, and were the catalysts to the production of the F. Mark 4, given the type number G.41F. Furthermore the F.4 was to be fully tropicalized and pressurized so that it might be able to perform above its operational ceiling.

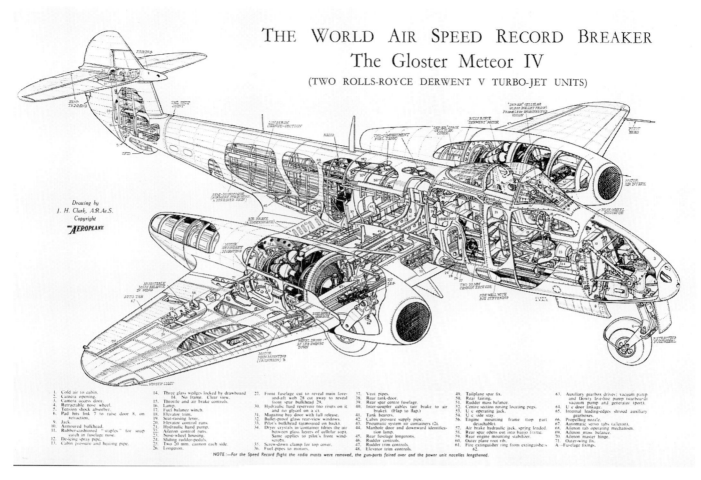

THE WORLD AIR SPEED RECORD BREAKER
The Gloster Meteor IV
(TWO ROLLS-ROYCE DERWENT V TURBO-JET UNITS)

Drawing by
J. H. Clark, A.R.Ae.S.
Copyright
Aeroplane

J.H.Clark's cut-away, drawn for *Aeroplane* at the time of the 1945 record. *Aeroplane Monthly.*

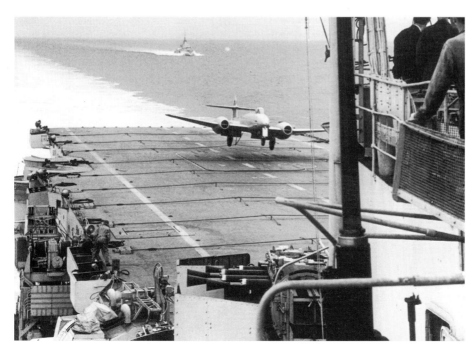

EE387, with Derwent 5s in short nacelles, was one of two F.3s fitted with 'A'-frame hooks; it is seen here catching the third arrester wire on HMS *Implacable*, during the trials in 1948. Derek N. James.

Gloster Aircraft received Contract No. 6/ACFT/SB1490/CB7(b) for the production of 170 aircraft in five batches, with the serials EE517 to EE554, EE568 to EE599, RA365 to RA398, RA413 to RA457 and RA473 to RA493 inclusive. This was followed by Contract No. 6/ACFT/658/CB7(b), dated 22 November 1946, covering the manufacture of another 210 aircraft, also in five batches, with the serials VT102 to VT150, VT168 to VT199, VT213 to VT247, VT256 to VT294 and VT303 to VT347 inclusive. A third Meteor F.4 contract, No. 6/ACFT/1389/CB7(b), dated 2 August 1947, was agreed for the building of a further sixty-one aircraft in two batches, with serials VW255 to VW315 for the first batch, and VW780 to VW791 inclusive for the second. And for the first time, Meteor production went outside Gloucestershire: fellow Hawker-Siddeley Group member Sir W.G. Armstrong Whitworth Aircraft Limited, at Baginton outside Coventry, who had been making various Meteor components for some time, was given two contracts to produce complete F.4s. The first was Contract No. 6/ACFT/1389/CB7(b), an extension of Gloster's third contract, covering forty-six aircraft with serials VZ386 to VZ429 inclusive; the second was Contract No. 6/ACFT/2430/CB7(b) and covered two aircraft, VZ436 and VZ437. The F.4 was also the first Mark of Meteor to be built for export, with aircraft being supplied to Argentina, Belgium, Denmark, Egypt and the Netherlands.

The first production Meteor F.4, EE517, made its maiden flight on 12 April 1946 and this, together with the next six aircraft, was used by various establishments, although EE518 was lost before being delivered, on 9 May, when it disintegrated at high speed over TFU's airfield at Defford, killing Gloster's chief production test pilot, Llewellin Moss. The Meteor's riveted box-structure centre-section was vulnerable to rivet failure, and this induced transfer loads onto the next set of rivets, which in turn could not cope. In this case it caused a rapid forward movement of the centre of pressure, which created a pitch-up that shed both wings. It quickly became evident that, although the airframe had been strengthened compared with earlier Marks, it was still suspect when it came to handling the greatly increased operating speeds. Mr J. Cuss, senior stressman at Gloster's, undertook considerable research in the quest to cure the problem, and it was looking as if a major redesign of the wing

EE457, the F.3 test aircraft for long-chord nacelles, being flown here by Eric Greenwood. Author's collection.

would be necessary. In view of the delay that this would cause to deliveries, a compromise was sought and it was decided to remove 2ft 10in (86.3cm) from each wing-tip, as tests had shown that the majority of the stress was being absorbed by the wing structure. The cropping of the wings went a long way to solving the stress problem and gave the added benefit of improving the aircraft's rate of roll. The penalties were an increase in landing speed, together with a reduction in the rate of climb and service ceiling. With the shorter span, the modified F.4 carried the maker's type number G.41G.

Nearly fifty of the first production batch had come off the lines with the long wingspan and these were put into storage

EE545, an early production F.4 with long-span wings, which went to the Royal Naval air station at Bramcote in October 1953. It had the additional Royal Navy instructional airframe serial A2332, which was later changed to E3108 as shown here. It was scrapped two years later. Mike Hooks.

Two long-span F.4s of No. 263 Squadron tuck away their undercarriages nice and early as they climb out of RAF Acklinton. Derek N. James.

until their wings could be modified. A small number went to various establishments, and as far as can be gleaned from records, none of these aircraft went into RAF squadron service fitted with the original long-span wings. EE525, the first aircraft to have the modified wings (which gave it a span of 37ft 2in (11.3cm) compared with the 43ft 0in (13.1cm) of all previous Meteors), was retained by the manufacturer to undergo trials at the A&AEE, before going to No. 207 Advanced Flying School (AFS) at Full Sutton in Yorkshire; it was written off on 12 April 1954. In December 1947, Nos. 74, 245 and 263 Squadrons at Horsham St Faith in Norfolk (now Norwich airport) started receiving short-span Meteor F.4s, as did No. 222 Squadron at Tangmere, all four squadrons losing Meteor F.3s. Two months later, in February 1948, Horsham St Faith's other tenant, No. 257 Squadron, accepted its first F.4 to replace

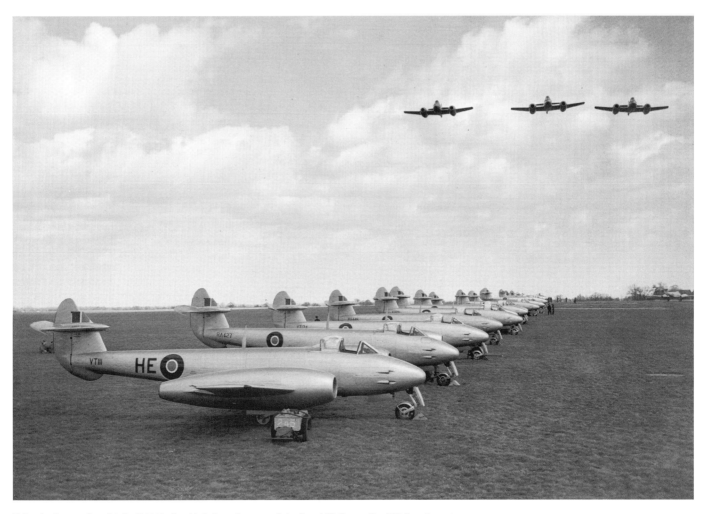

Taken in the morning of 1 April 1948, the thirtieth anniversary of the Royal Air Force, No. 263 Squadron at Horsham St Faith display their full complement of short-span F.4s. Author's collection.

their F.3s, and No. 266 Squadron at Tangmere followed suit in the same month.

The ex-Battle of Britain airfield of Duxford in Cambridgeshire, from where the 'Big Wing' operated in September/October 1940, had hosted Nos. 56 and 92 Squadrons with their Meteor F.3s since the spring of 1947. In May 1948, both replaced them with F.4s, while No. 1 Squadron at Tangmere, having flown Harvards and Oxfords for a year, took delivery of its short-span Meteors in June. The following month, one of Thorney Island's two units, No. 63 Squadron, started receiving F.4s, with the other one, No. 56 Squadron, being similarly equipped in September, both squadrons replacing their Meteor F.3s. By the end of 1948, eleven front-line RAF fighter squadrons were flying the Mark 4.

Gloster had recognized that there was a requirement for a two-seat Meteor early in 1947, and they commenced design work on a private-venture basis. In order to accomodate a second crewman in a conventional style – as opposed to simply squeezing an observer into the magazine bay, as was arranged in EE215 during its reheat trials! – a 30in (76.2cm) increase in fuselage length was proposed. The two-seat Meteor prototype was partly constructed from a previously damaged demonstrator, G-AIDC; being a private venture, it carried the civil registration

No. 222 Squadron received RA481 at Tangmere, early in 1948, but it was written off in July 1949 when the squadron was at Thorney Island. Aeroplane Monthly.

G-AKPK when it made its first flight on 19 March 1948. To everyone's surprise it was found that the directional instability that had dogged the Meteor since day one and that had never been completely eradicated, had virtually disappeared.

In order to discover if this betterment would apply to the single-seat Meteor, the aircraft RA382, from the third batch of the first Mark 4 production contract, was modified to have a 30in (76.2cm) plug inserted in the fuselage, just behind the cockpit. The improvement was so marked that the decision was made to introduce the longer fuselage – which as a bonus provided the space for an additional 95-gallon (432-litre) fuel tank – into all future single-seat Meteors. The first would be the F. Mark 8, which will be featured in a later chapter. Some references have stated that the modification was introduced into F.4 production, but this has never been substantiated.

Deliveries of the Meteor F.4 continued in 1949, No. 43 Squadron becoming Tangmere's fourth when the new aircraft started to arrive in February, replacing Spitfire VIIIs, while No. 504 (County of Nottingham) Squadron at Wymswold in Leicestershire – which in 1948 had its Meteor F.3s replaced by Spitfire F22s – received its first F.4 in October. Four more Meteor F.4 squadrons were formed in 1950: the first was No. 600 (City of London) Squadron at Biggin Hill, which had been flying Spitfire F.22s for eighteen months prior to that; then fellow Biggin Hill tenant, No. 615 (County of Surrey) Squadron, also with the Spitfire F.22 on charge, received its first F.4s in September, while in December 1950 ATA pilots deliv-

A busy scene, showing F.4 RA440 HI-H of No. 66 Squadron with two anonymous F.4s on one side and a pair of Vampire FB.5s on the other. Miscellaneous Meteors are dotted around, together with a couple of Wellington T.10s and a Mosquito NF.XIII. Author's collection.

ered Meteor F.4s to the Yorkshire base of Linton-on-Ouse, home to Nos. 64 and 65 Squadrons, which had been operating de Havilland Hornet F.3s since the spring of 1948. In January 1951 the squadrons based at Church Fenton, another Yorkshire airfield – Nos.19, 41 and 609 (City of Glasgow) Squadrons – gave up their Vampire FB.5s, in the case of No. 609, and Hornet F.3s for the others, so as to commence operating with Meteor F.3s. Two months later, in March, No. 611 (West Lancashire) Squadron, based at Woodvale in Lancashire, replaced Spitfire F.22s with Meteor F.4s, and the original Meteor F.1 operator, No. 616 Squadron, having been reformed at Finningley in 1946, took Meteor F.4s to replace F.3s. The last two F.4-operating squadrons – No. 500 based at West Malling in Kent with Meteor F.3s, and No. 610 (County of Chester) Squadron at Hooton Park, flying Spitfire F.22s – received their new aircraft in July, so that by the summer of 1951 twenty-four front-line squadrons had been issued with the Meteor F. Mark 4, as had another seven units, such as Advanced Flying Schools (AFS) and Flying Training Schools (FTS). Many of the squadrons became elements of the British Air Force of Occupation (BAFO) over the years and supplied detachments to operate from former Luftwaffe bases.

Sir W.G. Armstrong Whitworth Aircraft (AWA) had been supplying components to Gloster Aircraft's production lines for some time, and their undertaking to build forty F.4s started a long association between the company and the Meteor. VZ389, the fourth aircraft to come off the Baginton line, was heavily involved in tests to perfect the flight refuelling system; these were conducted by the Alan Cobham-founded company known as Flight Refuelling Limited, based at Tarrant Rushton in Dorset. Eventually AWA would take over Meteor development and production completely, leaving Gloster free to concentrate on their massive Javelin night fighter.

With 489 Meteor F. Mark 4 aircraft produced for RAF service, plus a considerable number built for export, it is quite understandable that many were used to enhance the type's operational performance even further. EE519 tested underwing rocket projectiles and 1,000lb (453.5kg) bomb installations, while in 1948 EE578 was employed by Gloster to test-fly various wing extensions, with a

Meteor F.4s VT114 FX-X of No. 266 Squadron and RA481 ZD-T of No. 222 Squadron, together with an anonymous F.4 in the foreground, photographed in April 1948. Author's collection.

This photograph shows No. 63 Squadron's F.4s at Thorney Island in 1950, displaying their yellow/black check colours to advantage; it is particularly interesting in that the Armstrong Whitworth Apollo prototype G-AIYN has paid the base a visit. Author's collection.

view to producing a truly high-altitude Meteor; these plans were abandoned, however. RA421 went by sea and rail to the Royal Canadian Air Force (RCAF) Winter Experimental Establishment at

Edmonton, Alberta, arriving on 14 October 1947. During transit, damage was sustained to the front fuselage, and a considerable quantity of coal, soot and grit penetrated the airframe during the rail journey from the docks, which necessitated a very thorough cleansing of the whole airframe interior. Flying commenced on 10 November 1947, and in a total flight-time of 5 hours 40 minutes taken over the following ten days, seven landings were made on an ice-covered runway. Particular note was taken of the aircraft's behaviour in the landings, with notes being made regarding skidding and brake segment condition. An average landing with an approach speed of 126.5mph (203.5km/h), a wind speed of 18mph (28.96km/h) and with a touch-down of 325ft (99m) achieved a total run length of 3,743ft (1,140.8m). Brake segments inspected afterwards were found to be unaffected.

Additional testing was made 850 miles (1,368km) further north, at Watson Lake in the Yukon. Before making the flight north, RA421's outer wings and tail-plane were sprayed yellow in accordance with the

A crowded Horsham St Faith tarmac, as an F.4 of No. 257 'Burmese' Squadron is manoeuvred by manpower, with the two aircraft on the right displaying the unit's emblem of a Burmese Chinthe on their noses. *Author's collection.*

Meteor F.4s of No. 203 AFS based at Driffield, fly against a dramatic cloud formation in the summer of 1951. VT309 FMJ-A served with No. 63 Squadron and was a Waterbeach Station Flight aircraft, before going to Driffield. Author's collection.

VZ429 LJ-Q of No. 600 (City of London) Squadron touches down. This was the third to last F.4 built, and it went to No. 205 AFS when the Biggin Hill squadron started receiving F.8s in 1952. *Aeroplane Monthly.*

regulations that governed aircraft operating within the Artic Circle. The destination landing was in a valley 2,245ft (684.2m) above sea level and surrounded by the Rocky Mountains, but the aircraft made a perfect first-time touch-down, with a considerable length of runway to spare. In daily temperatures averaging –20 degrees centigrade, cannon-firing tests were carried out, both on the ground and in the air. No stoppages of any kind occurred and in engine run-ups conducted during heavy snowfalls the Derwent 5s lit up instantly. Most of the flying was carried out at 30,000ft (9,144m), with an outside air temperature of –50 degrees centigrade. The aircraft eventually returned to Britain and was used by RAE Farnborough for the development of the later Meteor drones.

Britain had an undisputed lead in turbojet propulsion in the mid-1940s, and the Gloster Sales Department realized that there was great potential for selling the Meteor abroad. The company took an

Gloster Aircraft's beautifully finished Meteor Mark 4 demonstrator G-AIDC, which executed demonstration flights on the European mainland before its landing accident at Melsbroek in May 1947. Author's collection.

early standard Mark 4 that had come in for overhaul and converted it into a very potent demonstration aircraft. All arma-ment was removed and a 180-gallon (819-litre) ventral fuel tank was installed, as well as a pair of 100-gallon (455-litre) underwing tanks. The aircraft was finished in a striking carmine red, with a thin white line running from lightning graphics on the nose to the tail, broken by the letter-ing 'GLOSTER METEOR MKIV ROLLS ROYCE DERWENT V ENGINES' and the civil registration G-AIDC. On 14 April 1947 the aircraft, piloted by Gloster test pilot Sq Ldr Digby Cotes-Preedy, left Moreton Valence to commence an exten-sive planned tour of European countries in order to stimulate sales, starting at Valkenburg in the Netherlands. This was to have been followed by demonstrations at Melsbroek and Kastrop, but these were cancelled at the last minute because of the death of the King of Denmark. Further displays held in Sweden and Norway were curtailed in favour of a return the follow-ing month to Melsbroek in Belgium (which had been airfield B 58 when the No. 616 Squadron detachment first landed on the European mainland in January 1945). There, an experienced Belgian Air Force pilot was flying the air-craft when the port mainwheel became partially extended while G-AIDC was fly-ing at well over 500mph (804.6km/h). The aircraft started a series of uncontrolled upward rolls, and this so weakened the oleo that, on touching down, the port leg collapsed. Damage sustained by the wing and tail-plane in the crash-landing was sufficient to put an end to the tour, and the wreckage was brought back to Moreton Valence; later it would be resurrected as Gloster's second private-venture Meteor, the prototype T. Mark 7 trainer G-AKPK.

The oldest known Meteor F. Mark 4 is EE531: built at Hucclecote, it is today on permanent display in the Midland Air Museum (MAM) at Baginton, repre-senting the Mark which was AWA's first production variant. It never saw squadron service because it was made with long-span wings and was one of those put into store. When it was modified to short-span config-uration it was retained by Gloster Aircraft for company trials programmes, and then it went to A&AEE Boscombe Down where, amongst other programmes, it was employed in folding wing experiments, aimed at possible Fleet Air Arm (FAA) use

A No. 245 Squadron pilot climbs aboard his F.4, which carries the squadron crest on its nose and a pair of Union flags on the upper cannon panel. Author's collection.

On August 22, 1949 a goodwill air display was made by eight F.4s of No66 Squadron, at Stockholm's Barkarby airbase, which the official news agency says was 'greeted by a parade of military music, etc.' Author's collection.

(which did not materialize in that form). It was struck off charge on 25 August 1953, and was installed at Lasham as an ground-handling instructional airframe, with the number 7090M. Before long, its impor-tance was recognized and in 1973 it was rescued by the MAM. It stands in their Sir Frank Whittle Jet Heritage Centre, resplendent in gloss-finished camouflage, opposite the de Havilland Vampire F.1 No.

Meteor F.4 EE549, Group Captain Donaldson's record-breaking aircraft, which is currently in the Tangmere Military Aviation Museum, attracted interest when statically displayed at Abingdon's Battle of Britain Day in September 1980. Mike Hooks

The former *Reaper* G-7-1 was converted into the Meteor T.7 demonstrator G-ANSO in 1954 and was seen at Baginton in the late 1950s without its tip tanks, before eventually being sold to Sweden as SE-DCC. Mike Hooks

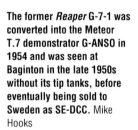

Photographed at Colerne in October 1975, Meteor F.4 VT229/60 carries the markings of No. 209 AFS, Weston Zoyland. Mike Hooks

Meteor T.7 WF791, photographed at Brize Norton in 1981, was part of the *Vintage Pair* before its airframe life expired and WA669 joined the popular air show act in October 1982 as its replacement. Author's Collection

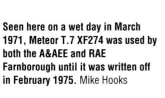

Seen here on a wet day in March 1971, Meteor T.7 XF274 was used by both the A&AEE and RAE Farnborough until it was written off in February 1975. Mike Hooks

On the strength of the IWM at Duxford, Meteor F.8 WK991 carried the markings of No. 56 Squadron when on display in April 1996. George Pennick

VW417, the seventh production Meteor T.7, was sold to the RNethAF as I-320, but was in a very sorry state in June 1969. Mike Hooks

Meteor NF.14 WS760/P of No. 1 Air Navigation School (ANS) Stradishall carried plenty of day-glo strips when seen at Coltishall in October 1964. George Pennick

Leuchars Station Flight's Meteor T.7 WA725/Y wore the markings of Nos. 43 and 151 Squadrons, as well as underside target-tower stripes, for Wethersfield's Battle of Britain Day in 1958. Mike Hooks

Stradishall Station Flight's Meteor T.7 WL459 was seen in the sunshine, alongside an NF.14, at the base in October 1959. George Pennick

Meteor F.8 WF654 served with Nos. 29, 56, 64 and 85 Squadrons, but was devoid of markings when seen here in August 1967. Mike Hooks

Meteor NF(T).14 WS774/D was present at Duxford in August 1960, carrying the markings of Thorney Island's No. 2 Air Navigation School. George Pennick

There was plenty of day-glo red present in September 1964, when Meteor T.7 WH166 joined a Varsity, Gnat and Meteor NF(T).14 on a Stradishall dispersal. George Pennick

In June 1971, Meteor NF(T).14 WS774/D was silver, with day-glo strips, possibly as displayed on the gate at the RAF Hospital, Ely. Mike Hooks

Typical of French electronics trials conversions was Meteor NF.11 NF11-5 of the Bretigny-based *Centre d'Essais en Vol* (CEV), which was photographed at the *Musée de l'Air et de l'Espace*, Le Bourget, in March 1990. NBS Aviation

Meteor NF(T).14 WS842/B had been flown by the All Weather Operational Conversion Unit (AWOCU) as an NF.14 before its conversion to a trainer. It flew with Nos. 1 and 2 ANS with the 'B' coding and was struck off charge in November 1967. Mike Hooks

No. 2 Air Navigation School had Meteor NF(T).14 WS788/C on charge at Thorney Island, with liberal amounts of day-glo orange when seen in 1960. Mike Hooks

Photographed in the late 1950s while serving with No. 264 Squadron, Meteor NF.14 WS810/B later served with No. 60 Squadron before ending up on the fire dump at Tengah in September 1961. Mike Hooks

Meteor F.8 WH301/T went for storage as 7930M in February 1967, but the number was never worn and in June of the same year the aircraft was brought out into the sunlight wearing No. 85 Squadron markings and lots of day-glo strips. It is currently on display at the RAF Museum, Hendon. Mike Hooks

Seen at Biggin Hill in May 1975, Meteor WD592/864 had served with Nos. 125, 141 and 264 Squadrons as an NF.11 before conversion to TT.20 standard for the Royal Navy, who flew it with No. 728 Squadron at Hal Far, Malta. In June 1975 it went across the Atlantic, to become N94749 with Al Letcher and Associates at Mojave. Mike Hooks

The Royal Navy operated Meteor T.7 WS116/935 in the Lossiemouth Station Flight, with a blue rudder, before the aircraft was scrapped in 1965. Mike Hooks

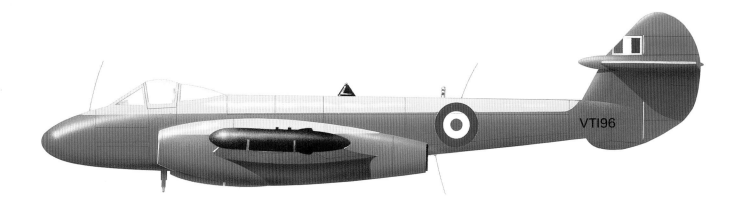

Meteor F.4 VT196 had a busy engine-testing career, starting with Rolls-Royce on Derwent 5 reheat in 1948 and then the Division of Mechanical Engineering in Ottawa, test-flying the Orenda reheat system in 1953. In 1959 it went to Flight Refuelling Limited (FRL) for conversion to U.15 drone standard as shown, operating with RAE Llanbedr where it flew the final U.15 sortie on 9 February 1963. Author's artwork

Basking in brilliant sunshine at Abingdon in June 1968, Meteor F.8 WH364/U carries the markings of No. 85 Squadron, having previously served with the Malta Communications and Target Towing (MC&TT) Squadron. It is currently stored at Kemble for the Gloucestershire Aviation Collection. Mike Hooks

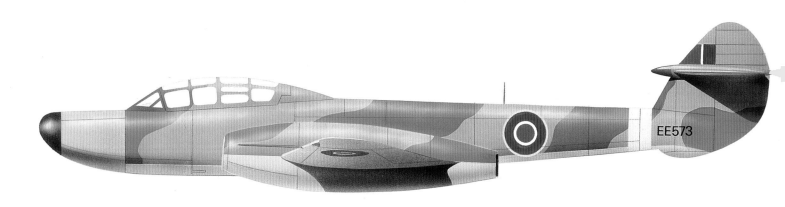

Meteor EE573 was built as an F.4 in the early 1950s, but was converted to T.7 standard to be operated by the Telecommunications Research Establishment (TRE) where it was fitted with various nose configurations. As shown, it was employed on guided weapon head trials and had an experimental tail 'wave-horn' installation, testing the detection of centrimetric AI transmissions to counter rear-end air attacks for the forthcoming V-bombers. The aircraft was finally scrapped in May 1958. Author's artwork

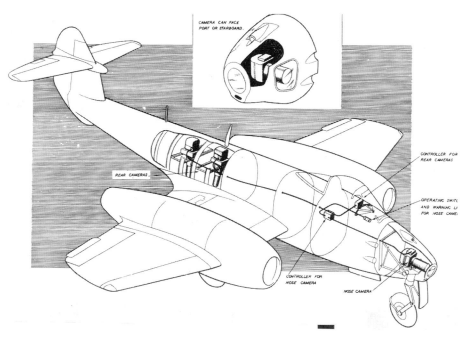

CAMERA CAN FACE
PORT OR STARBOARD.

CONTROLLER FOR
REAR CAMERAS

REAR CAMERAS

OPERATING SWITC
AND WARNING LI
FOR NOSE CAME

CONTROLLER FOR
NOSE CAMERA

NOSE CAMERA

Gloster Aircraft's *Technical Publications* drew this proposal for the Meteor FR.5, which became null and void with the disintegration of VT347. Author's collection.

VF301, and an example of America's first operational jet, 51-4419, a two-seat T-33A variant of Lockheed's P-80 Shooting Star.

The last aircraft from the fifth batch covered by Contract No. 6/ACFT/ 658/CB7(b), VT347, was taken off the production line to act as the prototype for the next Mark of Meteor. Tests made with nose-mounted cameras on F.3 EE338 and F.4 EE568 had not proved entirely effective due to icing forming on the camera windows, as well as problems with the camera mountings. However, the Air Ministry informed Gloster that there was an RAF requirement for a fighter-reconnaissance variant, which encouraged the company to put in hand the G.41H Meteor FR. Mark 5. Oblique and vertical cameras were installed in a modified nose-pack, which retained the standard armament and was designed to be a replacement/alternative nose-section for squadron F.4s. Two vertical cameras were also positioned in the fuselage, aft of the

An aerial view of Moreton Valence in the spring of 1951, with thirty-three Meteors of various Marks and finishes parked around the tarmac area. Derek N. James.

main fuel tank. The prototype was completed at the end of May 1949, and on 15 June, Rodney Dryland, who had been a production and development test pilot since joining Gloster Aircraft in 1946, took VT347 off from Moreton Valence for its maiden flight. During the flight, a high-g manoeuvre made over the airfield led to the failure of the centre-section tank-bay side skin; this caused the aircraft to disintegrate and Rodney Dryland was killed in the subsequent crash. This accident was very similar to the one that had killed Llewellin Moss, flying F.4 EE518 over Defford, on 9 May 1946. VT347's catastrophic break-up resulted in a certain amount of redesigning, and further strengthening modifications were introduced to production Meteors, but plans for manufacturing the FR.5 were discarded. However, the installation had provided useful information, and this was incorporated in the later design of the Meteor FR. Mark 9.

Before leaving the first five single-seat Meteor designs, mention must be made of the G.41J F. Mark 6, which had a slightly larger fuselage than previous Meteors. This type did not progress further than the design stage, and it was thought to have been drafted with swept wings; however, this has never been confirmed, and the only drawing to be released of the aircraft's general arrangement showed it to be substantially so similar to the F. Mark 8, that the latter could be considered a scaled-down G.41J, to standard Meteor size. By the time the design was on the drawing board, the revised tail unit of TX148, the second E.1/44, had been proven on this aircraft and was incorporated in the Mark 6's profile. With the slightly larger fuselage, internal fuel capacity was greater than previous production Meteors, but this was lost when the design was scaled down to produce the F. Mark 8.

The basic Meteor F.4 was flown at three SBAC displays. EE525 appeared in 1946, when the event was staged at Handley Page's Radlett airfield in Hertfordshire, and the same venue was used in 1947 when RA449 flew. In 1948 the SBAC display moved to the RAE airfield at Farnborough in Hampshire, where it has remained, and VT256 occupied a flying slot.

Meteor F. Mark 4	
Span:	37ft 2in (11.3m)
Length:	41ft 0in (12.49m)
Height:	13ft 0in (3.9m)
Wing area:	350sq ft (32.5sq m)
Weight empty:	11,217lb (5,088kg)
Weight loaded:	14, 545lb (6,597kg)
Max speed at 10,000ft (3,048m):	580mph (933km/h)
Climb to 30,000ft (9,144m):	6 minutes
Service ceiling:	44,500ft (13,563m)

CHAPTER SEVEN

A Meteor Built for Two

In 1947 Argentina purchased 100 Meteor F. Mark 4s, and a dozen pilots from the *Fuerza Aerea Argentina* (Argentine Air Force) were sent over in order to be type-converted at Moreton Valence. To do this, Gloster's test pilots had to give the Argentinian pilots ground-handling instructions by sitting astride the fuselage immediately behind the cockpit, from which the canopies had been removed in order for the shouted instructions to be heard. Not very high-tec! This sad state of affairs stimulated Gloster's design office into putting extra momentum into the project to produce a two-seat Meteor. Another catalyst was the crashing of G-AIDC by a Belgian pilot: the company

could not afford to keep donating aircraft for prospective customers to fly on their own, unsupervised.

In order to get a two-seat prototype into the air as soon and as economically as possible, the remains of G-AIDC, which had languished behind a hangar at Moreton Valence since its return from Melsbroek, were brought out, and a careful examination of the damaged airframe was conducted so as to ascertain just how much could be recycled. The cost of constructing a two-seat prototype would have to be met by Gloster Aircraft, as no official approval had so far been given for it, although the RAF had expressed interest. Richard Walker, who became chief designer in

1948, had been responsible for all the Meteor's development since July 1943, and he produced the G.43 two-seat Meteor in a remarkably short time. He was supported by some excellent, quick engineering work by the experimental department who completely refurbished G-AIDC's centre-section, rear fuselage and tail assembly, together with both outer wings, to a point where it could be mated with a newly designed front fuselage. New Derwent 5 engines producing 3,500lb (1,587kg) thrust were installed, and by the beginning of March 1945 the prototype was ready for ground-testing. It was finished in the overall carmine-red colour-scheme first introduced on G-AIDC, and carried the

G-AKPK, the carmine red, private venture trainer demonstrator, flying in May 1948, the crossed flags on the nose being a Union flag and a Gloster Aircraft 'G' logo. Author's collection.

new civil registration G-AKPK; it was 30in (76.2cm) longer than single-seat Meteors, and had no provision for armament. All the essential controls were duplicated, and the crew would sit under a heavily framed, sideways-opening canopy.

In 1947 'Bill' Waterton – who had been a member of the High Speed Flight at Tangmere as a squadron leader in the summer of 1946 – succeeded Eric Greenwood as Gloster's chief test pilot, and the new two-seat Meteor was to be the first prototype that he would take on a maiden flight. This took place on 19 March 1948, when he lifted G-AKPK off the Moreton Valence main runway that ran parallel with the A38 Cheltenham to Gloucester trunk road. The lengthened fuselage reduced the requirement for ballast that had always existed with single-seat aircraft, and its removal, together with the Hispano cannon, plus their ammunition tanks, gave the new aircraft a faster rate of climb than operational F. Mark 4s. Waterton also found that the handling in general was superior to previous Meteors.

A production T.7 on test before it is passed through the paint shops, showing an additional window-frame member on the port side of the rear cockpit, added since **G-AKPK** first flew. Author's collection.

The T. Mk7

The Air Ministry followed the early flights with great interest, and the feedback they received encouraged them to issue specification T.1/47, for an aircraft adapted to RAF training requirements, concerning only internal equipment. Initial contracts were issued, and the foundations were laid for the Gloster G.43 Meteor T. Mark 7 production lines; these would construct a total of 640 examples of the variant for the British services, plus another fifty-four that were exported.

The first contract, numbered 6/ACFT/1389/CB7(b), was an extension of the last F. Mark 4 contract, shared with Armstrong Whitworth. The extension covered the production of seventy T. Mark 7 aircraft, built in two batches, with the serials VW410 to VW459 and VW470 to VW489 inclusive. Contract No. 6/ACFT/2430/CB7(b) dated 4 September 1948 followed, this being for forty aircraft, VZ629 to VZ649 inclusive, to be built in one batch. The third, Contract No. 6/ACFT/2982/CB7(b) dated 25 November 1948, was for 137 aircraft, WA590 to WA639, WA649 to WA698 and WA707 to WA743, all inclusive, and built in three batches. Contract No. 6/ACFT/5044/CB7(b) issued on 1 May

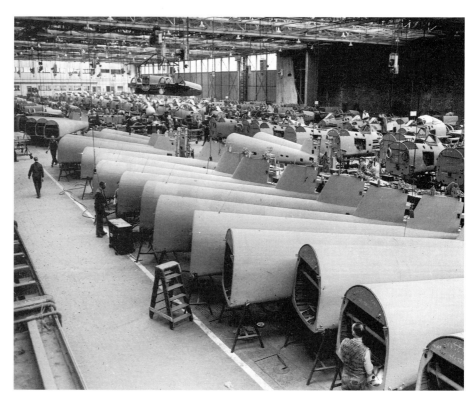

T.7 rear fuselages include, in the foreground, WF830, which went to the RAF Flying College at Manby, while the gentleman in the pullover attends to WF832, a T.7 that became a member of the Gütersloh Meteor Flight and finished up in France on 2 July 1953. Derek N. James.

1950, the fourth contract, was for eighty-nine aircraft produced in three batches, with serials WF766 to WF785, WF813 to WF862 and WF875 to WF883, all inclusive. This was followed by Contract No. 6/ACFT/5621/CB7(b) dated 8 August 1950, covering the160 aircraft WG935 to WG950, WG961 to WG999, WH112 to WH136, WH164 to WH209 and WH215 to WH248, all inclusive, manufactured in five batches. The sixth, Contract No. 6/ACFT/6066/CB7(b), issued on 15 January 1951, was for 139 aircraft, made in four batches, with serials WL332 to WL381, WL397 to WL436, WL453 to WL488 and WN309 to WN321, all inclusive. The seventh order, for the Royal Navy, covered fifteen aircraft, WS103 to WS117 inclusive, built in one batch against Contract No. 6/ACFT/6410/CB7(b) dated 28 April 1951; while the eighth and last, Contract No. 6/ACFT/6411/ CB7(b), issued on the same date, was also for the RN, with a total of nine aircraft WS140 to WS141 and XF273 to XF279 inclusive being ordered in two batches. (Some references have included the additional aircraft originally ordered for either the RAF or RN and subsequently exported; however, as they were not issued to British services, they are included in the chapter covering foreign air force orders.)

Prototype G-AKPK was demonstrated in many countries, and was instrumental in Gloster Aircraft receiving several export orders; then in November 1948 it was itself sold, with the number I-1, as the first two-seat Meteor in the *Koninklijke Luchtmacht* (Royal Netherlands Air Force), who had been operating F.4s since June 1947. It did not last with the RNethAF very long, however, as it was written off in an accident within a few weeks. The first production T. Mark 7 VW410 had its maiden flight on 26 October 1948, and was retained by the company for type trials; it was sold to the Royal Australian Air Force (RAAF) three years later, on 9 November 1951, when it was registered as A77-2. (The RAAF have a unique system of giving each aircraft type an individual number, prefixed by 'A', and this is included in an aircraft's serial, the number 77 being allocated to the Meteor.) The next five aircraft were used for trials and testing at just about every establishment in the United Kingdom, so were never issued for squadron service. Therefore, it was the seventh production T.7 VW415 that

The student's cockpit, showing the small clear-view window open on the left, and the fact that the standard fighter's control column is fitted, although the aircraft had no armament. Derek N. James.

became the RAF's first example, when No. 203 Advanced Flying School (AFS), a unit formed for the purpose of training raw pilots up to OCU standard, received it at their Driffield base in the spring of 1949. Within two years, several hundred T.7s were operating with the RAF.

In Service

While the RAF was pleased to operate a two-seat Meteor, finding it easy to fly and

having a good performance (although many will remember it as being draughty), the aircraft was found to fall short of true operational training requirements in quite a number of departments. One major fault was that it could not accept external ordnance such as bombs or rocket projectiles, nor could it be fitted with the four-cannon armament of the fighter variants, and these presented a distinct limitation in the training of a fighter pilot. Furthermore the instructor's station in the rear was not equipped with the means to relight an engine in the event of a flame-out, and because he did not have fuel gauges on his panel, he was totally unaware of the state of the fuel load without asking the pupil. Also, the cabin was not pressurized, and this meant that the RAF had to limit the aircraft's operating ceiling to 5,000ft (1,524m) below the designed ceiling of 45,000ft (13,716m). Some of these restricting features were rectified later in production, but the T.7 was never pressurized, nor was it able to operate in simulated anger.

Besides being issued to the training and conversion units, T.7s were starting to come on the inventories of operational squadrons, where they were utilized for air experience flights, continuation training, check-outs for new pilots joining a squadron, and instrumentation rating. Before the dedicated T.T. Mark 20 was produced, squadrons often used their T.7s as target tugs. The 175-gallon (795-litre) capacity ventral fuel tank and two 100-gallon (455-litre) underwing tanks, augmenting the internal tanks' capacity of 325 gallons (1,567 litres), gave it an operational time nearly 50 per cent better than the squadron F.4s. Each squadron had one or two Mark 7s on their charge, although attrition took its toll and individual aircraft were often rotated between several units, an example being WH127 which served with nine different units.

Because the Meteor had been in service with the RAF since 1944, with more and more squadrons becoming equipped with them every year, by the time the first T.7 was received in 1949, experience with operating and handling them was virtually second nature so that, with servicing not really being a problem either, reliability was very good. When the Hunter began replacing the Meteor in fighter squadrons they were all single-seaters, so the T.7 was kept on charge for three or four years until a two-seat Hunter – coincidently also a T. Mark 7 – became available. Units serving in BAFO, the Mediterranean and Middle East (MEDME), plus the Far East, flew them operationally, then as squadron 'hacks', up to the early 1960s. By then, however, Fighter Command was contracting with indecent haste and starting to use the English Electric Lightning, and so the T.7's days were definitely numbered; the last two squadrons to employ them – for target-towing – are believed to have been No. 23 Squadron at Coltishall, operating with the Javelin

The instructor's cockpit behind the student contains the hood jettison lever, and a warning not to lower the undercarriage over 175 knots ASI. Derek N. James.

FAW.7, and No. 85 Squadron at West Malling, which moved to West Raynham on 6 September 1960, taking their Meteor with them, together with their front-line Javelin FAW.8s.

Changes were introduced into the T.7 production line fairly late, the first being the Derwent 8: this produced the same 3,500lb (1,587kg) thrust as the earlier series 5 but more efficiently and, in order to increase the airflow to the series 8, the nacelle diameter was increased. And during the building of later batches at

Hucclecote, the tail assembly which had been found so beneficial on the E.1/44 was installed on some production T.7s; it was also retro-fitted to a few aircraft with the original tail units.

Two Meteor T.7s that were in use long after the type had been withdrawn from regular service were WA669 and WF791. In the early 1980s the CFS formed a display team with the title 'Vintage Pair', composed of the two T.7s in turn, and de Havilland DH115 Vampire T.11 XH304; the DH aircraft, built in the mid-1950s,

WA634 was an early recipient of the E.1/44-type tail unit; following trials at Boscombe Down, it went to Martin-Baker Aircraft for several years, before going to the Aerospace Museum at Cosford. Derek N. James.

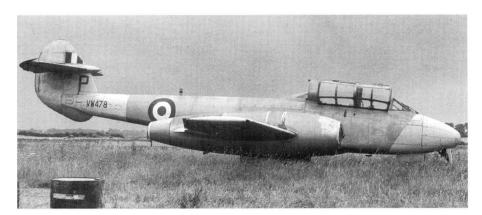

Meteor T.7 VW478, in a rather dilapidated condition on the Kemble fire dump, carries the 'P' code and markings worn when it was on the strength of 3/4 CAACU. *Aeroplane Monthly*.

On 28 March 1951 the Minister of Supply visited Gloster's test facility at Moreton Valence, and an impressive line-up of marks was assembled for the occasion, with twenty-five of them being visible here. Author's collection.

The Advanced Flying Schools which are known to have operated Meteor T.7 at some time, are as follows:

Unit	Location	Example aircraft
No.202 AFS	Valley, Anglesey	WG983
No.203 AFS	Driffield, Yorkshire	VW422
No.205 AFS	Middleton St George, Durham	WG995
No.206 AFS	Oakington, Cambridgeshire	WH192
No.207 AFS	Full Sutton, Yorkshire	WH121
No.208 AFS	Merryfield, Somerset	WG960
No.209 AFS	Weston Zoyland, Somerset	WL371
No.210 AFS	Tarrant Rushton, Dorset	WA717
No.211 AFS	Worksop, Nottinghamshire	WL474
No.215 AFS	Finningley, Yorkshire	WL371

Meteor T.7s were operated at seven Operational Conversion Units (OCU), seven Flying Training Schools (FTS) and two Air Navigation Schools (ANS):

Unit	Location	Example aircraft
No.226 OCU	Stradishall, Suffolk	WG943
No.228 OCU	Leeming, Yorkshire	WH239
No.229 OCU	Leuchars, Fife	WL349
No.231 OCU	Bassingbourn, Cambridgeshire	WE795
No.233 OCU	Pembrey, Carmarthen (now Dyfed)	WA602
No.237 OCU	Bassingbourn, Cambridgeshire	WA660
No.238 OCU	North Luffenham, Rutland	VZ638
No.2 FTS	Church Fenton, Yorkshire	VW418
No.4 FTS	Middleton St George, Durham	WH166
No.5 FTS	Oakington, Cambridgeshire	WH186
No.8 FTS	Driffield, Yorkshire	WH120
No.12 FTS	Weston Zoyland, Somerset	VZ635
No.19 FTS	Cranwell, Lincolnshire	WH118
No.211 FTS	Worksop, Nottinghamshire	WN319
No.1 ANS	Stradishall, Suffolk	WF826
No.2 ANS	Thorney Island, Sussex	WL349

This No. 203 AFS line-up at Driffield, photographed on 18 October 1949, contains eleven T.7s and a pair of F.4s, while a solitary Vampire FB.5 looks on from the other side of the taxiway. Author's collection.

Meteor T.7s were employed at many various other service units and establishments, among them being the following:

Unit	Location	Example aircraft
Air Practice Station (APS)	Acklington, Yorkshire	WA599
(APS)	Sylt, Western Germany	WA610
Armament Practice Camp (APC)	Butterworth, Malaya	WA683
Central Fighter Establishment (CFE)	West Raynham, Norfolk	WK340
Central Flying School (CFS)	Little Rissington, Gloucestershire	WH166
Central Gunnery School (CGS)	Leconfield, Yorkshire	VZ635
College of Air Warfare	Manby, Lincolnshire	VW427
Empire Test Pilots School (ETPS)	Boscombe Down, Wiltshire	WA638
Fighter Weapons School (FWS)	Leconfield, Yorkshire	WL410
Middle East Air Force Instrument Training Flight	Nicosia, Cyprus	WF849
No.101 Flying Refresher School (FRS)	Finningley, Yorkshire	VW449
No.102 FRS	North Luffenham, Rutland	VW419
No.103 FRS	Full Sutton, Yorkshire	WF831
Royal Aircraft Establishment (RAE)	Farnborough, Hampshire	WL468
RAF College	Cranwell, Lincolnshire	WA619
RAF Flying College	Manby, Lincolnshire	WA654
RAF Germany Instrument Training Flight	Gutersloh, West Germany	WA656
RAF Instrument Rating Flight	West Raynham, Norfolk	WL349
RAF Jet Conversion Unit	Binbrook, Lincolnshire	WG942
Tactical Weapons Unit (TWU)	Brawdey, Pembrokeshire (now Dyfed)	WA669

WH231 of the Empire Test Pilots' School has the smaller-diameter intakes for its Derwent 5s, while the unmarked aircraft on the right shows the larger intakes required for Derwent 8s. With a Fairey Gannet behind the Meteors, a Vickers Varsity at the end of the runway, and a Hastings, complete with cargo pannier, in the far background, this photograph was possibly taken at Farnborough before the ETPS moved to Boscombe Down. Author's collection.

WH224, seen here at Wethersfield on 28 May 1960 as a T.7 coded 'Z' of No.223 Squadron, was at one time part of the Duxford Station Flight. George Pennick.

T.7 WG964 on the strength of Headquarters Malta Section, seen at Ta Kali in 1960. Author's collection.

All the station flights and squadron 'hacks', due to their constant interchanging, are difficult to confirm, but the following stations are known to have had the aircraft listed at some time:

Station Flights:

Abu Sueir, Egypt	WA613
Acklington, Yorkshire	WF819
Ahlhorn, Western Germany	WF862
Benson, Oxfordshire	VW449
Biggin Hill, Kent	VZ638
Binbrook, Lincolnshire	VW451
Brawdy, Pembrokeshire (now Dyfed)	WS117
Brüggen, Western Germany	WA610

Station Flights:

Church Fenton, Yorkshire	WA740
Coltishall, Norfolk	VW471
Coningsby, Lincolnshire	WH188
Cranwell, Lincolnshire	WA619
Duxford, Cambridgeshire	VW450
Fassberg, Western Germany	WA693
Gaydon, Warwickshire	WA697
Geilenkirchen, Western Germany	WN310
Gütersloh, Western Germany	WA656
Hemswell, Lincolnshire	WH224
Horsham St Faith, Norfolk	VW430

Station Flights:

Khormaksar, Aden	WL348
Laarbruch, Western Germany	WF836
Leuchars, Fife	WA725
Linton-on-Ouse, Yorkshire	WA671
Lossiemouth, Morayshire	VW447
Nicosia, Cyprus	WA736
North Weald, Essex	WA599
Odiham, Hampshire	VW486
Oldenburg, Western Germany	WL464
Scampton, Lincolnshire	WA592
Seletar, Singapore	WH218

Station Flights:

Stradishall, Suffolk	WL459
Tangmere, Sussex	VW425
Thorney Island, Hampshire	VZ644
Waterbeach, Cambridgeshire	WA639
Wattisham, Suffolk	VW473
West Malling, Kent	WL470
West Raynham, Norfolk	VZ640
Wildenrath, Western Germany	WA714
Wroughton, Wiltshire	WH188
Wunstorf, Western Germany	WF779
Wyton, Huntingdonshire	WL366
Yeovilton, Somerset	WS103

The following squadrons are known to have had the numbered aircraft listed on charge at some time:

Squadron	Example aircraft	Squadron	Example aircraft	Squadron	Example aircraft	Squadron	Example aircraft
No.1	VW487	No.64	WG979	No.151	WG949	No.504	WF823
No.2	WA685	No.65	WA728	No.152	WA727	No.600	WA628
No.3	WL346	No.66	WF769	No.153	WA615	No.601	WA655
No.4	WL338	No.67	WF792	No.208	WF855	No.602	WA629
No.6	VW482	No.71	WF856	No.213	WA622	No.603	WG949
No.19	WF791	No.72	VZ629	No.222	VZ633	No.604	WL462
No.23	WA721	No.73	WA618	No.234	VW485	No.605	WA598
No.25	VW422	No.74	WL380	No.245	WA725	No.607	WF833
No.26	WF791	No79	WG987	No.247	VZ634	No.608	WA672
No.28	WA675	No.81	WA681	No.249	WA627	No.609	WA601
No.29	VW487	No.85	VZ638	No.256	WG929	No.610	WH127
No.33	WA659	No.87	WH204	No.257	VZ634	No.611	WA718
No.34	WL422	No.89	WA620	No.263	WA733	No.612	WF842
No.41	WF848	No.92	WA659	No.264	WG970	No.613	WA637
No.43	VW488	No.96	WA710	No.266	WL464	No.614	WG991
No.46	VW452	No.111	WA612	No.421	WA742	No.615	WA687
No.54	VW416	No.125	VW425	No.500	VW427	No.616	VZ640
No.56	VW473	No.141	WF816	No.501	WA594		
No.63	WA722	No.145	WH236	No.502	VZ637		

Photographed at Wyton in September 1962, T.7 WH127 was at one time a member of the Wattisham Station Flight. George Pennick.

was a much younger airframe than either of the Gloster aircraft. The first Meteor used in the 'Pair', WF791, came to the end of its fatigue life within a couple of years, and its place was taken by WA669. The latter was kept flying by the use of parts from WD790, a Meteor NF.11 which became the airframe with the longest life (just over thirty years) as a radar research aircraft, before it was dismantled at Leeming, in November 1981. WA669 and XH304 continued together, operating from Scampton, until 25 May 1986 when the Mildenhall Air Fete was witness to disaster: the Meteor touched one of the Vampire's twin booms, and both aircraft crashed outside the airfield perimeter. The T.7's crew, Flt Lt Andrew Potter, a CFS instructor, and ground crewman Cpl Kevin

WL415 aligns with Russell Adams' viewfinder showing the slotted airbrakes and larger-diameter intakes, indicating that it is powered by Derwent 8 engines. This aircraft later went to the Belgian Air Force as ED-10. Author's collection.

Four T.7s from the Fleet Requirements Unit of No. 728 Squadron, Fleet Air Arm, based at Lossiemouth; WL350/574 in the foreground was previously a Lossiemouth Station Flight aircraft. The three other aircraft are WS116/410, WA600/573 and VW446/412. Author's collection.

Airwork FRU WL350/044 comes in to land at the Unit's Hurn base; this aircraft was also an ex-Lossiemouth
Station Flight member. It was written off on 13 February 1969, in Dorset. Author's collection.

Central England, circa 1953: the Gloucestershire countryside, four T.7s up from Little Rissington, and an
artist with a camera by the name of Russell Adams. Author's collection.

A Pair of Trainers

The first two jet-powered trainers operated by the RAF and RN were the Gloster G.43
Meteor T.Mark 7 and the de Havilland DH115 Vampire T.11 (T.22 in the RN). They
were different in nearly every aspect, and it can be fairly said that the Vampire T.11,
being produced some three years later than the Meteor T.7, benefited from the latter's
shortcomings.

Meteor T.7

Span:	37ft 2in (11.3m)
Length:	43ft 6in (13.2m)
Height:	13ft 0in (3.9m)
Wing area:	350sq ft (32.5sq m)
Powerplant:	Two R-R Derwent 5 or 8 turbojets, each producing 3,500lb (1,587kg) thrust
Armament:	None
Seating:	Two, in tandem
Ejection seat:	None
Weight, empty:	10,645lb (4,829kg)
Weight, loaded:	14,230lb (6,454kg)
Max speed:	585mph (941.4km/h) at sea level
Rate of climb:	7,900ft/min (2,407.9m/min)
Service ceiling:	45,000ft (13,716m)
Range:	580miles (933km)

Vampire T.11/T.22

Span:	38ft 0in (11.58m)
Length:	34ft 6.5in (10.52m)
Height:	6ft 2in (1.87m)
Wing area:	262sq ft (24.3sq m)
Powerplant:	One DH Goblin 35 turbojet, producing 3,500lb (1,587kg) thrust
Armament:	Two 20mm Hispano 404 cannon. Provision for underwing bombs or rocket projectiles
Seating:	Two, side-by-side
Ejection seat:	Two
Weight, empty:	7,380lb (3,346.8kg)
Weight, loaded:	11,150lb (5,056.5kg)
Max speed:	538mph (865.8km/h) at sea level
Rate of climb:	4,500ft/min (1,371.6m/min)
Service ceiling:	40,000ft (12,192m)
Range:	840miles (1,351.8km)

Turner, were both killed. The Vampire's crew, Sqn Ldr David Marchant, also a CFS instructor, and ground crewman Sergeant Alan Ball, were fortunate that the de Havilland aircraft had been fitted with Martin Baker ejection seats, and both men escaped with only minor injuries.

Royal Navy (RN) interest in the Meteor dated back to DG202/G's deck-handling trials on HMS *Pretoria Castle* in August 1945. These were followed in 1948 by the arrester hook-equipped F.3s EE337 and EE387, which made over thirty landings on the carriers HMS *Illustrious* and HMS *Implacable* in the summer. After these, both aircraft went to Fleet Air Arm (FAA) land stations, EE337 to No. 778 Squadron at Ford and EE387 to No. 771 Squadron, based at Lee-on-Solent, in Hampshire, where they served until 1955, when they were both scrapped.

With the arrival of the T.7, the Admiralty appreciated that they could update their pilot training programmes, and in 1948 an order was placed for forty-three examples of the Mark. Contract No. 6410, mentioned earlier, covered fifteen new aircraft, and the balance of twenty-eight was made up from RAF orders. Two FAA units, No. 702 Squadron at Ford, with at least WS103, WS105 and WS106 on charge, plus No. 759 Squadron at Culdrose, flying WS104, WS107, WS108 and WS109, were the main operators. Ford's other tenant, trials unit No. 703 Squadron, also operated T.7s for a short time. In October 1953, because Culdrose was being increasingly used by other units, No. 759 Squadron moved to Lossiemouth, and here the two-seat Meteor's operations were gradually taken over by Vampire T.11s; the Gloster aircraft therefore became dispersed among other FAA establishments. No. 728 Squadron, based at Hal Far on the George Cross island of Malta, received WS111, WS115 and WS116 for jet conversion plus continuation training, while Airwork's Fleet Requirement Unit (FRU), operating from Brawdy's satellite at St David's, had at least two, WL332 and WL350. The FRU moved to Hurn, in Hampshire, and was still using its T.7s in 1970. Royal Navy association with two-seat Meteors occurs later, when the T.T.20 is featured.

In December 1953, the Ferranti Flying Unit (FFU), based at Turnhouse, received T.7 VW470 for a series of trials concerning accurate gunsight tracking, with auto-stabilization. In February 1954, the aircraft

The *Vintage Pair* taxiing out to fill their display slot at the 1982 Mildenhall Air Fete. WF791 was the first T.7 used by the duo, and it came to the end of its fatigue life later in that year. Vampire T.11 XH304 was joined in 1983 by Meteor T.7 WA669, and they operated together until 1986. Author's collection.

went to Airwork, at Blackbushe, for modifications required to further Ferranti's testing. When it returned to Turnhouse in the second week of July, it sported an E.1/44 tail unit, and because the F.Mark 8s in squadron service were similarly equipped, VW470 was irreverently dubbed a Meteor 7 1/2 by the Unit.

As well as supplying the RAF with many hundreds of trained jet pilots, the Meteor T.7 supplied tens of thousands of aircraft enthusiasts with some of the best air-to-air images ever published. Russell Adams was a technical research assistant with Gloster Aircraft, attached to the flight test department: from taking pictures of instruments and aircraft skin deformation in flight, he persuaded company test pilot Jan Zurakowski to take him, together with a Speed Graphic camera, in a T.7 flying in a formation loop with WL364, another similar aircraft. The resulting photograph was printed in a total of 120 publications throughout the world, and it heralded many years of Gloster aircraft being presented, via 5in x 4in (12.7cm x 10.1cm) pin-sharp glass negatives, in advertisements and editorial articles in just about every aviation magazine. His prowess was such that the company allowed him to build a camera of his own design in their technical unit. He is quoted as confessing to feeling slightly anxious on taking off on first flights with aircraft straight from the production line, hoping they had been screwed together correctly – the first manoeuvre pilots would perform when airborne was a slow roll, to ensure that no spanners or screwdrivers had been left behind!

The prototype G-AKPK was flown at the 1948 Farnborough SBAC Display, and production T.7s appeared on four other occasions. VW482 flew in 1949, and WL453 was in the static park in 1952. In 1953 WS141 was flown, and the type's last appearance was in 1954, when G-ANSO was static.

The Meteor T.7 was purchased by a total of nine foreign countries, as the first jet-powered trainer for their respective air forces; these are detailed in a later chapter.

G-ANSO, the 1954 conversion to T.7 configuration of Gloster's private venture, single-seat, ground-attack aircraft which was sold to Sweden as SE-DCC. Derek N. James.

CHAPTER EIGHT

The Mighty Eight

The Gloster Meteor's development as a single-seat fighter reached its zenith with the G.41K F.Mark 8. From the delivery of the first production aircraft in December 1949, to the arrival of the Hawker Hunter in July 1954, the Meteor F.8 operated as Fighter Command's principal single-seat day fighter, serving with a total of thirty front-line squadrons, as well as ten auxiliaries.

During 1947, Gloster's were aware that several other air forces were receiving fighters which had been conceived when the F.3 was already in squadron service, and which therefore had superior performances. The arrival of the MiG-15 was an eye-opener to the Western Allies, although the USA had the F-86 starting on North American's Inglewood production line. Great effort was therefore put into a programme of development, so as to enhance the Meteor's performance as soon as possible. Insertion of the additional 30in (76.2cm) plug in the fuselage of F.4 RA382 as part of the T.7's development had improved longitudinal stability dramatically, and experience gained with the trainer in service had proved that the longer fuselage was essential. A considerable amount of redesigning was

The pristine third production F.8 presents its underside to the camera. VZ440 served with Nos. 43 and 66 Squadrons, before being scrapped in August 1959. Author's collection.

GLOSTER METEOR F.8

1 Cockpit fresh air intake
2 Camera aperture
3 Access hatch
4 Gun camera
5 Nose undercarriage pivot mounting
6 Nosewheel leg door
7 Shock absorber strut
8 Trailing axle nosewheel suspension
9 Aft retracting nosewheel
10 Fixed mudguard
11 Nosewheel bay doors
12 Nose undercarriage mounting sub-frame
13 Hydraulic retraction jack
14 Armoured cockpit front pressure bulkhead
15 Cannon muzzle apertures
16 Ground power and ground/flight switch

17 Cannon barrel recoil mountings
18 Engine throttle levers
19 Control column
20 Instrument panel
21 Instrument access panel
22 Retractable gyro gunsight
23 Armoured windscreen panels
24 Sliding cockpit canopy
25 Ejection seat face blind firing handle
26 Headrest and drogue container
27 Martin-Baker Mk.2E ejection seat
28 Sliding canopy side rail
29 Canopy external release
30 Kick-in boarding steps
31 Oxygen charging point
32 Pull-out step
33 Cartridge case and link ejector chutes and airflow deflector

34 20mm British Hispano Mk.5 cannon
35 Ammunition feed drums
36 Ammunition magazines, 190 rounds per gun
37 Cockpit pressure seal
38 Hydraulic reservoir
39 Ammunition loading ramp
40 Forward/centre fuselage joint bulkhead
41 Fuselage top longeron attachment joint
42 Sliding canopy rear centre rail
43 Fuel tanks (3), total internal capacity 420 Imp gal (1,909 lit)
44 Centre fuselage frame and stringer structure
45 Fuel tank retaining straps
46 Tank bay access hatches
47 Fuel fillers
48 Starboard airbrake panel, open, upper and lower surfaces

49 Starboard mainwheel, stowed position
50 Engine rear suspension link
51 Rolls-Royce Derwent 8 centrifugal flow engine
52 Engine oil tank
53 Starter unit
54 Engine-driven accessory gearbox with Heywood compressor
55 Generator
56 Starboard nacelle air intake
57 5in high-velocity aircraft rockets (HVAR), carried by Israeli aircraft
58 Starboard navigation light
59 Homing antennae
60 Aft facing recognition light
61 Starboard aileron
62 Aileron hinge control link, torque shaft operated
63 Aileron internal mass balance weights
64 Balance tab

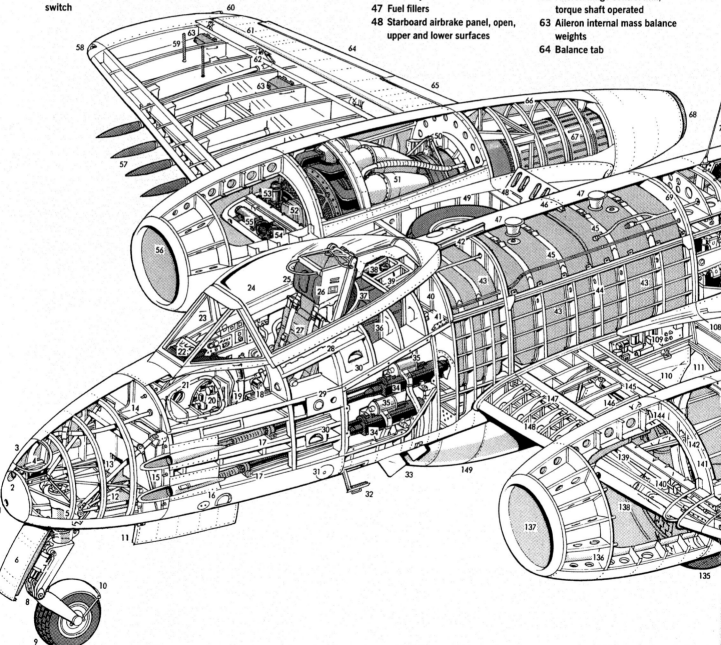

65 Additional spring tab on rocket
carrying aircraft
66 Nacelle tailcone
67 Jet pipe
68 Exhaust nozzle
69 Centre/aft fuselage joint frame
70 Radio equipment bay
71 VHF antenna
72 Stowage compartment, off-base
and tropical equipment
73 IFF antenna
74 Aft fuselage upper main
longeron
75 Aft fuselage frame and stringer
structure
76 Lower fin segment
77 Two-spar and rib lower fin
segment structure
78 Fin/tailplane fairing
79 Tailplane spar bolted
attachment joints
80 Starboard tailplane
81 Starboard elevator
82 Upper fin segment rib structure

111 Main undercarriage wheel bay
112 Engine nacelle access hatches
113 Rear engine mounting
114 Rear spar ring frame and
engine bay rear bulkhead
115 Nacelle tailcone frame
structure
116 Jet pipe rear suspension
mounting
117 Exhaust nozzle shroud
118 Nacelle trailing edge fairing

83 Upper rudder segment
84 Rudder rib structure
85 Rudder interconnection, upper
and lower segments
86 Elevator hinge control
87 Tail navigation light
88 Elevator trim tab
89 Port elevator rib structure
90 Tailplane spar and rib torsion
box structure
91 Lower rudder segment with
trim tab
92 Semi-span tailplane front spar
93 Fuselage tailcone
94 Rudder hinge control link
95 Tail bumper
96 Elevator hinge control link
97 Tailplane spar mounting
bulkheads
98 Tailcone joint frame
99 Control cable access panels
100 Tailplane control cable runs
101 Remote compass transmitter
102 Pneumatic air bottle
103 Wing root trailing edge fairing
104 Radio equipment bay ventral
access hatch

119 Outer wing panel rear spar
attachment bolted joint
120 Starboard aileron
121 Aileron rib structure
122 Aileron balance tab
123 Aft recognition light
124 Wing tip fairing rib structure
125 Port navigation light
126 Pitot head
127 Retractable landing light
128 VHF homing antennae
129 Outer wing panel rib structure
130 Rocket rail mounting
hardpoints (four)
131 External tank pylon mounting
and release unit
132 Jettisonable external fuel tank,
capacity 100 Imp gal (455 lit)
133 Leading edge rib structure
134 Outer wing panel front spar
bolted attachment joint
135 Port mainwheel with fixed
mudguard
136 Detachable nacelle intake nose
cone structure
137 Port engine air intake
138 Intake duct spar fairing
139 Aileron push-pull control rod
140 Main undercarriage leg with
trailing axle suspension
141 Engine bay forward main
bulkhead
142 Main engine mounting
143 Engine bay mainframe upper
segment, detachable for engine
removal
144 Mainwheel leg pivot mounting
145 Leg mounting semi-span false
spar
146 Hydraulic retraction jack
147 Wing main spar, front and
rear spars continuous through
fuselage
148 Inboard detachable leading
edge rib structure
149 Ventral fuel tank, capacity 175
Imp gal (796 lit)

105 Split trailing edge flap
106 Flap hydraulic jack
107 Airbrake hydraulic jack
108 Port upper airbrake panel, open
109 Electrical equipment panel
110 Port mainwheel door

Mike Badrocke/05

©MIKE BADROCKE 2005

entailed to further strengthen the centre-section so it would accept the Rolls-Royce Derwent 8s for fighter operations, with high-tensile steel being introduced into the spar webs and centre-section, as well as some rear fuselage components. VT150, the last airframe from the first batch of the Meteor F.4's second production contract, which had been retained by the manufacturer and operated at Boscombe Down, was assigned to be the new Mark's prototype. The aircraft was taken back into Gloster's experimental department so that modifications for improving performance could be put in hand; and for the first time, an operational Meteor was equipped with a Martin-Baker Mk1E ejector seat. To accommodate it the cockpit had to be somewhat enlarged and the windscreen repositioned slightly more forward, and a large, powered canopy hood was fitted, the rear portion of which was faired in with metal to provide additional strength. Later production aircraft were fitted with a fully transparent canopy, which gave the pilot a greatly improved field of vision. Another improvement on the new Mark was that the gunsight was made retractable.

The additional 30in (76.2cm) fuselage plug caused the four-Hispano cannon armament to move forward by the same amount, and an additional 95-gallon (432-litre) fuel tank was installed in the resultant space. Still fitted with its original F.4 tail unit, VT150's conversion to the F.Mark 8 prototype was completed in the autumn of 1948, and on 12 October it was given a maiden flight by Jan Zurakowski. 'Zura', as the Polish-born aviator was popularly known, flew as Gloster's chief development test pilot from 1947 to 1952; with a sound engineering background and a natural test-flying ability, he became a display pilot of great international repute. At the beginning of 1949 the aircraft was delivered to the A&AEE at Boscombe Down where it was subjected to a month of testing; however, it was found to be inferior to the preceding F.4 and the Establishment would not pass it for squadron service. Originally it had been proposed to manufacture the first 100 F.8s, retaining the F.4 tail; but the A&AEE report encouraged Gloster to bring forward the installation of the 'E.1/44-type' tail assembly, and VT150 was so modified when it went back to Boscombe Down eight months later. It received a much better handling assessment than it had been given previously:

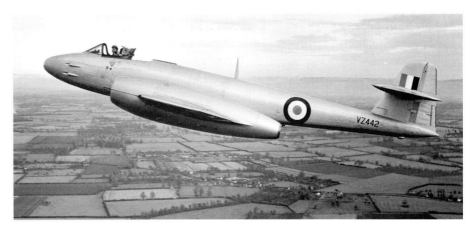

VZ442, the fifth production F.8, was designated for A&AEE service at Boscombe Down, to be employed on a variety of trials programmes, including forms of canopy fastenings and jettisoning which sometimes required it to fly without a hood. Rocket-projectile test-firings were also conducted, and a battery of four 60lb (27.2kg) RPs are shown under each wing. For some reason the Meteor was never cleared for RP firing by the RAF. Author's collection.

the limiting Mach number was raised from 0.80 to 0.82, while the lighter rudder forces reduced the minimum speed for safe control in the event of an engine failure by about 17mph (23km/h). The elevator was more pleasant, and the mechanical operation of the trim tabs was improved. The spinning and recovery characteristics were considered satisfactory, but pilots were warned that heavy stick forces would be encountered in two spins at any altitude, with recovery from a two-turn spin from 40,000ft (12,192m) frequently being very unpleasant due to the combinations of snaking, yawing,

nose-down pitch and associated negative 'g', which could occur simultaneously when rotation ceased. They also stated that while the use of airbrakes would be unlikely, should an aircraft be spun with them extended, it was recommended that they should not be retracted until recovery was completed.

Problems had arisen due to the re-positioning of the armament and the additional fuel tank positioned just aft of the cockpit, because once the ammunition and the additional fuel had been exhausted, the aircraft's centre of gravity moved to an unacceptable extent, creating instability in the longitudinal direction. The fitting of the new tail assembly went a long way towards a rectification of this trouble.

On 4 September 1949, Contract No. 6/ACFT/2430/CB7(b) was issued for the production of 118 Gloster G.41K Meteor F.Mark 8 aircraft in four batches. Serials VZ438 to VZ485 inclusive were allocated to the first batch of forty-eight aircraft, and VZ493 to VZ517 inclusive to the second batch of twenty-five. Both batches were built by Gloster Aircraft at Hucclecote. The third batch, consisting of fifteen aircraft with serials VZ518 to VZ532 inclusive, and the fourth, of thirty aircraft numbered VZ540 to VZ569 inclusive, were built by Sir W.G. Armstrong Whitworth Aircraft at Baginton. Contract No. 6/ACFT/2983/CB7(b) followed, dated 25 November 1949, for the production of 210 F.Mark 8s in eight batches: the first batch of forty aircraft was allotted the serials WA755 to WA794 inclusive, and the second batch of five aircraft, WA808 to WA812 inclusive; they were all built at Baginton. The third batch of forty-five aircraft, WA813 to WA857 inclusive, the fourth batch totalling forty-three aircraft, WA867 to WA909 inclusive, and the fifth batch of forty-five aircraft WA920 to WA964 inclusive, were all made by Gloster. Armstrong Whitworth returned with the sixth batch, covering five aircraft WA965 to WA969 inclusive, as well as batch number seven, nineteen aircraft with serials WA981 to WA999 inclusive, and the eighth batch, covering eight aircraft with serial numbers WB105 to WB112 inclusive.

The third contract, numbered 6/ACFT/4040/CB7(b) and dated 29 December 1949, covered the building of 120 aircraft. Armstrong Whitworth kept in the story with the first batch of forty aircraft, allocated serial numbers WE852 to WE 981 inclusive, and the second batch, eight aircraft with the serials WE895 to WE902 inclusive; all were built at Baginton. The remaining two batches covered by the contract were constructed by Gloster Aircraft, thirty-seven aircraft, WE903 to WE939 inclusive being the third batch, and the fourth, of thirty-five F.8s WE942 to WE976 inclusive. On 4 May 1950 the fourth contract was issued, this being No. 6/ACFT/5043/CB7(b) for eighty-nine aircraft; the production was to be undertaken in four batches, the first two going to Baginton and the last two for

VZ460 was engaged in rocket projectile and bomb trials, including a double-tier eight-missile battery under each wing. The combined elements of this lovely photograph are VZ460's pilot Jan Zurakowski, Gloster Aircraft's photographer Russell Adams and his T.7's pilot, Brian Smith. Author's collection.

Hucclecote. Batch one covered twenty-four aircraft numbered WF693 to WF662 inclusive, and batch two, twelve aircraft with serials WF677 to WF688 inclusive. The third batch contained twenty-eight aircraft, WF689 to WF716 inclusive, and the fourth, twenty-five aircraft numbered WF736 to WF 760 inclusive.

Later in the same year, Contract No. 6/ACFT/5621/CB7(b) dated 8 August

Tangmere early in 1951, and No.1 Squadron parades fourteen F.8s, a miscellany of groundcrews and pilots and a bull terrier. VZ551/J and WE947/L were both Armstrong Whitworth-built aircraft: the latter was written off in August 1952 while still with the squadron, whilst VZ551 finished up as a U.16 at Llanbedr, in 1959. *Aeroplane Monthly*.

Photographed on 13 April 1983 WK991, a late production F.8 with large-diameter intakes, did serve with No56 Squadron but became a non-effective airframe in April 1961 and went to Duxford, two years later, with the Instructional Airframe number 7823M. Over the years, it was repainted in No56 Squadron markings and is currently retained by the Duxford Aviation Society. George Pennick.

1950 was for the supply of 200 F.Mark 8s, to be supplied in seven batches, all being made by Armstrong Whitworth. Batch one contained fifteen aircraft, WH249 to WH263 inclusive and batch two, forty-nine, with the serials WH272 to WH320 inclusive. The third batch of forty-five aircaft were allocated numbers WH342 to WH386 inclusive, while the fourth was thirty-two aircraft with the serial range WH395 to WH426 inclusive. Batch number five was for just three F.8s, WH442 to WH444 inclusive, while the sixth contained forty aircraft, WH445 to WH484 inclusive. The seventh and last batch produced sixteen aircraft, with the serials WH498 to WH513 inclusive.

The final contract for Meteor F.8 production, numbered 6/ACFT/6066/CB7(b) and dated 15 January 1951, was the largest: a total of 343 aircraft was ordered in nine batches, the second and fifth batches to be built at Baginton, while Gloster produced the rest at Hucclecote. Batch number one contained fifty aircraft with serials WK647 to WK696 inclusive being allocated. The second batch was also fifty aircraft, numbered WK707 to WK756 inclusive. Serial numbers WK783 to WK827 inclusive were allotted to the forty-five aircraft in the third batch, while another forty-five aircraft made up batch number four, with serials WK849 to WK893 inclusive. Armstrong Whitworth were to build the fifth batch, serial numbers WK906 to WK934 inclusive being given to the twenty-nine aircraft involved. Batch number six contained the twenty-one aircraft numbered WK935 to WK955 inclusive, and a further twenty-nine made up the seventh batch, with serials WK966 to WK994 inclusive. Forty aircraft constituted the eighth batch, to which the numbers WL104 to WL143 inclusive were given, while batch nine covered the last thirty-four F.8s built, to which serials WL158 to WL191 inclusive were allocated.

The F. Mk8 in Service

It has to be admitted that when the first production Meteor F.8 VZ438 made its maiden flight it was bordering on obsolescence compared with the equipment of many foreign air forces. The armament was identical to that carried by No. 616 Squadron's aircraft back in 1944 –

This Baginton-built F.8 WH291 had a mixed life: it started with No. 257 Squadron; the RAF Flying College and the College of Air Warfare followed; then it was operated by No. 85 Squadron, before going to No. 229 OCU, where it carried the markings of No79 Squadron; and after this O. Haydon-Baillie purchased it in February 1976. From No. 5 MU, Kemble, WH291 was prepared for transportation to Lasham where the Second World War Aircraft Preservation Society unloaded it – and still retain it today. *Aeroplane Monthly.*

although the four 20mm cannon provided more fire-power than the F-86's six 0.50 machine guns. The fact that the F.8 was produced in such large numbers is really a reflection on the failure of the Supermarine Swift as an operational fighter, coupled with the airbrake and gun-gas ingestion problems that delayed the Hawker Hunter's introduction to Fighter Command. Gloster began deliveries in June 1950, when No. 245 Squadron at Horsham St Faith started replacing its Meteor F.4s with F.8s, the earliest being VZ449; it is believed that this squadron was the first to be fully equipped with the new Mark. Two months later, in August 1950, Tangmere-based No. 1 Squadron received its first F.8, with its neighbour at the Sussex airfield, No. 43 Squadron, doing the same the following month. Also in September, both No. 257 Squadron at Horsham St Faith and No. 222 Squadron at Leuchars started exactly the same operation, replacing F.4s with F.8s. Three more units took Meteor F.8s on charge in October 1950: Nos. 74 and 263 Squadrons, both also at Horsham St Faith – and when they received their new

The only unit to have the majority of its aircraft converted for air-to-air refuelling was No. 245 Squadron at Horsham St Faith, and WA829/A is here hooked up during the proving trials. Later this aircraft went to the Armament Practice Station at Sylt, before being struck off charge on 15 April 1959. Derek N. James.

Not the sharpest of photographs, but it shows the sole 'three-pointer' Boeing YKB-29T, modified by FRL, refuelling No. 245 Squadron F.8s WA826/F and WA829/A from wing-tip points and FRL's F.4 VZ389 hooked up to the ventral drogue. The F.4's final conversion, by its operators, was into a U.15 drone, which was shipped to Woomers in 1955. Mike Hooks.

aircraft, this became the first base to replace *all* its Meteor F.4s with F.8s; and No. 92 Squadron at Linton-on-Ouse, which again was relinquishing F.4s. Lastly the two Waterbeach-based units, Nos. 56 and 63 Squadrons, went through a similar exercise in December.

World tension escalated on 25 June 1950 with the outbreak of hostilities in the Korean peninsular, and this led to an expansion of the RAF's turbojet-powered fighter strength – in 1951, ten more squadrons re-equipped with Meteor F.8 aircraft. Linton-on-Ouse hosted four fighter squadrons: No. 92 had already changed its aircraft in October 1950, and then in January 1951 No. 66 Squadron, followed by No. 65 Squadron in February and No. 64 Squadron in March, all

replaced their Meteor F.4s with F.8s – although by August, Nos. 64 and 65 Squadrons had taken their new charges to Duxford. No. 41 Squadron at Biggin Hill handed over its F.4s in April, and in June the Royal Auxiliary Air Force's No. 609 (West Riding) Squadron at Church Fenton did the same. Wittering in Northamptonshire was base to No. 19 Squadron, which in fact had only held Meteor F.4s for three months before replacing them in August 1951, and No. 615 (County of Surrey) Squadron at Biggin Hill followed suit a month later. In November, No. 500 (County of Kent) Squadron at West Malling and No. 600 (City of London) Squadron at Biggin Hill both replaced their F.4s, and the year of change was rounded off in December,

when the pioneer Meteor operator, No. 616 (South Yorkshire) Squadron at Finningley, which had been equipped with both of the earlier single-seat Marks, received its first Meteor fitted with an ejector seat.

Deliveries of the F.Mark 8 maintained their momentum in 1952. Three auxiliary units re-equipped in March, No. 504 (City of Nottingham) Squadron at Wymeswold, plus No. 610 (County of Chester) Squadron and No. 611 (West Lancashire) Squadron, both based at Hooton Park, all giving up the Meteor F.4. At Odiham in Surrey, both No. 54 and No. 247 Squadrons had been flying the twin-boom Vampire F.3 and FB.5 for three years before taking their first Meteors on charge, the F.8s starting to arrive in April. It was a similar case at North Weald, in Essex, where No. 74 Squadron had operated the de Havilland aircraft until July 1952, when their first F.8 was delivered. At the same location, both No. 601 (County of London) Squadron and No. 604 (County of Middlesex) Squadron had flown Vampire F.3s before receiving their first Gloster-built aircraft in August.

By the following year, the torrent of Meteor F.8 deliveries had reduced to a trickle; one of the last to be equipped with the F.8 was No111 Squadron, a former Spitfire IXE operator that was disbanded in Italy on 16 May 1947, and reformed at North Weald on 2 December 1953. The very last front-line squadron to receive this Mark was No. 34 Squadron, also a unit which had been reformed, on 1 August 1954 at Tangmere, having been disbanded in July 1951 when it flew Beaufighter TT.10s.

Before we leave the squadron service Meteor F.8, it is interesting to recount an experiment undertaken in 1952, when Nos. 257 and 263 Squadrons were at Wattisham. Although 'Fog Investigation and Dispersal Operation' (FIDO) was not installed at the base, it was decided to investigate the possibility of the heat from turbojets *en masse* doing a similar job. With visibility down to 50yd (45.7m) or so, over a dozen aircraft were taxied out and lined up on each side of the operational runway, with their tails angled inwards by about 30 degrees. The engines were run at idling revs for some time, but this had no effect, so orders were given to open the throttles wide – and within a few minutes, a tunnel of clarity was burned in the fog. The green light was given and another Meteor taxied onto the runway threshold, ready for take-off down the tunnel. The stationary aircraft shut their engines down to idling, in order to give the Meteor less turbulence to negotiate – and the fog rolled back again! The experiment was judged to be a dead loss, and everyone went back to the Mess!

During the trials to improve performance, the nacelle air intakes were redesigned to give a 4.5in (11.43cm) enlargement of the frontal diameter, and the increased airflow to the Derwent 8s produced an additional 200lb (90.7kg) thrust from each engine; the larger intake diameter was therefore introduced early in the F.8's production, and was also applied to later production T.7s. Time was also given to resolving a comparatively minor

Taxiing along Duxford's perimeter track, 'R' of No. 64 Squadron is a late production F.8 with larger-diameter intakes, while 'U', behind it, has the smaller intakes; both aircraft are fitted with one-piece canopies. The line-up being refuelled has a mixture of hoods, and the squadron shows the reversion to camouflage which came into force when relations between the Western Powers and the Communist bloc deteriorated, although the carrying of the red/blue trellis squadron markings was allowed. Author's collection.

problem that had occurred since the ventral fuel tank had been introduced to the F.4: spent 20mm cartridge cases were ejected via slots in the underside of the front fuselage, and these were causing

damage to the external tank. In tests, the fitting of substantial ejector chutes was found to give good results, so these too were incorporated in production F.8s and retro-fitted on some earlier aircraft.

In-Flight Refuelling Trials

The Meteor's involvement in flight refuelling is included in a later chapter, but it is relevant to mention No. 245 Squadron at Horsham St Faith here, as it was the only unit to have nearly its entire complement of F.8s fitted with receiver probes for air-to-air refuelling. At least thirteen of the squadron's sixteen aircraft are known to have gone to Flight Refuelling Limited's (FRL) establishment at Tarrant Rushton, near Blandford in Dorset for modifications, these being VZ476, VZ477, VZ528, WA823, WA826, WA827, WA829, WA830, WA832, WA834, WA836 and WA837, all built by Gloster Aircraft, plus Baginton-built WE934. Code-named *Pinnacle*, the trials officially started on 8 May 1951, with three converted Avro Lincolns – RA657, SX993 and RE293 – being scheduled as tanker aircraft, although RE293 arrived too late to be involved, and FRL's Lancaster G-33-2 had to be used when RA657 was grounded for inspection. The five-month trials finished at the end of October and were considered to be a success, although the importance of timing was made very obvious at least once. The tankers were grounded at Horsham St Faith, being refuelled, when a section of Meteors arrived overhead, with their fuel loads approaching zero. A rapid 'scramble' of the Lincolns was accomplished – in just nine minutes! – and the first Meteor engaged its receiver probe at well below 1,000ft (304.8m), as the tanker was commencing its climb from Tarrant Rushton's runway.

American interest in FRL's system, led by Colonels Bill Ritchie and Dave Schilling of the USAF, was instrumental in four Boeing B-29 Superfortresses being sent to Tarrant Rushton for conversion to the tanker role. Their arrival generated huge interest amongst the local aircraft enthusiasts, and enterprising coach companies in the area organized tours to the base, until large canvas screens were put up. (I bet this did nothing to stop the ardent spotter!) Somewhat unwisely, as it turned out, FRL undertook the conversions at a pre-agreed fixed-price bid, an agreement that was made in order to get the work. However, when the bomb-doors were opened and the service panels removed, the company was astounded at how complex the B-29 was, compared with the relatively uncomplicated Lancaster. The costs involved in

When No. 615 (County of Surrey) Squadron received its F.8s at Biggin Hill, it was quick to form an aerobatic team, the pilots being, from left to right, Flt Lt J.W.C. Judge (leader), Fg Off J.A. Vivian, Fg Off G.I. Smith and Flt Lt P.V. Pledger. WE949 had served with No. 41 Squadron before going to Biggin Hill, and finished as instructional airframe number 7319M at No.10 School of Technical Training, Kirkham, in February 1956. *Aeroplane Monthly.*

'Best blues' was the order of the day when Emperor Haile Selassie of Abyssinia (now Ethiopia) visited No.64 Squadron at Duxford. The F.8s lined up for inspection had all been retrofitted with one-piece clear canopies. *Aeroplane Monthly.*

With the Meteor F.8 being produced in greater numbers than any other Mark, it is quite understandable that a large number of service units and establishments employed the aircraft for a great variety of activities. While not professing to be a complete list – which would be very difficult to compile, in view of the common practice of units borrowing aircraft on an unofficial basis that went unrecorded – the following bases are known to have been involved with the aircraft at some time during its active life.

Unit	Location	Example aircraft
Air Attaché,	Paris Le Bourget	WA926
Air Practice Station	Acklington, Yorkshire	WK752
Central Fighter Establishment (CFE)	West Raynham, Norfolk	
AFDS		VZ500
AWFCS		WK654
Communications Flight		WB112
DFC School		WL106
DFC Squadron		WK754
DFLS		WL968
Fighter Command ITS		WF815
Handling Squadron		VZ493
CGS	Leconfield, Yorkshire	WE917
Communications Squadron	Colerne, Wiltshire	WL113

Unit	Location	Example aircraft
Communications Squadron	Turnhouse, Midlothian	WL116
ETPS	Boscombe Down, Wiltshire	WK660
Far East Air Force Training Squadron	Butterworth, Malaya	WH410
Fighter Command Communications Squadron	Bovingdon, Cambridgeshire	WL347
FWS	Leconfield, Yorkshire	WH395
Handling Squadron	Manby Lincolnshire	VZ464

Unit	Location	Example aircraft
Malta Communications Flight	Takali, Malta	WH256
Middle East Air Force		
ITF	Nicosia, Cyprus	WK946
No.27 APC	Butterworth, Malaya	WL180
No.5 CAACU	Llanbedr, Merioneth (now Gwynedd)	WK914
No.4 FTS	Worksop, Nottinghamshire	WE962
No.211 FTS	Worksop, Nottinghamshire	WK860

F(TT).8 VZ467/A is believed to have been the last Meteor in RAF service, having been operated by No. 229 OCU at Chivenor, which became No. 1 TWU following the move to Brawdy in October 1974. The aircraft was struck off charge on 22 October 1982. Author's collection.

the operation nearly finished the company, and they were only kept solvent by selling the probe/drogue manufacturing rights to the United States. One aircraft, the unique YKB-29T 521734, was modified to be a 'three-point' tanker, with a Hose Drum Unit (HDU) installed in the rear fuselage and an electrically driven HDU at each wing-tip. For testing this installation, FRL had their own Meteor F.4 VZ389, a Baginton-built aircraft, and the two USAF colonels, flying a pair of Republic F-84 Thunderjets that had been converted to

receivers with a probe under the port wing, were to join in the trials. But the officers were recalled to the United States, so elements of No. 245 Squadron took over for the first triplicate flight-refuelling sortie. The company had appreciated the great publicity potential of the event, and had organized a Lancaster, crowded with fourteen cameras, to accompany the trials' participants: they were correct, and photographs of the unique 'hook-up' were published in the world's aeronautical press.

The Korean War

Five years after its Hispano-cannon armament had last been fired in anger, the Meteor went to war again in 1950. The comparatively remote land of Korea had been part of the Rising Sun Empire, and when Japan surrendered on 15 May 1945 the country was promised independence by the Allies; with the latitudinal 38th Parallel constituting a border, the Russians occupied the land to its north. South of the

Unit	Location	Example	Unit	Location	Example	Station Flights	
No.11 GCF	Martlesham Heath, Suffolk	WA991	RAE	Bedford, Bedfordshire	WE855	Biggin Hill, Kent	WA965
No.12 GCF	Newton, Nottinghamshire	WK680		Farnborough, Hampshire	VZ460	Church Fenton, Yorkshire	WE876
No.226 OCU	Stradishall, Suffolk	WH352				Coltishall, Norfolk	WE913
No.229 OCU	Chivenor, Devonshire	WK721	**Sector Flights**			Duxford, Cambridgeshire	WA983
No.233 OCU	Pembrey, Carmarthen (now Dyfed)	WE887	Caledonian	Turnhouse, Midlothian	WA933	Geilenkirchen, West Germany	WK803
			Eastern	Horsham St Faith, Norfolk	WA773	Habbaniya, Iraq	WK946
No.238 OCU	Colerne, Wiltshire	WA816	Northern	Linton-on-Ouse, Yorkshire	WA909	Hooton Park, Cheshire	WA908
No.1 TWU	Brawdy, Pembroke (now Dyfed)	VZ467	Scottish	Leuchars, Fife	VZ555	Horsham St Faith, Norfolk	VZ559
			Southern	Tangmere, Sussex	WA764	Leuchars, Fife	VZ468
OFU	Chivenor, Devonshire	VZ525	Western	Wymeswold, Somerset	WA844	Linton-on-Ouse, Yorkshire	WA921
						North Weald, Essex	WK689
						Odiham, Hampshire	WA987
						Ouston, Northumberland	WA931
						Stradishall, Suffolk	WH305
						Tangmere, Sussex	VZ542
						Waterbeach, Cambridgeshire	WA812
						Wattisham, Suffolk	WL108
						West Malling, Kent	WH262
						SHQ Flight	
						Butterworth, Malaya	WA760
						Kai Tak, Hong Kong	WF736
						Seletar, Singapore	WA899
						TT Flight	
						Changi, Singapore	WA880

WK887 was once a Geilenkirchen Station Flight aircraft. It was consigned to the Manston dump on 31 July 1972; before this it was a Duxford Station Flight aircraft coded 'PW', and is shown here standing alongside WE927/JR, as other elements of No. 64 Squadron taxi in front of them. *Aeroplane Monthly.*

38th parallel, American forces administered Southern Korea, and when the two wartime allies withdrew from their respective territories, it was naively believed – by America, at least – that a single self-governing country would be formed. But political arguments generated a mutual distrust so that in 1948 two separate states – the northern Democratic People's Republic and the Republic of Korea (ROK) in the south of the peninsula – were established. Two years later, on 25 June 1950, the armies of the Communist North

Korea marched south, across the border, forcing the much weaker ROK forces to withdraw, in a very short time, to a small region in the south-east corner, around Pusan.

Within twenty-four hours of the start of the conflict, the United Nations (UN) Assembly condemned North Korea's actions and demanded that the country withdraw its troops back across the border. There was no response, and so the United States President, Harry Truman, promptly committed American land, air and naval

units to assist South Korea. This led to the assembling of a UN force, commanded by the charismatic General Douglas MacArthur, with components of the armed forces from sixteen member countries, including the USA, Britain, Australia and South Africa. The enclave around Pusan had only three airfields, and although considerable air strength was based in Japan, its distance from the battleground meant that only a limited period could be spent actually providing air support to the ground troops. Furthermore, the sophisticated jet-fighter forces of the USAF and US Navy were designed to operate from 6,000ft (1,829m) or more concrete runways or carrier decks, with the prime role of engaging in air combat; here, the runways were on the Japanese mainland, and because of the shallow Korean waters, the carriers could get no nearer than about 70miles (112.6km) from the coast. Furthermore, the F-80 Shooting Stars, F-84 Thunderjets, F2H Banshees and F9F Panthers were not ideal for ground-attack operations – although the lessons learned at the start of the Korean conflict led to certain modifications to these aircraft that made them better equipped for such operations.

Five days from the outbreak of hostilities, the Australian Prime Minister, Robert Menzies, proposed No. 77 Squadron of the RAAF for immediate operations in Korea; three days later, on 2 July, the squadron's P-51D Mustangs were flying escort to USAF transport aircraft which were evacuating casualties out of the war zone. The squadron had been formed on 16 March 1942 at Perth's Pearce airbase with Curtiss P-40E Kittyhawk 1A fighters, and it operated against Japanese forces with these for the next three years. At the end of World War II, the squadron joined with Nos. 76 and 82 Squadrons of the RAAF at Hunshu in Japan, forming the 81st Fighter Wing, and re-equipped with Mustangs. As had been proven over Europe in 1944/45, the Mustang was an excellent ground-strafing aircraft and the squadron soon racked up a good tally of North Korean armoured equipment, including three dozen tanks. But changes were about to happen, because the Australian Government had purchased a quantity of Meteor F.8s – much to the consternation of RAAF Korean-experienced pilots, who had encountered Chinese-flown MiG-15s and were hoping to receive the F-86 Sabre.

Fifteen F.8 and two T.7 Meteors were prepared for their long sea journey by 43 Group at Abbotsinch, and arrived at Hiroshima Bay, on the Japanese mainland of Honshu, secured to the flight deck of the Royal Navy light carrier HMS *Warrior* on 24 February 1951. The aircraft were then transported ashore in threes, by lighter – there being no harbour installations – and were taken to No. 77 Squadron's base at Iwakuni; this was a British Commonwealth unit shared with Nos. 86 and 391 Squadrons of the RAAF, and a detach-

The wintry atmosphere of this photograph does not seem to have dampened No. 19 Squadron at Church Fenton. The Squadron Leader's WE863, WA969/E, WB108/F and WE870/G were all Baginton-built aircraft. *Aeroplane Monthly.*

No. 19 Squadron look much more picturesque when flying above the murk. *Aeroplane Monthly.*

ment of the RAF's No. 88 Squadron from Seletar, flying Short Sunderland GR.5s. An RAF handling party, commanded by Flight Lieutenant John Fleming, administered operations, over eight hours having to be spent on each airframe to remove its

anti-corrosive coatings. Another consignment of Meteors arrived in March, consisting of twenty F.8s, plus a further two T.7s; and four seasoned RAF pilots accompanied them, to oversee the conversion of RAAF pilots from Mustangs to Meteors.

Three Wattisham-based No. 263 Squadron F.8s, with Baginton-built VZ567 fitted with intake guards. This aircraft went on to serve with Nos. 64, 66, 85, 245 and 500 Squadrons before being scrapped in November 1971. WA894 crashed in August 1952 while still with the squadron, while WA896 was scrapped in August 1959, after being on charge to Nos. 56 and 64 Squadrons. *Aeroplane Monthly.*

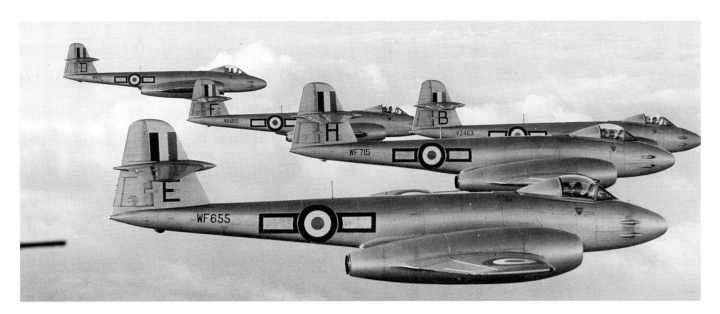

This formation of No. 66 Squadron aircraft is led by VZ463/B, only the twenty-sixth F.8 to come off the Hucclecote lines, while WF655/E and WB112/D were both Baginton-built. WA850/F went to provide spares for U.16 drones, and the other four were scrapped at the end of their operational lives. *Aeroplane Monthly.*

No. 77 Squadron, commanded by Sqn Ldr Richard Cresswell, continued operating with Mustangs over Korea while their jet fighters were being prepared, and the RAF pilots, unable to get on with the conversion programme because no RAAF pilots were available, applied for operational flying. They were Flt Lts Joe Blyth, Frank Easley and Max Scannel, and Sgt Bob Lamb, and they were posted to Pusan where they flew Mustangs on sorties for nearly a month. Back at Iwakuni, Sqn Ldr Cresswell became the first to check out on the Meteor – which was not too difficult as he had already flown USAF F-80s over Korea. Flt Lt Compton, the squadron's engineering officer, became the second RAAF Meteor-converted pilot, and so he was able to test-fly the aircraft as they became available. The four T.7s were heavily utilized, as the Australian pilots were enthusiastic to accumulate as many jet-flying hours as possible, and the trainer's airframe hours had to be carefully logged in case they were exceeded before their principal job was completed. All four arrived at Iwakuni with RAF serials, these being WA731, WA732, WG974 and WG977, but these were changed to the RAAF numbers A77-229, A77-305, A77-380 and A77-577 respectively. Later these were changed again, the new numbers being A77-701, A77-702, A77-703 and A77-704. Ten weeks later, on 4 May 1951, No. 77 Squadron bade a fond farewell to

Iwakuni, circa January 1951. Meteor F.8s WH251, WA961 and WA946, registered in No.77 Squadron RAAF as A77-510, A77-189 and A77-911 respectively, have received their radio compasses prior to moving on to South Korea. Of the three aircraft, A77-510 returned to Australia after the end of hostilities, but the other two were lost in action. Three of the T.7s employed on type-conversion can also be seen in the photograph. John Cummings.

Hamilton Standard Hydromatic propellers, and became the RAAF's first all-jet fighter squadron.

Shortly after the changeover, Flt Lt Daniels, an RAF pilot on detachment to the USAF, spent two days at Iwakuni flying an F-86 Sabre in a comparative-performance trial with an F.8. From these trials, as was expected, the American aircraft proved better in a dive or when flown straight and level, but the Australian pilots were pleased to learn that the Meteor had a better sustained climbing performance and could out-turn the F-86. Before these findings could be tested against the MiG-15, Lt Gen Sir Horace Robertson, the Australian commander of the British Commonwealth occupation force in Japan, issued a directive in June 1951, that each Meteor would have to be fitted with a radio compass before it could be accepted for service in the Korean theatre of operations; early in June, a consignment of ARN-6 radio compasses arrived. Problems arose when it came to the location of the loop aerial, which could not operate under metal. The Sabre's fully transparent canopy could accommodate its aerial just aft of the pilot's seat, but the Meteor's hood, with its metal rear portion, made it impossible for a similar installation to be made. After much deliberation, the Meteor's aerial mast mounting was modified to take the loop aerial, which was then encased in an Australian-produced perspex blister. During the compass's check-flight in WA944, the pilot, Sgt Stone, was the unexpected participant in a demonstration of the Martin-Baker ejector

In the markings of the Acklington-based Armament Practice Station, VZ494/L was photographed at Bovingdon in July 1956. An early, second batch production F.8 which first served with No. 222 Squadron, it has been retrofitted with a one-piece cockpit hood, cartridge ejector chutes and underwing fuel tanks. Aeroplane Monthly.

The red chevrons on WK987/D proclaim it to be a No. 65 Squadron F.8, based at Duxford. This aircraft was written off and scrapped on 29 June 1958, while still operating with the squadron. Author's collection.

seat, the first knowledge of which was his projection through the canopy. Luckily he sustained only minor injuries, and a later examination failed to deduce how, or why, the incident occurred.

No. 77 Squadron departed from Iwakuni on 30 June 1951 and relocated on the Korean airbase of Kimpo, commanded by Colonel John Tipton of the USAF, from where an element of the 4th Fighter Interceptor Wing operated with F-86s. Nearly the whole of July was spent flying around the Kimpo area so that the Australian pilots could thoroughly familiarize themselves with the locality and its GCA facilities. On 30 July they were able to put their findings to the test, when eighteen Meteor F.8s, led by Sqn Ldr Cresswell, made their first Meteor operational flight at 35,000ft (10,668m) over the Yalu River. Three weeks later, on 18 August, their C.O. was posted and Wing Commander Gordon Steeg took over the squadron. They also lost two pilots in a mid-air collision later in the month, one of them being Sgt Lamb, who had been a member of the RAF quartet that came for the type-conversions at Iwakuni.

Escort missions for B-29 and RF-80 operations continued during August, and the first Meteor/MiG-15 encounter took place on 29 August; W/O Guthrie in A77-721 was shot down and spent the next two years as a prisoner-of-war. By the end of August, 354 sorties had been flown in twenty-five missions, and the squadron had logged 589 operational flying hours. On 5 September, twelve MiG-15s attacked the six-Meteor escort of a USAF 15th Squadron RF-80 reconnaissance mission, and A77-726 was brought back to Kimpo by its pilot, W/O Michelson, with, amongst other damage, a 24in (61cm) hole in its tail-plane. The aircraft was repaired at Iwakuni and returned to operations a month later. A very successful attack against an enemy convoy was made on 9 September, although several aircraft sustained damage from anti-aircraft and

Instructional Airframe number 7214M receiving attention from a group of enthusiasts at No. 1 STT; it carries the yellow/black checks of No. 63 Squadron, and had the serial VZ464/H when it was a member of that unit at Waterbeach. Author's collection.

small-arms fire, which kept the airframe fitters busy back at Kimpo.

Whilst a very creditable time of sixty-five seconds was being taken to get eighteen F.8s airborne, the Australians noted that the USAF 4th Wing were getting their F-86s off the runway in pairs, and so No. 77 Squadron Meteors started doing the same, with a four-seconds interval between each pair. Another aircraft was damaged on 22 September, when Sgt Osborn landed A77-616 at Kimpo before the undercarriage had locked down; the incident occurring because his fuel-gauges had informed him that he was flying on vapour! Four days after this, a dozen Meteors were 'bounced' by MiGs in a three-to-one ratio, but the RAAF squadron had the satisfaction of driving the enemy aircraft off without receiving any casualties, thus enabling the USAF aircraft that they were escorting to complete their mission.

During a B-29 escort mission on 24 October, sixteen No. 77 Squadron aircraft came across an F-86/MiG-15 dogfight, and in the ensuing melée, six enemy aircraft evaded the Meteors and shot down a B-29. Three days later, Flying Officer Reading

Australia's No. 77 Squadron was commanded by Sqn Ldr Richard Cresswell when they started receiving Meteor F.8s at Iwakuni. Flt Lt Max Scannell was one of the small group of RAF instructors who assisted in converting the squadron to turbojet aircraft; he is seen talking with the Australian CO, who is in the cockpit. The metal fairing at the rear of the canopy and the absence of radio compass loop aerial indicates that this photograph was taken prior to the squadron going to Korea. *Aeroplane Monthly.*

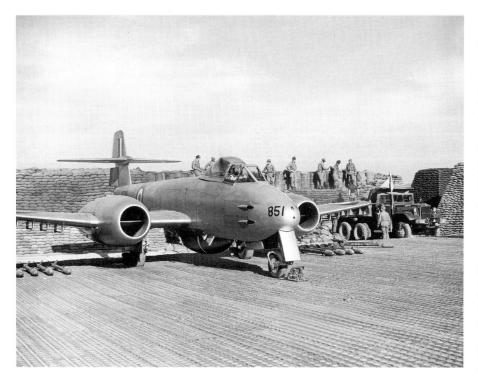

American troops build up the revetment around No. 77 Squadron F.8 A77-851 in Korea, the aircraft having been modified for rocket projectile operations and fitted with a radio compass loop aerial; before being shipped to the RAAF, the aircraft was built at Hucclecote as WK683. It survived the conflict to go to Australia and be converted to U.21A drone standard; it was scrapped in October 1965. *Author's collection.*

badly damaged a MiG-15 during an encounter, and on 2 November Flt Lt Blyth did likewise; but on the following day A77-811, flown by Sgt Robertson, was hit and, unable to lower its wheels to land, the aircraft was a write-off. Another air-to-air collision occurred on 11 November, when Sgt Robertson, this time flying A77-959, made contact with A77-587, piloted by Fg Off Blight, at 24,000ft (7,315m). Robertson ejected straight away, but Blight tried to get back to base; however, he was obliged to eject when his aircraft became uncontrollable at the approach speed.

The month of December started dramatically when twelve Meteors, flying at nearly 20,000ft (6,096m), were set upon by over fifty MiG-15s. In the ensuing dogfight two enemy aircraft were confirmed as destroyed, but for the loss of three RAAF aircraft, A77-29, A77-251 and A77-949. One MiG was credited to Fg Off Gogerly, and the other to the squadron, since several pilots claimed hits – including a certain George Hale, who went so far as to adorn his aircraft, named 'Halestorm', with the wording 'MiG killer'. But with only fourteen aircraft now

On their return to Australia, No.77 Squadron held an Open Day and their F.8s looked rather cleaner than when in Korea. No doubt the Air Cadets were wishing they were just a few years older! A77-897 in the foreground was built at Hucclecote as WK685 before going to Korea. It became an Instructional Airframe with No.22 Squadron RAAF before going to the Morrabin Air Museum. A77-397 was Baginton-built WE896 and it, too, became an Australian Instructional Airframe; it was struck off charge on 22 September 1958. Author's collection.

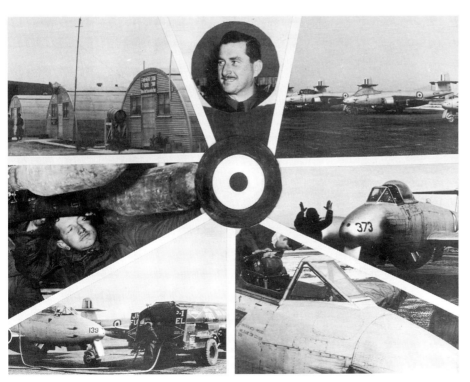

At the end of March 1952, the Headquarters, Far East Air Forces put out a montage depicting the activities of the RAAF's No. 77 Squadron in Korea, and acknowledging over 8,000 operational sorties flown. Wing Commander R.T. Susans was shown as the C.O and the groundcrews were not forgotten – and neither were their billets! Author's collection.

serviceable – this being the first week of December – No. 77 Squadron's role in Korea had to be reappraised. They were assigned the defence of Kimpo and the neighbouring Suwan airfields, and maintained this role until the end of 1951, when Wing Commander Ronald Susans took over as the squadron's new C.O. One of his first actions was to redirect the Meteor's utilization, believing that patrolling a couple of airfields in the rather forlorn hope that the enemy would put in an attack, was not good for his pilots' morale. The RAF had not cleared the Meteor F.8 for rocket-projectile operations, but by dint of careful argument, the wing commander managed to persuade the RAAF hierarchy that such a use made good sense. Engineering was put in hand at Iwakuni, and aircraft were adapted to take four rocket rails under the outer wings, on each of which a maximum of two 60lb (27.2kg) unguided rocket projectiles could be mounted, giving the aircraft a sixteen-missile armament that could be fired singly or in a volley. Activation was by an F-80 electrical tank release system, which had been modified to the Meteor's circuitry without affecting the Hispano cannon armament. The first ground-attack with the new installations was made on 8 January 1952, although in the event, only the cannon were used.

Attacks on important ground targets continued until the beginning of May, although accurate anti-aircraft fire made the missions anything but easy; in the first four months of 1952 the squadron lost nine aircraft, and four pilots. Then on 4 May the squadron was detailed to provide top cover for an American fighter-bomber mission: a dozen MiG-15s were encountered, and P/O John Surman scored a number of hits on one enemy aircraft. However, he could not claim it as a 'probable' because he had to take evasive action when his own aircraft was attacked. Fg Off Bill Simmonds had better results on 8 May, when the pilot of a MiG-15 on which he was scoring hits, baled out and his abandoned aircraft was seen to crash.

A cease-fire was negotiated on 27 July 1953. No. 77 Squadron's tally amounted to three enemy aircraft shot down by Mustangs, and a further three by Meteors. In a total of 18,872 sorties, over 1,500 vehicles, 3,800 ground installations and sixteen bridges were destroyed, for the cost of forty-two pilots, of which thirty-two, including at least two RAF loan pilots, were flying Meteors. Several RAF pilots flew with the squadron on exchange postings, with a full tour lasting six months.

The Meteor GAF

Although the RAF had not cleared the F.Mark 8 for operations with rocket projectiles when No. 77 Squadron used it in this role in Korea, it was not through any lack of thought by Gloster Aircraft, for they had produced such a version as a private venture in 1950. It was given the company type number G.44, and they resurrected one of their own chosen names on the list submitted to the MOS back in 1941: the 'Reaper'. Based on an F.8 airframe, the aircraft had strengthened outer wings and a span increased by 100-gallon (455-litre) fuel tanks on each tip. It had its maiden flight from Moreton Valence, in the hands of Gloster production test pilot Jim Cooksey, on 4 September 1950. Finished in the carmine red of the other PV Meteors, and carrying a white G-AMCJ civil registration and tip tanks, the aircraft went as a static display in the SBAC Show at Farnborough the following day. There it was fitted with eight 95lb (43kg) rocket projectiles under the starboard wing and a 1,000lb (454kg) bomb under the port, with a cluster of six dummy Rocket-Assisted Take-Off (RATOG) canisters around the fuselage centre-section. Two new centre-line installations under the fuselage were fitted, one carrying a 1,000lb (454kg) bomb, the other with four R.Ps. The official company designation was Meteor Ground-Attack Fighter (GAF). 'Reaper' just seemed to disappear.

The following year's Farnborough Display was one of those remembered and talked about by all who were lucky enough to be present; I know I will never forget it. G-AMCJ was re-registered G-7-1 in keeping with a new MAP Class B marking system for military private venture aircraft, or prototypes not produced to an official specification. The 'G' denoted Great Britain, and each company was allotted a number, '7' in Gloster's case. The last figure denoted the number of a particular company's airframe within the system: thus, the Meteor GAF being Gloster's first, the designation was G-7-1, displayed in black on an overall silver aircraft. The aircraft had been flown with a variety of external stores during 1951 by Jan Zurakowski and, with slide-rule in hand,

---

Aussie-operated Meteors

The following aircraft are confirmed as participating in RAAF activities during the Korean War, although not always in the theatre of operations. Individual RAF serials are followed in parenthesis by their original Australian serials and their renumbering, where applicable. *Indicates that the aircraft was lost, either through enemy action or flying mishap on operational service.

Meteor T.Mark 7.

VW410 (A77-2)	WF843 (A77-706)	WA680 (A77-705)
WG974 (A77-380/A77-703)	WA731 (A77-229/A77-701)	WG977 (A77-577/A77-704)*
WA732 (A77-305/A77-702)	WH118 (A77-707)	

Meteor F.Mark 8.

WA782 (A77-730)*	WE889 (A77-157)	WK670 (A77-860)*
WA783 (A77-446)	WE890 (A77-570)*	WK674 (A77-868)
WA786 (A77-744)	WE896 (A77-397)	WK682 (A77-858)*
WA934 (A77-354)*	WE898 (A77-134)*	WK683 (A77-851)
WA936 (A77-373)*	WE900 (A77-415)*	WK684 (A77-857)*
WA937 (A77-811)*	WE903 (A77-31)	WK685 (A77-867)
WA938 (A77-29)*	WE905 (A77-207)	WK686 (A77-856)*
WA939 (A77-587)*	WE906 (A77-251)*	WK688 (A77-859)*
WA941 (A77-163)*	WE907 (A77-734)	WK715 (A77-853)*
WA942 (A77-735)*	WE908 (A77-128)*	WK727 (A77-869)
WA944 (A77-231)*	WE909 (A77-959)*	WK728 (A77-855)
WA945 (A77-316)*	WE910 (A77-559)*	WK730 (A77-863)
WA946 (A77-911)*	WE911 (A77-15)*	WK735 (A77-864)*
WA947 (A77-741)*	WE918 (A77-385)*	WK748 (A77-870)
WA948 (A77-740)*	WE928 (A77-627)*	WK791 (A77-871)
WA949 (A77-139)*	WE969 (A77-193)	WK792 (A77-872)
WA950 (A77-982)*	WE971 (A77-436)*	WK796 (A77-873)
WA951 (A77-728)*	WF653 (A77-920)*	WK798 (A77-875)
WA952 (A77-368)	WF746 (A77-46)*	WK800 (A77-876)
WA954 (A77-721)*	WF750 (A77-422)	WK821 (A77-879)
WA956 (A77-616)*	WH251 (A77-510)	WK907 (A77-878)
WA957 (A77-726)*	WH252 (A77-793)	WK909 (A77-874)
WA958 (A77-464)*	WH254 (A77-258)	WK910 (A77-880)
WA960 (A77-949)*	WH259 (A77-11)*	WK912 (A77-883)
WA961 (A77-189)*	WH274 (A77-343)*	WK913 (A77-877)
WA964 (A77-17)	WH405 (A77-865)	WK931 (A77-884)
WA998 (A77-802)	WH414 (A77-866)*	WK937 (A77-882)
WE874 (A77-953)*	WH417 (A77-862)*	WK938 (A77-886)
WE877 (A77-393)*	WH418 (A77-861)	WK944 (A77-881)
WE880 (A77-120)*	WH475 (A77-65)	WK973 (A77-885)
WE886 (A77-643)*	WK650 (A77-854)	

WA935 (A77-300) never received its allocated RAAF serial number, as the aircraft was lost in transit; it is believed to have come down in the Middle East.

---

he prepared a routine to be flown at the SBAC Show. On 11 September he made the first display, loaded with twenty-four 95lb (43kg) R.P.s and two 100-gallon (455-litre) tip-tanks. Following a low-level high-speed run up the runway, he pulled the aircraft up into a pure vertical climb. As the speed dropped off to the stall, he simultaneously kept one throttle fully open

and shut the other right down, at the same time spinning the Meteor round its vertical axis and holding the rotation through several cycles during the descent. The manoeuvre was christened the 'cartwheel' and, with 'Zura' being a qualified engineer, the stress loads had been fully worked out before the spectacular demonstration was made. The days of the Meteor's structural

A keen interest in Frank Whittle's labours is being shown when A77-880 is open for inspection back home. The aircraft was built by Armstrong Whitworth as WK910 and transferred to the RAAF on 10 March 1953 as a brand-new aircraft. It stayed with No. 77 Squadron until it was scrapped on 14 January 1959. Mike Hooks.

problems had long since disappeared.

Gloster's efforts to get a ground-attack Meteor into the RAF fell on deaf ears – the Air Ministry was far more interested in getting swept-wing fighters into service. By the time No. 77 Squadron's F.8s were pouring R.P.s into Communist troops in Korea a few months later, Hunters were flashing around the skies – but without airbrakes! G-7-1 was used by Gloster Aircraft for various experimental trials, including the perfecting of spring-tab ailerons, and was then refurbished with a grafted-on T.7 front fuselage in place of the single-seat configuration. The tip-tanks were retained, but with stabilizing fins at either end, and the aircraft was once again put on the civil aircraft register, this time as G-ANSO. It appeared at another SBAC Display in 1954, resplendent in a larkspur-blue and ivory colour scheme, before eventually being sold to Sweden.

When the F.8 came into squadron service, target-towing was mainly supplied by the Bristol Beaufighter TT.10 and Hawker Tempest TT.5. The large number of F.8s produced enabled the type to take over from its piston-engined predecessors, and by utilizing the ventral tank for the target's tow-line attachment point, an acceptable, if unsophisticated, conversion was made.

Fairly early in its life, VZ438, the first production F.8, went to RAE Farnborough where the first T T conversion and flying trials were conducted. These were later flown in conjunction with F.8 WA830, an ex-No. 245 Squadron aircraft that had the additional modification of a camera installed in its nose for recording the said trials. The Armament Practice Stations (APS) at Acklington and Sylt were the first to operate the type, designated the F(TT).8, followed in 1954 by No. 229 OCU at Chivenor. Target-towing aircraft were attached to just about every Station Flight in the United Kingdom, together with the overseas bases at Changi, Gibraltar and Malta, which also operated their own TT Flights. For these operations, the F(TT).8s had their under-surfaces painted in the broad black and yellow stripes that had adorned target-towing aircraft since the beginning of World War II.

With the arrival of Lightnings in squadron service, the inadequacy of the

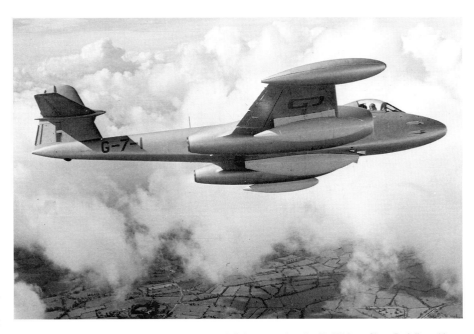

Gloster's one-off private venture G.44 ground-attack fighter, carrying the Air Ministry Class B civil markings G-7-1, flew with many combinations of external stores; one of these was this fuel load which, including the aircraft's internal tankage, gave a maximum of 820 gallons (3,731 litres). Author's collection.

A casual-looking Jan Zurakowski (right) certainly belies his great test- and display-flying abilities, which were well proved to everyone attending the 1951 SBAC display. He is here shown taking off in the Reaper, with red-painted tip-tanks and RP load, prior to executing his unique 'cartwheel' manoeuvre. Author's collection.

No. 229 OCU F(TT).8 WK941/E went to Tarrant Rushton on 16 May 1972 for conversion to U.16 drone standard, and was placed on charge to RAE Llanbedr. Author's collection.

Gloster G.44 Meteor Ground-Attack Fighter

In 1950, Gloster Aircraft produced an impressive brochure extolling the virtues of a 'new, special version of the Meteor'. To the standard Meteor F.8, with what the company described as 'a particularly generous power-to-weight ratio that has always been an outstanding characteristic of the basic Meteor airframe', additional tactical armament and equipment was added, while retaining the full 20mm cannon and ammunition, as follows:

Four 1,000lb (454kg) bombs, with two 100-gallon (455-litre) tip-tanks

or

Twenty-four 95lb (43kg) rocket projectiles, with two 100-gallon (455-litre) tip-tanks

or

580-gallon (2,639-litre) additional fuel in ventral, underwing and tip-tanks, giving a ferrying or operational range of 1,500 miles (2,414m)

or

Two 1,000lb (454kg) bombs and ventral pack containing two additional 20mm cannon, plus ammunition, with two 100-gallon (455-litre) tip-tanks

or

Sixteen 95lb (43kg) rocket projectiles and ventral pack containing two additional 20mm cannon, plus ammunition, with two 100-gallon (455-litre) tip-tanks.

Combinations of these loads could be devised as required.

The brochure stated that 'In order to ensure practical operation with maximum loads from improvised or forward airfields, full provision is made for the installation of RATOG, whilst an arrester hook can also be fitted.'

Without RATOG, a fully laden Meteor GAF was specified as taking off from a runway of less than 1,800 yards (1,646m). With RATOG, an airstrip of under 500 yards (457m) would be sufficient to ensure a take-off in order to clear a 50ft (15.5m) obstacle within 1,000 yards (914m). The principal aircraft engaged in the development of the Meteor GAF were Mark 3 EE254, Mark 4 EE519 and Mark 8 VZ460.

Reaper and Russell Adams: nothing more needs to be said. Author's collection.

The last Meteor to be built at Hucclecote was F.8 WL191, seen here taking to the air for the first time on 9 April 1954 in the hands of Jim Cooksey, Gloster's chief production pilot. It did not see RAF service, but was delivered to the Egyptian Air Force as number 1426, on 6 June 1955. Derek N. James.

F(TT).8 became very apparent and the type started disappearing, in company with a reduction in operational fighter squadrons, together with their bases. The Chivenor OCU moved to Brawdy in October 1974 and became No. 1 TWU. They took F(TT).8 VZ467 with them, and it continued to be used until it was struck off charge on 22 October 1982; it was therefore the longest-serving target-tug Meteor.

The last Meteor F.8 to go into RAF squadron service was WL190, the penultimate example of the Mark, built at Hucclecote; it joined No. 34 Squadron at Tangmere in July 1954.

The type was flown in standard form at two SBAC Displays at Farnborough, namely VZ438 in 1949 and WA878 in 1950. The aircraft was sold to a total of eight foreign counties, to serve in their respective air forces.

CHAPTER 9

The Cameramen

The FR. Mk9

Despite the fatal break-up of the one-and-only Meteor FR.5 on 15 June 1949, the Air Ministry were not deterred, and Richard Walker's design department had produced a fighter reconnaissance aircraft based on the Meteor F.8 to replace the RAF's long-in-the-tooth PR Spitfires. The nose was basically identical to that of the FR.5, but the design allowed for the installation of a remotely controlled F.24 camera, posi-tioned on a universal mounting attached to the nose-wheel bulkhead. With the full four 20mm cannon armament retained, Perspex panels on either side of the nose, together with one directly ahead, allowed oblique photographs to be taken in three independent directions. Hot air ducted from the compressor casing of the star-board engine provided heating to prevent condensation on the windows and camera lens. In fact the F.24 was a rather cumber-some piece of photographic equipment, and later in 1954 the much neater F.95 camera was produced by Vinten; this was small enough to allow three to be installed in place of the F.24.

The company was awarded Contract No. 6/ACFT/1389/CB7(b), dated 2 August 1947, to produce twelve Gloster G.41L Meteor FR. Mark 9 aircraft in one batch, the serials running from VW360 to VW371 inclusive. The first aircraft acted as the prototype, and this made its maiden flight from Moreton Valence on 22 March 1950, in the hands of Jan Zurakowski. A short spell of handling trials, starting in

The FR.9 had the small-diameter intakes of earlier F.8s, and three clear-view panels for the F.24 camera carried. A product of the second FR.9 contract, VZ605 is photographed before delivery to No. 2 Squadron of the 2nd Tactical Air Force, based at Buckeburg, early in 1951, where it carried the coding 'B-S'. The aircraft was scrapped at the end of December 1957. *Aeroplane Monthly.*

No. 541 Squadron's WH552/E-B, with WH548 in the background, stand on a rain-soaked tarmac. Both were scrapped in the winter of 1957. *Aeroplane Monthly.*

July, was conducted at Boscombe Down, where the camera's operating capabilities were assessed in the low-level tactical role for which the aircraft was designed. Ferranti checked out their camera-control system and VW360, which was always on charge to its manufacturer, is believed to have ended its days with the Proof and Experimental Establishment (PEE) at Shoeburyness, in September 1957.

Five further contracts for FR.9 production were received over the next four years. Contract No. 6/ACFT/2430/CB7(b), dated 4 September 1948, covered the manufacture of thirty-five aircraft in one batch with serial numbers VZ577 to VZ611 inclusive, and this was followed by the contract numbered 6/ACFT/2983/CB7(b) signed on 25 November 1948, to build a total of twenty-three aircraft in two batches. The first batch was twelve aircraft numbered WB114 to WB125 inclusive, while the second contained eleven, with serials WB133 to WB143 inclusive. The

fourth contract was No. 6/ACFT/5621/CB7(b), issued on 8 August 1950, for a single batch of twenty-five aircraft, the serial numbers WH533 to WH557 inclusive being alloted to them. On 15 January 1951, contract No. 6/ACFT/6066.CB7(b) was signed, covering eleven FR.9s in one batch, with serials WL255 to WL265 inclusive. The sixth and last was contract No. 6/ACFT/7252/CB7(b), dated 17 August 1951, for the production of a twenty-aircraft batch, numbered WX962 to WX981 inclusive. This made a total of 126 Meteor FR.9s, all being built at Hucclecote.

The first unit to receive the new fighter-reconnaissance Meteor was No. 2 Squadron, based in West Germany at Buckeburg as part of the 2nd Tactical Air Force (2TAF); they took on charge the second production aircraft, VW361, in December 1950 and operated the type, which included VZ587, VZ599 and WB114, for five and a half years. This

squadron moved its base of operations to Gütersloh in 1952, Wahn in 1953 and Geilenkirchen in 1955, where they replaced the Gloster aircraft with Swift FR.5s. No. 208 Squadron at Fayid in Egypt received the first of their FR.9s, VW363, in January 1951, and they used the type in a heavy flying schedule as an element of the Middle East Air Force (MEAF). They were the only tactical reconnaissance unit in the Canal Zone, with the tradition of being one of the best self-contained, independent units in the MEAF; they operated their Meteor FR.9s for seven and a half years, only changing them for the Hunter F.6. The tension that was building up in the area during the mid-1950s generated an increase in air activity, and the chiefs of staff in the MEAF drew up an outline plan on 29 July 1956 for operations against Egypt if that country went ahead with the threatened nationalization of the Suez Canal. Such were the seeds of Operation *Musketeer*, the Anglo-French intervention

FR.9s of No. 208 Squadron photographed in March 1958: WX978/Q, which later joined the Khormaksar
Station Flight, before being scrapped on 24 February 1959; and VZ601/D, which went to No. 8
Squadron before it, too, was scrapped, in March 1960. *Aeroplane Monthly.*

mounted in an endeavour to return the Canal to some form of international control; and as Egypt put its threat into action, so too was *Musketeer* activated on 31 October 1956. For the first time British-built and operated turbojet aircraft were in conflict with each other (the anti-Peron rebels in Argentina used three captured Meteors for a couple of days in 1955, but they were never used against Argentine Air Force Meteors). The island of Cyprus became the hub of air operations, with the airfield at Nicosia, at the height of *Musketeer*, holding 127 aircraft, while a further 112 were at Akrotiri. Because of this over-crowding, and because No. 208 Squadron's FR.9s did not have sufficient range to enable them to operate from Cyprus with any worthwhile time over an Egyptian target, the squadron was withdrawn to Malta. Republic RF-84Es of the French *Armée de l'Air* supplied the necessary photo-reconnaissance requirements during the seven-day operation.

The Meteor FR.9 was operated by two other front-line units: No. 8 Squadron, based at Khormaksar in Aden, received its first in January 1958, and subsequently the Arabian Peninsula Fighter Reconnaissance Flight was formed as a separate element from the squadron, using FR.9s in conjunction with some de Havilland Venom FB.1s and FB.4s until they took delivery of their first Hunter FGA.9 in January 1960. The other squadron was No. 79: during World War II they operated Republic Thunderbolt Is and IIs from India until moving to Burma, where, while based at Meiktila, they were disbanded on 30 December 1945. Reformed on 15 November 1951 at Gütersloh, the new No. 79 Squadron became a fighter-reconnaissance unit, flying Meteor FR.9s, including VZ590 and WL265, until these were replaced in June 1956 by the Swift FR.5, the squadron then operating from Wunstorf. Stradishall-based No. 226OCU also employed a few FR.9s, among them WB125 and WB137, while it is known that one, VW366, was flown by the CFE at West Raynham. The aircraft was generally liked by service pilots, and in low-level mock combats they easily outmanoeuvred the Hunter. But it was accepted that air-to-ground gunnery was a very hit-and-miss affair, with emphasis on the miss! The aircraft's notorious snaking behaviour, which occurred at roughly 30kt bands, made the range operations very much of a lottery, so that

hitting the target at all was accepted as being good, and scoring a 'bull' was miraculous.

Besides the prototype, VW360, at least three other Meteor FR.9s were used on non-operational activities. The third production aircraft, VW362, was engaged in heating trials associated with the Mark and was then loaned to Ferranti at Turnhouse; and VZ608 is featured in the engine testbed chapter. WH535 was used in September 1955 by the Ballistic Trials Flight, Armament and Instrument Unit at Martlesham Heath, for rocket projectile

trials, operating on the Orfordness range; it is possibly the only FR.9 fitted with RPs and is known to have been flown by Flt Lt J. Gibson from the Flight. The type was too long-in-the-tooth to qualify for any SBAC display, but it was exported and three foreign air forces operated FR.9s for varying periods.

The PR. Mk10

By way of complementing the FR.9 and going down the Hucclecote production

A quartet of silver-finished FR.9s from No. 208 Squadron go into a loop in the Middle East sunshine in the spring of 1952. VW368/S was written off in an accident the following year; both VZ606/Z and VZ593/Q stayed with the squadron until they were scrapped in February 1958. Author's collection.

lines at the same time, Gloster Aircraft developed the high-altitude photo-reconnaissance Meteor PR.10. This was a contemporary aircraft, utilizing old Meteor elements. The original long-span wings of the F.3 were married to an FR.9 fuselage, minus cannon armament, with the old F.3/F.4 tail assembly, that everyone was so pleased to get rid of when the E.1/44 unit was introduced. With a service ceiling of 47,000ft (14,326m), the 43ft 0in (13.1m) span wings are understandable, but the reason for fitting the older tail has often been queried. The aircraft had a Type 24 camera in the nose, as originally installed in its predecessor, plus two F52 cameras in ventral positions, aft of the ventral fuel tank; these were protected from stones and mud during take-off by metal plates, which were jettisoned once the aircraft was airborne.

Gloster received five contracts for the building of fifty-nine G.41M Meteor PR. Mark 10 aircraft at Hucclecote. The first, No. 6/ACFT/658/CB7(b) dated 22 November 1946, was for one batch of twenty aircraft, alloted the serial numbers VS968 to VS987 inclusive. Contract No. 6/ACFT/1389/CB7(b), signed on 2 August 1948, covered a batch of four aircraft, VW376 to VW379 inclusive, while the third was Contract No. 6/ACFT/2430/CB7(b), dated 4 September 1948, ordering twenty-one T.7s but including one PR.10, VZ620. Twenty-nine aircraft in one batch was the requirement of Contract No. 6/ACFT/2983/CB7(b) dated 25 November 1948, their numbers being WB153 to WB181 inclusive. The fifth and final contract for PR.10s was also Gloster's

The installation of the bulky F.24 camera in the nose of an FR.9 and its positioning on the universal mounting, in this instance for photography via the port side window. *Aeroplane Monthly.*

A mixed trio of 2nd TAF PR aircraft, circa 1955. The French RF-84E leads FR.9s VZ611/B-Z of No. 2 Squadron and PR.10 WB156/A-B of No. 541 Squadron, showing heavy weather-wear on its starboard underwing tank. The latter aircraft went to the Proof and Experimental Establishment in June 1960. Author's collection.

last Meteor order, Contract No. 6/ACFT/5621/CB7(b), issued on 8 August 1950 covering five aircraft, WH569 to WH573.

As was the case with the FR.9, the first production PR.10, VS968, served as the prototype and trials aircraft. It was first flown from Moreton Valence by Jan Zurakowski on 29 March 1950, just six days after he had flown the first FR.9, and was then taken through the company handling trials programme before going to the A&AEE in August. It was fitted with a ventral tank and two 100-gallon (455-litre) underwing tanks. Heating for the oblique camera in the nose was the same as on the FR.9, while the two ventral cameras benefited by hot air ducted from the port engine's compressor casing, the heat being retained in the camera-bay by a canvas curtain around the whole installation. Following its Boscombe Down trials, in December 1950 VS968 was delivered to No. 541 Squadron at Benson, which had re-formed at the Oxfordshire base on 1 November 1947, operating with Spitfire PR.19s. With the arrival of further Meteor PR.10s, including VS972, VS973 and VS975, the Spitfires gradually disappeared, the last going in May 1951, leaving Benson with a full jet complement; this it took to Buckeburg a month later, on 7 June 1951. The squadron moved around 2TAF during its four years of operations in West Germany, spending periods at Gütersloh, Laarbruch and Wunstorf, where it was disbanded on 7 September 1957.

Another 2TAF unit, No. 2 Squadron, based at Buckeburg and equipped with Meteor FR.9s, received PR.10s from March 1951, the two Marks operating together for three months, until June, when the PR.10s left. Then in December 1951 No.13 Squadron at Kabit in the Canal Zone started replacing their Spitfire PR.11s with Meteor PR.10s; the new jet-powered photo-reconnaissance arrivals, including WB161, WB162 and WB165, operated until February 1956, when they were replaced by the Canberra PR.7 while the squadron was based at Akrotiri, on the island of Cyprus. With the Meteors, the squadron had flown in conjunction with No. 208 Squadron, and their combined field of operations had extended down to Nairobi during the Mau Mau uprisings.

The last unit to replace Spitfire PR.19s with Meteor PR.10s, in January 1954, was No. 81 Squadron, operating out of Seletar on Singapore island, with detachments at Butterworth in Malaya and Kai Tak on Hong Kong. WB153, WB159 and WB169 are known to have served with the squadron, who used the type until February, when it too re-equipped with the Canberra PR.7. Another Benson-based unit, No. 237 OCU, accepted PR.10s on charge in April 1951, taking them when it moved to Bassingbourn six months later, where No. 231 OCU was based with its own PR.10s. No. 237 became absorbed into No. 231 OCU in December 1951, and the Meteor PR.10 was utilized for nearly five years, until the OCU became an all-Canberra operator in October 1956.

Both the FR.9 and PR.10 were equipped with Martin-Baker ejector seats, and the PR.10 was the highest-operating Meteor

A fine portrait of VS968, the first PR.10, on air test before going to Boscombe Down for evaluation, following which it served with No. 541 Squadron. It was scrapped on 7 July 1958. Author's collection.

WB156/A-B of No. 541 Squadron, which operated PR.10s in Germany from December 1950 until the unit was disbanded at Wunstorf, on 7 September 1957. Mike Hooks.

Meteor FR. Mark 9

Span:	37ft 2in (11.3m)
Length:	44ft 7in (13.5m)
Height:	13ft 0in (3.9m)
Wing area:	350sq ft (32.5sq m)
Weight empty:	10,790lb (4,894kg)
Weight loaded:	15,770lb (7,153kg)
Armament:	Four 20mm Hispano 3 cannon
Reconnaissance equipment:	One F.24 camera in nose, later replaced by three F.95 cameras
Max speed at sea level	598mph (962.3km/h)
at 30,000ft (9,144m)	550mph (885.1km/h)
Climb to 30,000ft (9,144m)	6.5 minutes
Service ceiling:	41,000ft (12,497m)

Meteor PR. Mark 10

Span:	43ft 0in (13.1m)
Length:	44ft 3in (13.4m)
Height:	13ft 0in (3.9m)
Wing area:	374sq ft (34.7sq m)
Weight empty:	10,993lb (4,986kg)
Weight loaded:	15,400lb (6,985kg)
Armament:	None
Reconnaissance equipment:	One F.24 camera in nose, two ventral F.52 cameras
Max speed at sea level	575mph (925.3km/h)
at 30,000ft (9,144m)	541mph (870.6km/h)
Climb to 30,000ft (9,144m)	6.2 minutes
Service ceiling:	47,000ft (14,326m)

(the long-spanned F.4 has sometimes been specified as having a 50,000ft (15,240m) ceiling, but it came nowhere near that in squadron service). With a maximum endurance of 3hr 40 min – although this was less for aircraft fitted with the larger-diameter intakes – the PR.10 had a useful range of operations. There were no direct export orders, although it is known that WB165, having served with No. 81 Squadron, was sold for service with the Royal Malaysian Air Force. Many of them finished in either No. 29 MU at Aston Down or No. 38 MU at Llandow, where some were refurbished with fully transparent canopies, such as VZ584 and VZ606, to join 2TAF in West Germany.

The last production PR.10 was WH573, completed early in 1952 – but the last Meteor of all to be built at Hucclecote was WL191, an F.8 that finished its life in the Egyptian Air Force. Taking off from Moreton Valence with Jim Cooksey at the controls, it ended ten and a half years of continuous production, totalling over 2,500 aircraft, including the F.9/40 prototypes. By this time Gloster's shop-floor space was becoming swamped by acres of delta wings, as the G.A.5 Javelin was being turned out to meet the 'Super Priority' category production instigated by Prime Minister Winston Churchill at the time of the Korean War – although in reality this high priority categorization did nothing to speed up the delivery of new aircraft. With contracts ordering over 430 Javelins to be built at Glosters, Baginton-based Armstrong Whitworth Aircraft was handed all further Meteor design and production which was to take the type into another sphere of operations: interception in the dark.

CHAPTER TEN

The Bats from Baginton

It has long been a subject of debate as to why, when the RAF had a surplus of jet day-fighters in the late 1940s, and knowing how long it takes to get an aeroplane from the drawing board to the threshold of a squadron runway, it was not until 1947 that the Air Ministry even issued a specification for a turbojet-powered day/night all-weather fighter. By the middle of World War II, Britain was in the lead with AI radar development, and when centrimetric radars – perfected in conjunction with the United States – were installed in Mosquito night fighters, met all their squadron's requirements. Maybe it was because, crude as they were, they operated so well, especially in the Mosquito NF.36, that the Service was quite happy to continue relying on them – although only about 160 had been built. The war had been won, and the fact that North American Aircraft were churning out all-weather versions of

the Sabre, the F-86D, while even Avro Canada had designed the mighty CF-100 Canuck in 1946/47 – and goodness knows what was happening on the other side of the Iron Curtain – none of this disturbed the mandarins from resting on their laurels.

Gradually a light started piercing the Stygian corridors of Whitehall, to the extent that in January 1947 Specifications F.43/46 for a single-seat day-fighter, and F.44/46 for a two-seat day/night all-weather fighter, were issued. F.43/46 went on to form the basis for Specification F.3/48, from which the P.1067 Hunter would emerge – in fact, Hawker Aircraft's project office carried out a number of design studies for both specifications. The majority were based on the use of two Rolls-Royce AJ.65 axial-flow engines giving about 6,500lb (2,947kg) thrust, which in 1948 became the Avon. There

was a very limited knowledge of swept-wing design in Britain at that time, but Hawker submitted proposals using moderate sweep, with one of them incorporating intakes on either side of the nose, jet outlets aft of the wing-roots, a two-man crew in tandem and a high-set tail-plane.

Gloster and de Havilland were among other companies that tendered designs, but the Air Ministry did not consider that anything submitted by any firm was instantly acceptable. However, both the Gloster and the de Havilland proposals were deemed worth developing, the latter eventually seeing operational service as the Sea Vixen. Gloster's development of F.44/46 would crystallize as the G.A.5 Javelin, and because the Air Ministry knew how long it would take for the aircraft to evolve from design to operational status, the company was requested to consider producing a night-fighter variant of the Meteor for more immediate service. Gloster knew it could not handle both, and in view of Armstrong Whitworth having already produced over 450 Meteors, it was decided within the Hawker Siddeley Group that Gloster would concentrate on perfecting their F.44/46 submission, while all future Meteor development would be concentrated with AWA at Baginton.

The starting-point for any Meteor night-fighter, with its pilot/radar-operator crew, would have to be the T.7, already in production at Hucclecote. Specification F.24/48 was drawn up, outlining the Air Ministry's requirements for the new Meteor variant, and H.R.Watson, Armstrong Whitworth's chief designer, headed the team that would undertake the work. VW413, the fourth production T.7, was ear-marked as the aerodynamic test airframe for the night-fighter, and a full-size wooden mock-up of the whole new, much longer, front fuselage section was completed by December 1948. The only available radar was the AI Mk 10 – the

VW413, the fourth production T.7 was transferred to Armstrong Whitworth for conversion into the aerodynamic trials aircraft for their proposed NF.11 adaptation of the Meteor. Derek N. James.

same equipment as fitted in the Mosquito NF.36, which the Meteor night-fighter was being developed to supersede. Furthermore, the only available armament was the 20mm Hispano Mk5 cannon, again the same as the Mosquito's. Well, at least it would be a lot faster.

Once again the long-span wings, as used on the F.3 and the first few F.4s, and also the PR.10, were incorporated into the design. VW413's short-span wings were removed and, fitted with its new 43ft 0in (13.1m) wings, it went to AWA's experimental facilities at Bitteswell, the ex-No. 105 OTU airfield six miles north of Derby, which the company had shared with the RAF for test-flying Lancasters built at Baginton during the war. Test-flying of VW413 was started on 23 December 1948, first to establish the effects on the centre of gravity (cg), to be moved further forward by the proposed longer radar-equipped nose, would have on the aircraft's handling. By the middle of January 1949, the first metal-fabricated nose had been completed, and this was fitted to the airframe at the nose-wheel armoured bulkhead. It encased a mock-up of an AI Mk10 28in (71.12cm) diameter dish, together with ballast to simulate the production-equipment's weight. The new nose increased the aircraft's length to 47ft 6in

As Baginton's first prototype NF.11 banks to port, it shows the repositioned four-cannon armament in standard Meteor long-span wings, and also the bulge under the radar nose-cone, required to house the scanner's lower bracket. Author's collection.

(14.47m). On 28 January 1949, AWA's test pilot William 'Bill' Else flew the aircraft for a 25-minute maiden flight. Since the airframe was basically a T.7, complete with that Mark's tail assembly,

'snaking' occurred during the flight. Subsequent flights led the pilot to believe that there was too much play in the rudder controls, but following the fitting of a replacement complete with its bearing, he did find an improvement, although directional stability still deteriorated in turbulent air conditions.

In March 1949, an E.1/44-type empennage was fitted in place of the original, which increased the length by 12in (30.4cm), to an overall 48ft 6in (14.7m). VW413 was first flown in this configuration by AWA's chief test pilot Squadron Leader Eric Franklin, on 8 April 1949. When the design office got down to details, it was found that the bottom bearing bracket of the radar scanner was too deep to be accommodated in the new nose. A neat blister housing was therefore incorporated to cover the protruding bracket, and flight-testing found that, although some slight vibration was encountered at Mach 0.72, it was acceptable, having no effect on the limiting Mach number. VW413 became longer again when a new 15in (38.1cm) longer nose was fitted, to take an AI Mk9C radar test installation. The overall length became 49ft 9in (15.16m), further test-flying in December found that this made no difference to the aircraft's performance.

Following six months of intensive test-

On 21 February 1952, No. 85 Squadron, at West Malling, had a Press Day, but there were notices on the canopies stating 'It is regretted that photos of internal fitments are forbidden'. Of the four NF.11s shown, WD625, WD617 and WD615 all later went to No. 29 Squadron, while WD618 went to No. 228 OCU. All four aircraft were scrapped in the first half of 1958. Author's collection.

Two later NF.11s, WM176 and WM177, join this No. 85 Squadron formation, photographed in 1953. Later, WM176 also went to No. 29 Squadron, while WM177 crashed in August 1953 when still serving with No. 85 Squadron. Author's collection.

flying at Bitteswell, VW413 was flown to Boscombe Down by Bill Else on 18 July 1950, and on the following day A&AEE pilots gave the aircraft over three and a half hours of trials. At the end of July, yet another nose was fitted. An example of the American APQ43 AI radar had been delivered to Bitteswell, and fitting it increased the nose by a further 9.5in

(24.1cm): thus VW413's overall length became 50ft 6in (15.39m), as compared with the 43ft 6in (13.2m) when AWA first received the aircraft; once again the handling was not affected. Having been engaged on test-flying at Bitteswell for over three years, VW413 then went to RAE Farnborough, where it put in another three and a half years flying for the

Establishment; lastly it went to No. 20 MU at Aston Down, and it was eventually scrapped there in March 1958.

The NF. Mk11

With the transference of Meteor work to Armstrong Whitworth, the aircraft's type number changed and the Baginton-based company received Contract No. 6/ACFT/3433/CB5(b) in 1949, covering the building of three G.47 Meteor NF.Mark 11 prototypes, given the serials WA546, WA547 and WB543, as well as 200 production aircraft, to be produced in four batches of fifty aircraft; these serial numbers would be WD585 to WD634, WD640 to WD689, WD696 to WD745 and WD751 to WD800, all inclusive. All aircraft would be powered by two Rolls-Royce Derwent 8 engines, each producing 3,600lb (1,632.6kg) static thrust. A further order, Contract No. 6/ACFT/6164/CB5(b) followed, to build 107 NF.11s in three batches: the first comprised fifty aircraft numbered WM143 to WM192 inclusive; the second was also for fifty, numbers WM221 to WM270 inclusive; and the third was a smaller batch of eleven aircraft, WM292 to WM302 inclusive. Four additional aircraft, WM372 to

A busy No. 87 Squadron hangar scene at either Wahn or Brüggen, with WD681's wing cannon panel open for servicing. This aircraft was struck off charge on 6 March 1953. *Aeroplane Monthly*.

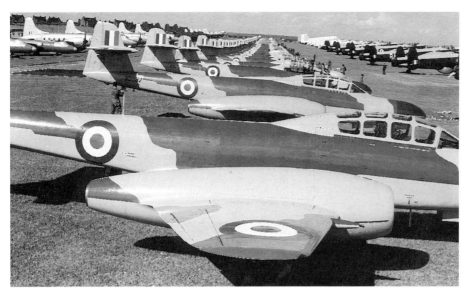

A galaxy of Meteors, together with nearly every other aircraft in the RAF, aligned at Odiham on 15 July 1953 for the Coronation Review. The second NF.11, WD592, served with several squadrons before being converted into a TT.20 for the RN, and eventually going to the USA as N94749. WM257 stands next in line: after the review it went to No. 29 Squadron; then it served with No. 228 OCU; and finally it was scrapped on 30 October 1963. Author's collection.

WM375 inclusive, were in a special MoS order on behalf of Fairey Aviation; these are detailed in the Trials Meteors chapter.

For the first time the Meteor armament had to be repositioned, the night-fighter's radar nose making it impossible to keep the standard front fuselage installation. Two 20mm cannon were fitted in each outer wing, adjacent to the engine nacelles, the outer guns being staggered more forward than the inner ones. As the ammunition tanks remained in their standard fuselage location, feeding the 160 rounds into each gun was via a Martin-Baker-designed flat ducting system, and firing was actuated electrically, with a synchronized cine camera installed in the starboard centre-section leading edge. Quick-removal, fully stressed access panels were constructed in the upper wing surface above the guns, to maintain the outer-wing torsional strength. The standard 325-gallon (1,478.7-litre) fuel tank was retained behind the fully pressurized cockpit. Here, the pilot occupied the front seat, with the radar operator in the rear. As on the T.7, no ejector seats were fitted; this was certainly a retrograde step, considering that all Marks since the trainer were equipped with a Martin-Baker seat. Additional fuel was carried in the 180-gallon (819-litre) ventral tank and two 100-gallon (455-litre) underwing drop tanks. Despite the trials made with the AI Mk9C and APQ43 radars, production NF11s were equipped with the old AI Mk10, so the fuselage length returned to 48ft 6in (14.7m).

At Baginton, metal was cut for the first prototype, WA546, in April 1949, with construction being completed early in May 1950. Ground-handling and taxiing trials followed, and on 31 May 1950, Eric Franklin took the first Meteor night-fighter for a maiden flight lasting thirty minutes. The smooth flight was followed by two more in the same day, the third flown by Bill Else. Although the ventral tank was fitted, it was not used, and neither was any on-board operational equipment, including the cockpit pressure system. A week later, on 6 June 1950, the aircraft was flown at the CFE, West Raynham, and by 29 June it was cleared for operation up to the 500mph (804.6km/h) design speed.

The fitting of further instruments was delayed so that WA546 could partake in the RAF Display held at Farnborough on 7/8 July 1950. On returning to Baginton, full instrumentation was completed, and on 21 July the aircraft flew to Bitteswell for the start of its flight-test programme. AI Mk10 checking was done in three days at TRE Defford starting on 23 October, after which it went to the manufacturer's airfield for two weeks; it then returned to Bitteswell on 11 November, to resume flight-testing in conjunction with the A&AEE. Three months later, on 12 February 1951, WA546 was given full CA.

WA547 was the second prototype, and it was fitted with AI Mk9C radar; Bill Else gave it its first flight on 11 August 1950. Although the AI Mk9C was not to become standard in operational aircraft, it was still installed when the second prototype became the first NF.11 to participate in an SBAC Display, held at Farnborough

No. 87 Squadron put up this formation when they changed from Meteor NF.11s to Javelin FAW1s in the autumn of 1957. WD795 went to No. 68 Squadron at Laarbruch, while WM168 was scrapped. Author's collection.

Following Gloster's attempts to have tip-tanks accepted via their GAF, Armstrong Whitworth showed NF.11 WD604 at the 1951 SBAC display with a similar installation; but economics prevented the system going into RAF service. WD604 later went to de Havilland for missile test trials. Author's collection.

between 5 and 10 September 1950. The pilot was J.O. 'Joe' Lancaster, the AWA test pilot who had been the first in the *world* to use the Martin-Baker ejector seat in earnest, when he had to make a hasty exit from the out-of-control AW52 proto-type TS363 on 30 May 1949. With the SBAC Display over, WA547 started armament testing on 26 September, flights being made from Bitteswell to evaluate the gun-heating's high altitude effectiveness. After this, firing trials were undertaken from Boscombe Down, when empty cases and links were once again the cause of slight skin damage, this time to the engine nacelles. The consensus of opinion was that the aircraft made a good gun platform, and rated well with other fighters in oper-ational service. When AWA's type-testing had been completed, WA547 was handed over to the A&AEE, who used it for a variety of trials.

The third of the trio of NF.11 prototypes ordered, WB543, was the first to have the strengthened, production-standard wings. Its first flight was made at Baginton a month after that of the second prototypes, Eric Franklin taking the aircraft up on 23

Three NF.12s of No. 25 Squadron, operating from West Malling in May 1954. WS622/K later served with No. 153 Squadron, after which it returned to No. 25 Squadron and was recoded 'R' before being broken up in April 1959. WS694 also went to No. 153 Squadron, where it was written off in a take-off accident on 16 April 1956. The leader in this formation, WS697/N, left for No. 72 Squadron and was consigned to scrap on the last day of 1959. Author's collection.

A mixed formation of NF.12s and NF.14s, carrying the markings of No. 46 Squadron in July 1955, when the unit was based at Odiham. All four NF.12s went on to serve with No. 72 Squadron at Church Fenton, as did three of the NF.14s. Only the leading aircraft, WS830 was written off, this being in an accident on 20 November 1957, while the rest of this formation was scrapped at various times. Author's collection.

September 1950. Because of the stronger wings, WB543 was chosen for under-wing drop-tank flight trials, but these were brought to an unexpected halt on 1 December. The practice of touching down on the over-shoot section, about 10 yards (9.14m) short of the runway itself, was quite common, but on this occasion it gave Bill Else a surprise, because the runway had recently been resurfaced and, unknown to him, it stood 6in (15.2cm) proud of the over-shoot section. On impact with the raised tarmac, the port main undercarriage collapsed and the resultant slide to the left removed the under-wing tank, which luckily was empty. It was another two months before WB543 was able to resume flying.

The drop-tank trials therefore had to be continued using WA546, and these were inevitably restricted because its wings were

not up to production strength; but by February 1951 WB543 was repaired, and the full programme was resumed. The manufacturer used the third prototype on various test flights for another eighteen months; then it went to RAE Farnborough to assist in their AI Mk17 trials, before being used by the CFE and Fairey Aviation as a chase plane. In November 1955 it was put into storage, and on 28 February 1958 it was eventually sold for scrap to Blackbushe-based Starvia.

Armstrong Whitworth's first production NF.11 – WD585 – took to the air on 19 October 1950, when Joe Lancaster flew it for the first time; it then went to the CFE, before joining No. 256 Squadron when this unit re-formed at Alhlorn on 17 November 1952. A year before this, in July 1951, No. 29 Squadron at Tangmere – previously a Mosquito NF.30 operator – became the

first to receive NF.11s, with WD598, WD600 and WD602 known to have been three of the early arrivals. A month later, Coltishall-based No. 141 Squadron, which had flown Mosquito NF.36s since January 1946, received WD607 and WD610 among its first NF.11s. Another Mosquito NF.36 operator since January 1946 was No. 85 Squadron, which took delivery of WD615, WD617 and WD620 in September 1951, when they were based at West Malling in Kent. One more unit became a Meteor NF.11 operator in 1951: this was No. 264 Squadron at Linton-on-Ouse, which also replaced Mosquito NF.36s, WD647 and WD650 being two of the early arrivals.

In 1952, four West Germany-based squadrons received NF.11s, first of all No. 68 Squadron, in February, and then No. 87 Squadron in March. Both of these re-formed at Wahn with the Meteor night-fighters, to become elements of 2TAF. WD656 and WD667 were among No. 68 Squadron's first, while No. 87 Squadron is known to have received WD651and WD667. In November 1952 Nos. 96 and 256 Squadrons re-formed at Alhlorn, both taking Meteor NF.11s on charge; among No. 96 Squadron's new aircraft were WD624 and WD628, while No. 256 Squadron had WD645 and WD689 in its early arrivals. The following year No. 151 Squadron received the first of their NF.11s at Leuchars in March; these included WD640 and WD670. In June 1953, Watton-based No. 527 Squadron had a mixture of aircraft, including Anson C.19s, Lincoln B.2s and Mosquito B.35s, but they are known to have received several Meteor NF.11s, WM221 being one of them. No. 125 Squadron had been disbanded on 20 November 1945 while operating Mosquito XXXs, but on 31 March 1955 they re-formed at Stradishall as a night-fighter squadron, equipping with Meteor NF.11s; however, they held these for only nine months before changing to Venom NF.3s.

In January 1959 two Meteor NF.11 operators were renumbered. First, while based at Laarbruch, No. 68 Squadron became No. 5 Squadron – they received WM156 among their additional aircraft. Then at Geilenkirchen, No. 256 Squadron was renumbered No. 11 Squadron, accepting WM238 and WM246 as two of

WM261, the first NF.14, was a converted NF.11 airframe; following manufacturer's trials it was sold to Ferranti, who placed it on the civil register as G-ARCX, which is here being pre-flight checked at Turnhouse. Author's collection.

its new NF.11s. No. 228 OCU at Leeming was the type's principal conversion unit, WD703, WD706, WD711, WD755, WD768 and WD778 being among over fifty NF.11s used. Of the 314 built for RAF service, several were exported after squadron use, while more became trials and research aircraft, all of which are covered in their respective chapters. The Meteor NF.11 appeared at three SBAC displays, WA547 flying in 1950, WD604 in 1951 and WM166 in 1952. Only the latter served with an RAF unit, this being No. 228 OCU, and it was written off when it undershot the runway at Leeming on 17 May 1953.

One aircraft, WD604 from the first production batch, was used for flight trials at Bitteswell in connection with a proposed 100-gallon (455-litre) wing-tip fuel tank installation. First flown on 20 July 1951, the tests proved them to be better than the under-wing tanks, although one did collapse during a dive, necessitating modifications to the vent valve. The tanks had a ventral fin on top of the front end, inclined at 10 degrees in order for them to fall away from the aircraft when jettisoned. The structural changes to the standard wing which were necessary in order for a tip-tank installation to be incorporated in the production run could not be made before over 75 per cent of the contracted airframes had been completed, and a retro-modification was considered far from cost-effective. The project was therefore cancelled in February 1952, and WD604 was handed over to Boscombe Down on 25 February, to be used by de Havilland for guided missile trials.

The NF. Mk12

Two aircraft from the second batch of the initial NF.11 production contract, WD670 and WD687, were used as the development aircraft for the next night-fighter variant, the NF.12. With the American

NF.14 WS760 served with No.64 Squadron before becoming Instructional Airframe 7961M at both Upwood and Brampton. It is seen here at Duxford on 13 April 1983 when painted all black as 'Z-14' for the BBC television series *The Aerodrome*. George Pennick.

APS21 AI radar proposed for the new Mark, a 17in (43.1cm) longer nose was needed; however, the equipment was smaller than the old AI Mk10, so a lower support bracket fairing was no longer required, and the new nose had a cleaner aerodynamic profile. The planned production NF.12 was to be fitted with the more powerful Rolls-Royce Derwent 9 turbojets producing 3,800lb (1,723.3kg) static thrust, but the two development aircraft retained the standard NF.11 Derwent 8s, which delivered 300lb (136kg) less. Flight trials with WD670 were made at Boscombe Down and they went reasonably well, apart from the fin having a penchant to stall at high altitude, thereby locking the rudder. Such a tendency gave the aircraft a thumbs-down for squadron service, so it was handed back to the manufacturer for investigation and remedy.

By the end of 1952, following much experimenting with WD687, it had been found that a fillet above and below the bullet fairing at the fin/tail-plane intersection, which increased the fin area by a square foot (0.09sq m), eliminated the problem. The aircraft went to the A&AEE in February 1953, and the type was passed for service operations. Armstrong Whitworth received Contract No. 6/ACFT/6412/CB5(b) for the building of 100 G.47 Meteor NF.Mark 12 aircraft, produced in three batches: there were fifty aircraft, WS590 to WS639 inclusive, in the first batch; forty-three, WS658 to WS700 inclusive, in the second; and the third batch was for seven aircraft, with serials WS715 to WS721 inclusive. Eric Franklin took the first production aircraft – WS590 fitted with Derwent 9s – into the air from Baginton on 21 April 1953, and after makers' trials it went to the All-Weather Operation Conversion Unit (AWOCU) section of the CFE at West Raynham.

The first front-line RAF unit to receive NF.12s was No. 25 Squadron at West Malling; they started replacing their Vampire NF.10s in March 1954, WS622 and WS637 being amongst the first to be installed. At the same base, No. 85 Squadron took WS602, WS604 and WS608 amongst the new Mark the following month, in place of the NF.11s that they had flown since September 1951. On 30 June 1954, WS674 and WS691 were two of the early arrivals when No. 152 Squadron was re-formed at Wattisham; it had been a Tempest F.2 operating unit when it was disbanded on 15 January 1947.

A lovely formation shot of seven NF.14s from No. 264 Squadron based at Linton-on-Ouse; it was taken in 1955 by Russell Adams. Author's collection.

Having previously operated with No. 72 Squadron, NF.14 WS793/5 is shown while serving with the Empire Test Pilot's School; after this it was broken up. Author's collection.

Two months later, on 15 August 1954, Odiham was the base where No 46 Squadron was reformed, to receive Meteor NF.12s, including WS609, WS611 and WS623. These were very different from the Dakotas that the squadron had been flying when they were disbanded at Oakington, on February 20, 1950.

Only one unit received NF.12s in 1955,

this being No. 153 Squadron when it was re-formed at West Malling on 28 February, with WS613 and WS662 being placed on charge. This too was a big change, as the squadron had operated with Lancasters when it had been disbanded at Scampton on 28 September 1945. In February 1956, No. 72 Squadron at Church Fenton had been a day-fighter squadron operating

Meteor F.8s, but when NF.12s arrived – including WS603 and WS628 – their role was changed. Another unit to do the same was Duxford-based No. 64 Squadron, which in September 1956 also gave up F.8s in favour of NF.12s; WS603 and WS623 were two of the earliest to arrive. One more operating squadron to receive NF.12s was No. 29: having moved to Acklinton on 14 January 1957 with their Meteor NF.11s, they received Javelin FAW.6s in November 1957 and three months later, in February 1958, a small number of NF.12s joined them; WS629 was one of these.

The Meteor NF.12 was operated by No. 228 OCU at Leeming – WS598 and WS605 are known to have served here – and also by No. 238 OCU at Colerne; this unit had WS594 amongst its aircraft. The CFE at West Raynham is also known to have received a few, two confirmed being WS698 and WS633, the latter later operating with No. 152 Squadron.

WS788/C NF(T).14 serving with No. 1 Air Navigation School at Stradishall in October 1965. It later became instructional airframe 7967M and is currently at the Yorkshire Air Museum, restored to WS788 markings. George Pennick.

The NF. Mk13

Numerically, the Meteor NF.13 is obviously the next Mark, but the prototype, WM308, had in fact been flown by Joe Lancaster on 21 December 1952, exactly four months before the first production NF.12. AWA received Contract No. 6/ACFT/6141/CB5(b) to build forty G.47 Meteor NF.Mark 13s in two batches, the first for the thirty-four numbered WM308 to WM341 inclusive, and the second for

six aircraft with serials WM362 to WM367 inclusive. Basically, the Mark was a tropicalized version of the NF.11, with two cold-air intakes in the fuselage, ahead of the ventral tank. Distance measuring equipment (DME) required additional aerials on the outer wings, and a radio compass loop – this is reminiscent of No. 77 Squadron RAAF in Korea – was fitted at the rear of the canopy fairing.

Being tropicalized, only two overseas units received the NF.13 as their main equipment, these being Nos. 39 and 219 Squadrons; both were based at Kabit when their new aircraft were delivered in March

1953. No. 39 Squadron had been flying Mosquito NF.36s since June 1949; their NF.13s including WM310 and WM333. No. 219 Squadron had been re-formed on 1 March 1951, and were also equipped with the Mosquito NF.36 until their Meteors arrived; two of which were WM323 and WM335, but the squadron only flew them for eighteen months before it was disbanded on 1 September 1954. No. 213 Squadron, a Vampire FB.5 operator in the Canal Zone, has been reported as holding at least two NF.13s, WM337 and WM341, before the aircraft were sold to Syria. Over 40 per cent of the NF.13 production is known to have been exported, and at least one, WM318, is known to have served for a while at the RAF Flying College.

The NF. Mk14

The last fighter Mark of Meteor was the NF.14, which was physically the largest to be operated by the RAF. Installation of the American APQ43 AI radar required a further 17in (43.1cm) extension of the NF.12 nose, bringing the fuselage overall length up to 51ft 4in (15.63m); but the earlier night-fighter wing-span was retained, while the Derwent 9 engines were housed in nacelles with the larger-diameter air intakes. The two-man crew sat under an entirely new, electrically operated, two-piece blown canopy, joined by a thin metal frame, replacing the heavily framed canopy of earlier two-seaters – which

WS760, shown previously as 'Z-14', also operated with No.1 ANS as 'P'. George Pennick.

personally I always felt looked as if they had been fabricated from a portcullis. The new cockpit cover included a revised windscreen, inclined at a slightly steeper angle with curved quarter panels, the port side incorporating a direct-vision (DV) window.

Meteor NF.11 WM261 was used as the aerodynamic trials aircraft, fitted with spring-tab ailerons plus an auto-stabilizer in order to eliminate the directional instability, which was still slightly evident when flying at high speed and high altitude. The aircraft went to the A&AEE for acceptance trials, but it was returned to Baginton for attention to the front canopy frame before it was cleared for operations. Armstrong Whitworth received an order for 100 production G.47 NF. Mark 14 aircraft, in the form of Contract No. 6/ACFT/6412/CB5(b). The aircraft were to be built in three batches: thirty-nine in the first two, with the serials WS722 to WS760 and WS774 to WS812, both inclusive; and the third containing twenty-two, numbered WS827 to WS848 inclusive. The NF.14 was destined to operate with eleven RAF squadrons, all of them finding it a very pleasant aircraft to fly, and pilots with experience of earlier Meteors considered it was the best of the lot. WS722, the first production aircraft, took off from Baginton's tarmac for the first time on 23 October 1953, piloted by Bill Else.

Deliveries of the NF.14 began in March 1954, when No. 25 Squadron at West

Meteor NF.11	
Span:	43ft 0in (13.1m)
Length:	48ft 6in (14.7m)
Height:	13ft 11in (4.2m)
Wing area:	374sq ft (34.7sq m)
Powerplant:	Two Derwent 8 producing 3,700lb (1,678kg) thrust
Armament:	Four 20mm Hispano 5 cannon, with 160 rounds per gun
Weight empty:	12,019lb (5,541kg)
Weight loaded:	20,035lb (9,058kg)
Max speed at 10,000ft (3,048m):	580mph (933km/h)
Service ceiling:	40,000ft (12,192m)

Meteor NF.12	
Span:	43ft 0in (13.1m)
Length:	49ft 11in (15.2m)
Height:	13ft 11in (4.2m)
Wing area:	374sq ft (34.7sq m)
Powerplant:	Two Derwent 9 producing 3,800lb (1,723kg) thrust
Armament:	Four Hispano 5 cannon, with 160 rounds per gun
Weight empty:	12,292lb (5,575kg)
Weight loaded:	20,380lb (9,244kg)
Max speed at 10,000ft (3,048m):	580mph (933km/h)
Service ceiling:	40,000ft (12,192m)

The last production NF.14, WS848, served with the Central Fighter Establishment, coded 'F' and the Fighter Command Communications Squadron; it was scrapped on 6 December 1963. *Aeroplane Monthly.*

Malling received the type at the same time as its NF12s; the fourth production aircraft, WS725, was its earliest example. The following month No. 85 Squadron, also based at West Malling, went through the same procedure, with WS723 and WS727 included in its allocation. On 30 June 1954 No. 152 Squadron was formed at Wattisham, receiving Meteor NF.14s at the same time as its NF.12s; WS735, WS749 and WS754 were three of the earliest. In August 1954, two more front-line units became NF.14 operators: No. 46 Squadron at Odiham, and a re-formed No. 527 Squadron at Watton. The Odiham-based squadron's aircraft included WS724 and WS790, which arrived at the same time as the NF.12s, while the few aircraft that went to Watton joined a mixed bag of Meteor NF.12s, Varsity T.1s and Lincoln B.2s. No. 264 Squadron at Linton-on-Ouse had been operating NF.11s since

Meteor NF.13

Span:	43ft 0in (13.1m)
Length:	48ft 6in (14.7m)
Height:	13ft 11in (4.2m)
Wing area:	374sq ft (34.7sq m)
Powerplant:	Two Derwent 8 producing 3,700lb (1,678kg)
Armament:	Four Hispano 5 cannon, with 160 rounds per gun
Weight empty:	12,347lb (5,600kg)
Weight loaded:	20,485lb (9,291kg)
Max speed at 10,000ft (3,048m):	585mph (940km/h)
Service ceiling:	36,000ft (10,972m)

Meteor NF.14

Span:	43ft 0in (13.1m)
Length:	51ft 4in (15.63m)
Height:	13ft 11in (4.2m)
Wing area:	374sq ft (34.7sq m)
Powerplant:	Two Derwent 9 producing 3,800lb (1,723kg)
Armament:	Four Hispano 5 cannon, with 160 rounds per gun
Weight empty:	12,620 (5,724kg)
Weight loaded:	21,200lb (9,626kg)
Max speed at 10,000ft (3,048m):	585mph (940km/h)
Service ceiling:	43,000ft (13,106m)

Built as WS829, an NF.14 that served with No. 228 OCU, the aircraft was purchased by Rolls-Royce and registered G-ASLW; following a period in camouflage with the RAF markings removed, it was repainted in a pale blue/dark blue livery, with white lettering. Derek N. James.

November 1951, when in October 1954 it traded them for NF.14s, with WS747 and WS765 being early arrivals. The type stayed with the squadron until it was renumbered No. 33 Squadron on 30 September 1957, retaining the NF.14s until August 1958.

On 28 February 1955, No. 153 Squadron was re-formed at West Malling and received Meteor NF.12s and NF.14s; WS722, WS757 and WS781 were three of the latter. The squadron operated with the two Marks until it was disbanded at Waterbeach on 2 July 1958. In February 1956, exactly a year later than No. 153 Squadron, Church Fenton-based No. 72 Squadron also received the same Marks of Meteor; WS779 and WS808 were early-numbered members of the squadron's complement. Later, in September 1956, No. 64 Squadron at Duxford was another to receive the two night-fighter Marks together; NF.14 WS797 is recorded as arriving early in the month. A Vampire and Venom operator at Tengah on Singapore Island, No. 60 Squadron had a detachment move to Leeming in Yorkshire, where it was to form the nucleus of a Meteor NF.14 squadron in October 1959; amongst these were WS728 and WS756. The detachment took the Meteors back to Tengah, operating over Malaya during the anti-Communist campaign, and they became the last squadron using the type, with WS787 making the unit's final RAF NF.14 operational sortie on 17 August 1961; the squadron then gave up its Meteors, replacing them with Javelin FAW.9s.

The last production Meteor NF.14, WS848, resplendent with Hawker Siddeley Group logos on its nose, took part in the 1954 SBAC Display at Farnborough. Several others were engaged in research programmes, as detailed in another chapter.

Fourteen NF.14 aircraft – WS726, WS737, WS739, WS744, WS760, WS774, WS788, WS792, WS797, WS802, WS807, WS840, WS842 and WS843 – were later converted to a training role for navigators, with the designation NF(T).14. These aircraft were exclusively used by air navigation schools (ANS), No. 1 at Stradishall and No. 2 at Thorney Island. In 1962, the latter became absorbed into the Stradishall school, which flew a mixture of de Havilland Dominie T.1s and Vickers Varsity T.1s with the Meteors.

CHAPTER ELEVEN

Targets and Tugs

The name of Alan (later Sir Alan) Cobham has been synonymous with aviation in Britain since the early 1920s and in 1934 he founded Flight Refuelling Limited (FRL). Air-to-air refuelling trials were conducted throughout the 1930s, and then the company's wartime activities included experiments on fire-proof fuel tanks, thermal de-icing of aircraft wings, and the towing of Spitfires or Hurricanes by Wellingtons as a proposed means of delivering fighters to Malta. Also during World War II, flight refuelling testing continued, including B-24 tanker/ B-17 receiver trials at Eglin Field, in April 1943.

A move to the former wartime airfield at Tarrant Rushton in 1949 gave the company much greater facilities, and here it started its association with the Meteor. In the early 1950s, flight refuelling trials led to the fitting-out of nearly all No. 245 Squadron's aircraft with receiver probes; moreover throughout the decade, FRL became heavily committed to Meteor maintenance and repairs, to the extent that the facilities were expanded to include overseas operators. Over 650 Meteors went through the Tarrant Rushton facilities, where all refurbishment and repainting work was carried out, and when the company became the design authority for several Meteor variants, the overhaul programme proved to be the mainstay of its finances.

The Meteor Drones

The advent of the guided missile, whether air-to-air or ground-to-air, proved to the RAF the inadequacies of the existing Fairey Firefly as a target in the development of their missiles and the education of their trainee pilots. With ship-borne missiles also being current standard armament, the Royal Navy, too, required more suitable targets. The target needed to have

the performance and the physical proportions of a potential enemy aircraft, as well as the capacity for pilotless remote control over its entire operational envelope. In 1954, the RAE was commissioned to undertake a series of test programmes at Farnborough, using a modified T.7, VW413 (before it became the aerodynamic test aircraft for the NF.11), fitted with an Ultra throttle-control unit, to evaluate the aircraft's potential as a target drone. Exploratory flight trials were made, with Flt Lt E. Pennie as pilot and Gordon Hamm of Ultra Limited in the rear, of various automatic system components, so that on 17 January 1955 the first fully automatic take-off was satisfactorily carried out. The results at the end of the RAE trials were encouraging. Furthermore, with Hunters coming into front-line squadrons in ever-increasing numbers, Meteor F.4s that had been in storage for some time at No. 5 MU Kemble and No. 33 MU Lyneham were being joined by Meteor F.8s – so there was no shortage of aircraft that could be adapted to a target-drone role.

Gloster Aircraft was fully preoccupied with existing development work, and was therefore in no position to put such a programme in hand; and the same applied to Armstrong Whitworth at Baginton. Flight Refuelling Limited, with its Meteor overhaul experience and with floor-space and manpower available, was regarded as being ideal to meet the new requirements, so the responsibility for the whole programme was placed at Tarrant Rushton, with FRL to work in close partnership with the RAE. In 1952 the company had been engaged on an RAE-requested programme to convert two Lancasters – out of a projected total of nine aircraft – into drones for use as targets in missile-firing trials. The first was PA343, on which the company completed the conversion, and it was flown five times by FRL's pilot Tom Marks, with Maurice

Jenkins as flight engineer. Difficulties with the Ultra-modified throttle box made the Lancaster unsuitable for the proposed drone role, and conversion of the second aircraft was not put in hand; had it been, the BBMF would have been short of a Lancaster, as the aircraft was PA474! Four years later, two Lincolns arrived at Tarrant Rushton for modification to U.Mark 5 standard and the first, RF395, flew in this configuration on 29 February 1956, but again, the system did not work too well and the Ministry dropped the whole idea.

However, in 1955 two new Marks of Meteor came into existence, both with the prefix 'U', for 'unmanned'. Modified F.4s became U.Mark 15s, some of which retained the ability to be piloted, and the designation U.Mark 16 was applied to target drone conversions of the F.8. Meteor F.4 aircraft started arriving at

Sir Alan Cobham photographed in 1935, a year after founding Flight Refuelling Limited. *Aeroplane Monthly.*

Former F.4 VT310, after conversion to U.15 standard for the RAE at Llanbedr, flying unmanned, with a group of three flares under each nacelle rear-end for firing when targeting for heat-seeking missiles. Derek N. James.

FRL's airfield towards the end of January 1955, and on 11 March 1955, RA421 – which in February 1948 had been engaged in the continuation of winterization trials at Edmonton, Canada – became the first U.15 to make a fully automatic, ground-controlled take-off from Tarrant Rushton. The landing was made by an on-board pilot, but later in March the first automatic landing was made, also by RA421. The reuniting with *terra firma* was too hard, and the undercarriage was projected up through the wings, writing off the aircraft. The FRL U.15 drone section was headed by a former Saunders Roe engineer, Ted Hall, while John Reid led a development team engaged on modifying old Elliott Brothers' control equipment for installation in the U.16. Some U.15s featured a modified nose-cone, originally tested on T.7 VW443, which had a large glass port-hole in its extreme tip.

At Tarrant-Rushton, flight command of the drones was undertaken by a pair of operators, one positioned parallel to the operational runway, and the other at its end. Equipped with binocular sights, the two operators transmitted input signals through a radio command link to the air-craft's throttles and control surfaces. A

high level of proficiency was soon achieved in both take-offs and landings, once a flying staff pilot had carried out a preliminary series of flight checks of the aircraft. (As a matter of interest, when vacancies once arose for extra flying staff pilots, one applicant was Sqn Ldr Neville Duke – and he was turned down!) The pre-assembled and tested automatic control system, known as the 'drone kit', was then installed in the airframe, following which the Special Equipment Section team, headed by Don Stubb, became responsible for an aircraft's operations.

Conversion of the F.8 into U.16 configuration incorporated lessons learned in the U.15 programme, and each aircraft was capable of being flown as a normal piloted aircraft with the automatic control system disengaged, as a radio-controlled aircraft carrying a pilot for systems checking, or as a pilotless target. The 30in (76.2cm) longer nose section was a redesigned and rebuilt unit, fitted with the majority of the required electronic equipment, together with a large door to give access for its main-tenance. While the full armament was not always removed during the U.15

A three-shot sequence showing a U.15 operating from Woomera, acting as the target for an Armstrong-Whitworth Seaslug ship-to-air missile. Mike Hooks.

conversions, all the F.8's standard electrical systems were rewired, with the new junction boxes being fitted in the unused gun bays. New generators and take-off gearboxes were installed on the engines, increasing the output from 4,000 to the 12,000 watts necessary to operate the additional electronics. RAE-developed flying controls were operated by a ground master-controller in a transmitter vehicle, handling the pre-set attitudes while the aircraft was out of sight. Once back in the airfield circuit, glide-path monitoring was shared with an additional pitch and azimuth controller. Take-offs were also a dual-control sequence, until the aircraft flew beyond visual sighting, when the master controller took over.

Wing-tip nacelles contained a pair of Australian-developed cameras which gave all-round coverage, which could be jettisoned prior to the drone being hit, using a parachute, buoyancy bag and homing beacon for survival, so that the film record could be saved. Flares in groups of three were carried under each engine nacelle, for firing if the drone was a target for infra-red heat-seeking missiles. Similar infra-red flares were sometimes trailed on a cable from a rear-fuselage housing fitted on some U.16s. All drones were painted in a vivid red/yellow colour scheme, with the wing-tip housings painted black.

Distribution of U.15s and U.16s was mainly to the RAE airfield at Llanbedr, which in those days was in the Welsh county of Merioneth but is now absorbed into Gwynedd; and to the Australian Weapons Research Establishment at Woomera. Some were also delivered to No. 728(B) Squadron of the RN at Hal Far in Malta. At Llanbder, U.16s often operated in conjunction with an Australian-designed and built drone, the Jindivik. A 1948 design from the Australian Government Aircraft Factories (GAF), it was first flown on 28 August 1952, powered by a single Rolls-Royce Viper Mk201 turbojet; of the original order for 486, the UK was scheduled to receive 234.

A few Meteor F.8s were converted to U.21/U.21A standard, these basically being U.16s, but incorporating modifications to meet operational techniques and environmental conditions peculiar to Woomera. The conversions were made by FRL for shipment to Australia, where the aircraft were re-assembled and tested by Fairey Aviation Australasia Pty. Limited.

WH344/O, an F.8 conversion to U.16, flying without a pilot in an air-test before it was delivered to RAE Llanbedr. Mike Hooks.

In addition, several ex-No. 77 Squadron RAAF aircraft were also converted to U.21/U.21As by Fairey Aviation, using modification kits and equipment sent to Australia by Flight Refuelling Limited.

Target Towing

Although deck-handling and flying trials were conducted for the Royal Navy, going right back to the first F.9/40 prototype DG202/G on HMS *Pretoria Castle* in August 1945, the Service found no operational use for the Meteor until 1957. In

that year, the RN recognized that there was a requirement for a high-speed target-towing aircraft, to be flown for shore-based operational use in the field of guided missile and ground-to-air gun firing, the Fairey Firefly TT.4 which had previously been utilized no longer being fast enough.

Armstrong Whitworth, as the development company for all Meteor applications, was contracted to convert a number of ex-RAF NF.11s to a target-towing configuration, with all armaments and magazine tanks removed. Earlier operations made with F.4s and F.8s, where a 30ft (9.14m) target was laid out on the ground

---

Gloster G.41G Meteor F.Mark 4 aircraft converted to U.Mark 15 drones

Aircraft delivered to Llanbedr:
EE521, RA371, RA373, RA397, RA415, RA420, RA421,* RA432 RA439, RA442, RA457, VT106, VT135, VT142, VT168, VT196,** VT268, VT270, VT291, VT332, VT338, VW280, VW285, VW293, VW299.
  * RA421 prototype U.15.
  **VT196 made the last U.15 flight, on 9 February 1963.

Aircraft delivered to Australia:
EE524, RA367, RA398, RA417, RA430, RA433, RA438, RA441, RA454, RA473, VT105, VT112, VT113, VT118, VT130, VT139, VT175, VT177, VT179, VT184, VT187, VT191,

VT192, VT197, VT219, VT220, VT222, VT226, VT230, VT256, VT259, VT262, VT286, VT289, VT294, VT316, VT309, VT329, VT330, VT334, VW266, VW273, VW275, VW303, VW308, VW781, VW791, VZ386, VZ389, VZ401, VZ403, VZ407, VZ414.

Aircraft delivered to Malta:
RA375, RA387, RA479, VT104, VT107, VT110, VT243, VT282, VT310, VW258, VW276, VZ415, VZ417.

A total of ninety-one Meteor F.4s were converted into U.15s.

Gloster G.41K Meteor F.Mark 8 aircraft converted to U.Mark 16 drones.

Aircraft delivered to Llanbedr:
VZ445, VZ485, VZ506, VZ508, VZ514, VZ551,
WA756, WA775,* WA842, WA982, WA991,
WE867, WE872, WE915, WE934, WE962,
WF706, WF707, WF711, WF716, WF743,
WF751, WF755, WF756, WH258, WH284,
WH286,** WH309, WH315, WH320, WH344,
WH349, WH359, WH365, WH369, WH372,
WH373, WH376, WH381, WH420, WH453,
WH469, WH499, WH500, WH505, WH506,
WH509, WK648, WK693, WK709, WK717,
WK729, WK738, WK743, WK745, WK746,
WK747, WK783, WK784, WK789, WK790,
WK793, WK795, WK807, WK812, WK852,
WK855, WK859, WK867, WK877, WK883,
WK885, WK911, WK925, WK926, WK932,
WK941, WK942, WK949, WK971, WK980,
WK989, WK993, WK994, WL110, WL124,
WL160, WL162, WL163.

*WA775 prototype U.16.
**WH286 last aircraft converted to U.16.

Aircraft delivered to Malta:
WE932, WK870, WL127.

Aircraft allocated for U.16 spares, but not all were converted:
VZ439, VZ448, VZ458, VZ462, VZ513, VZ520,
VZ530, VZ554, WA781, WA850, WA984,
WE881, WE919, WE924, WE925, WE946,
WF646, WF681, WF685, WF741, WH281,
WH419, WK675, WK716, WK721, WK731,
WK737, WK744, WL111, WL134.

A total of eighty-nine Meteor F.8s were converted to U.16s.
A total of thirty Meteor F.8s were allocated for U.16 spares.

Gloster G.41K Meteor F.Mark 8 aircraft converted to U.Mark 21/21A drones.

Aircraft delivered to Australia:
VZ455, VZ503, WE902, WE960, WF659,
WH460, WK710, WK797, WK799, WK879,
WL136.

Aircraft converted by Fairey Aviation with kits supplied by FRL:
WA998/A77-802,   WE889/A77-157,

WE969/A77-193,   WK683/A77-851,
WK728/A77-855,   WK730/A77-863,
WK792/A77-872,   WK796/A77-873,
WK800/A77-876,   WK937/A77-882,
WK973/A77-885.

A total of twenty-two Meteor F.8s were converted to U.21/U.21As.

NF.11s back in the shops, for conversion to TT.20 configuration – with Javelin XH959 joining the scene. Derek N. James.

behind the aircraft, to be lifted when the aircraft was about 50ft (15.2m) off the ground, was considered too cumbersome; furthermore, the target had to be jettisoned before the towing aircraft could land. AWA sought assistance from M.L. Aviation at White Waltham, who specialized in aircrew training equipment, including guided target aircraft. Their Type G fully-feathering windmill-driven winch, installed on a small aerodynamic pylon and fitted on the Meteor's top starboard centre-section, was capable of paying out and hauling in a 6,000ft (1,828.8m) long, 15cwt (762kg) Kilindo steel cable. Provision was made for installing four containers, two on each side, in the rear fuselage, each carrying a 3ft x 15ft (0.91m x 4.57m) high-speed, radar-reflective sleeve target, which could be streamed automatically. The aircraft was given the designation Meteor TT.Mark 20, and an ex-No. 141 Squadron NF.11, WD767, was modified to the new configuration, before going to A&AEE Boscombe Down for testing from July to October 1957; these trials occupied sixty flying hours.

With the pilot flying the aircraft from the front seat, the winch operator in the rear controlled the winch, together with target launching and exchanging. The towing cable was routed between a cocked spring-loaded cutter blade and an anvil. The remotely controlled blade trip mechanism could be activated by both the winch operator and the pilot. A streamlined wire tail-guard stretched from the tail-plane to a bracket around a rear fuselage buffer pad, to protect the tail unit from damage by the towing cable. In passing the TT.20 as suitable for operations, the conclusions and recommendations from the Boscombe Down trials stated that the aircraft's maximum speed should be limited to 322mph (481km/h) at 5,000ft (1,524m), with the safe towing endurance of a target on 6,000ft (1,828.8m) of cable, under these limitations, being 34 minutes. This endurance could be increased to 50 minutes if the towing speed was reduced to 259mph (416.8km/h). When not towing a target, the limiting Mach number, with the winch fitted, was M0.65.

Later targets carried SAAB near-miss recording equipment, including conductive cable and microphone on the towing cable, which produced a signal that registered on the winch-controller's instrument panel. In the summer of 1959, trials were made at the A&AEE Boscombe Down with a Brooklands Dart Mk3 high-speed target, the test aircraft again being WD767. The three-finned target was stowed on the underside of the aircraft's fuselage and was launched on a 25ft (7.6m), 3,200lb (1,451kg) nylon cable. With the Dart target installed, the limiting airspeed rose to 345mph (555km/h) at 5,000ft (1,524m). Mirrors fitted to the engine nacelles gave the winch operator a view of the target during its launching, and after it had been winched back into a casting-off position, it was released, following which a drogue extracted the main parachute, allowing the target to be retrieved after landing.

To help AWA in the early delivery of TT.20s, Gloster's Moreton Valence works undertook several conversions, while both the RNAS at Lossiemouth and RNAS Sydenham also handled a few. Late in their service, TT.20s WM167 and WM234 were allocated to target-towing trials of the American Hayes target, which FRL was going to manufacture under licence. It was found that significant modification to the unit was required, so the company thought it better to design their own: this resulted in the 'Rushton' target, equipped with hit-and-miss distance recorders and a flare pack. The under-fuselage attachment to the aircraft was similar to the Dart Mk3 installation, and the target itself resembled an air-to-air missile, with cruciform fins at its rear. Further development of the Rushton target was carried out by Canberra B.2 WJ632.

The RAF also operated a few TT.20s in the United Kingdom, through No. 3 Civilian Anti-Aircraft Co-operation Unit (CAACU) at Exeter, including WD610, WD630, WD645, WD647, WD678, WD679, WD702, WD706, WM223 and WM230, while No.1574 Target Facilities Flight was flown at Singapore. Royal Navy employment of eleven aircraft, WD649, WD652, WD657, WD780, WD785, WM151, WM159, WM242, WM255, WM260 and WM292 was handled by No.728 Fleet Requirement Unit (FRU) until its disbanding in May 1967, when the operations were given, under contract, to the Airwork Services Limited's FRU at Hurn, near Bournemouth, who used civilian pilots to fly Navy aircraft. The Service also employed the type, in the Station Flights at Brawdy, Sydenham and Yeovilton.

WM292/041, which had served with No. 527 Squadron as an NF.11 before joining the Royal Navy as a TT.20. After service it was displayed out-of-doors at Yeovilton; it is now stored at the FAA base for Phoenix Aviation, Bruntingthorpe. *Aeroplane Monthly.*

Six TT.20s were sold by the Royal Navy to the French Air Force; F-ZABD is shown taxiing for take-off. *Aeroplane Monthly.*

Gloster G.47 Meteor NF.Mark 11s converted by Armstrong Whitworth to T.Mark 20s.

WD585,	WD591,	WD592,	WD606,	WM159,	WM160,	WM167,	WM181,
WD610,	WD612,	WD623,	WD629,	WM223,	WM224,	WM230,	WM234,
WD630,	WD641,	WD643,	WD645,	WM242,	WM245,	WM246,	WM255,
WD646,	WD647,	WD649,	WD652,	WM260,	WM270,	WM292,	WM293.
WD657,	WD678,	WD679,	WD702,	A total of forty-four Meteor NF.11s were			
WD706,	WD711,	WD767,	WD780,	converted into TT.20s.			
WD785,	WM147,	WM148,	WM151,				

CHAPTER TWELVE

Engine Testbed Meteors

Because the Meteor was twin-engined, very rugged and available in considerable numbers, it played an integral part in the development of British gas turbine engines in the exciting decade 1945 to 1955 – and even French nationalism was temporarily shelved for a few years, to further their own propulsion programmes. While some engines took to the air for the first time on modified multi-piston-engined aircraft, the Meteor was the next logical step in view of it being able to test an engine in a more realistic operational flight envelope. Furthermore, in at least three cases it was the first airframe used to evaluate specialist engines in flight. Indicative of its versatility is the fact that it flew with three and even four engines, while at the prototype stage it was propelled by a pair of 1,400lb (635kg) thrust engines, and eventually the same basic design, albeit much stronger in construction, was powered by two 7,600lb (3,447kg) monsters.

The following is an abridgement of the principal aircraft/engine combinations that explored the abilities of the engine manufacturers' products.

GA.41A Meteor F.1, EE227

Much of the thinking in the early 1920s, excluding Frank Whittle's independent considerations, was orientated towards the turbine as a device that might drive a propeller, and the idea of having such an engine to drive a compressor, linked to a combustion chamber to produce a jet of air, was not generally recognized. Rolls-Royce's first exercise in propeller-turbine engines was the two-shaft 'Clyde', produced by a team at Barnoldswick headed by Dr S.G. Hooker and Mr A.A. Lombard; this was flown in VP120, the Westland Wyvern TF.2, which did not progress beyond the prototype stage. The second was a conversion of a production Derwent 2 engine, achieved by fitting a single-stage spur reduction gear and cropping the compressor to match the turbine, which was retained as produced. The engine was designated the Rolls-Royce RB.50 'Trent', and it was first run in a specially constructed test-rig at Barnoldswick, where it produced 750 shaft horse power plus 1,000lb (453.5kg) residual thrust; this was in March 1945. The next step was to flight-test the engine and, with Meteor F.3s being taken into squadron service, some F.1s had been struck off charge with No. 616 Squadron. One was EE227, flown as YQ-Y in squadron service, and it was transferred to the RAE, joining EE212 in the establishment's experiments to improve the Meteor's directional stability. EE227 became unique in that the upper fin and rudder was removed, thereby creating the only T-tailed Meteor – and, incidently, the first T-tailed British turbojet aircraft. The modification did virtually nothing for the instability investigations, and in February 1945 the removed tail area was replaced. With this restoration, the aircraft became a real oddity in the history of RAF markings: the striped tail markings on Meteors were positioned on the fin, above the tail-plane, so when the top fin/rudder sections were removed from EE227, the national tail stripes had to be resprayed on the remaining fin, under the tailplane – and when the top fin/rudder, complete with the original markings, was restored, the

The scene of so much of this chapter's events, Rolls-Royce's experimental facility at Hucknall, photographed in 1970. *Aeroplane Monthly.*

aircraft then had two tail stripes on each side. Then in March 1945, EE227 became even more unique when it was selected to become the world's first turboprop-powered aircraft. Rolls-Royce wanted to understand turboprop control systems more fully, and so on 7 March 1945 they accepted EE227 at Hucknall and started its conversion to take two Trents. In fact they decided to build three flight Trents, which gave them a spare for the Meteor's programmes, should it be necessary.

The reason that EE227 was selected was because it was one of the first Meteors fitted with the larger 'banjo' rear spars, so although considerable modification was necessary to install the Trents, none of it was major. A 2,200lb (997.7kg) increase in all-up weight, coupled with the ground clearance required to cater for the 7ft 11in (2.43m)-diameter propellers, dictated that the undercarriage required strengthening, and it also meant a 6in (15.2cm) increase in length; this in turn necessitated alterations to the wheel-wells. Even with these modifications, the clearance between the propeller arc and the ground was less than 12in (30.4cm). Ballast was installed to counter-balance the removed armament, and the cannon ports were covered over.

Six months after being delivered to Hucknall, the modified EE227 was transported to Rolls-Royce's airfield at Church Broughton, nine miles west of Derby and, following engine running, Gloster's Chief Test Pilot Eric Greenwood took the 'Trent Meteor' into the air for the first time on 20 September 1945. However, he soon found that the propwash and additional side area increased directional instability even more than before, making it advisable to return the aircraft to Moreton Valence. There, two small additional fins were fitted on the tail-plane, and in this configuration EE227 returned to Hucknall on 16 March 1946, to resume test-flying. The pilot mainly dedicated to the Trent Meteor programme was no stranger to the aircraft in its original form: it was Wg Cdr Andrew McDowell, No. 616 Squadron's CO when they were the first unit to receive Meteors.

Problems were still being encountered in the handling characteristics and the aircraft was grounded for a while. Rotol had produced a new five-bladed propeller with revised blade contours and a 40 per cent smaller diameter of 4ft 10in (1.46m). The new unit absorbed only 350hp, so the residual thrust was increased to 1,400lb (635kg) by reducing the size of the jet pipe.

A fine air-to-air shot of F.1 EE227, the 'Trent-Meteor', which was scrapped after being used at RAE Farnborough for fire test and struck off charge on 29 June 1949. *Aeroplane Monthly.*

By March 1948 Rolls-Royce had learned all that they required from the Trent: their new Dart turboprop engine had been flying in a nose installation on Lancaster NG465 since 10 October 1947, while the first aircraft to fly powered exclusively by the Dart, Vickers Wellington LN715, had also made its maiden flight.

Maurice Smith, the editor of *Flight* magazine, accepted the chance to fly EE227. He commented on its ease of handling when taxiing, the impressive acceleration provided by the combination of propeller/jet thrust, plus the engine's considerable advantage over contemporary pure jet aircraft, in giving the quick response and power build-up usually associated with piston-engined aircraft.

In April 1948 the aircraft was transferred to the A&AEE for a series of tests connected with the Royal Navy's interest at that time, namely in the deck operations and lower fuel consumption of turboprop-powered aircraft. The trials lasted over five months, during which time simulated deck-landings were made; and while it was at Boscombe Down, quite a number of test pilots from the Services, plus several from other aircraft manufacturers, flew EE227 in order to experience for them-

selves how a turboprop handled. On 22 September 1948 it returned to Hucknall once more, where the following month Rolls-Royce removed the two Trents after nearly fifty hours flying and the aircraft was restored to standard. From Hucknall it went back to RAE Farnborough, to suffer the indignation of fire destruction tests, until it was broken up in June 1949. Although the Trent was never intended to be a production engine, it did provide invaluable data for Rolls-Royce in the perfecting of the Dart, which is still in service today.

G.41G Meteor F.4, RA435

When RA435 came off the line at Hucclecote in the spring of 1947, it went straight to No. 39 MU at Colerne, where it remained for about two months. Then on 21 August, together with another from the same production batch, RA430, it was delivered to Hucknall, where both aircraft were to assist in the evolution of Rolls-Royce's Derwent 5 engine. RA430 was involved in an extended programme centred on the later Derwent 8, before going to No. 33 MU at Lyneham on 28 September 1952. Two years later it was converted into a U.15 by FRL at Tarrant Rushton.

RA435 was engaged on Derwent 5 development for twenty months, during which about 400 flying hours were accumulated; a lot of the testing was aimed at increasing the power output while improving the fuel consumption and it was quite paradoxical that the aircraft's next trials programme had no thought of fuel consumption whatsoever. Back in April 1945, the RAE had tested EE215 with a Power Jets-developed exhaust reburning system, and Rolls-Royce had been investigating 'afterburning' – a contemporary name for what nowadays is more usually referred to as 'reheat' – as a means of increasing the thrust of the Derwent 5. Although the system incurred prodigious fuelconsumption figures, they considered that these were justified by the anticipated improvement in performance during combat, plus much shorter take-off runs. In the spring of 1949, RA435 went into the experimental workshops at Hucknall to have its Derwents fitted with reheat units; this work was completed so that ground-running could commence at the end of May, and the aircraft had its first flight with the installations on 10 June.

The maiden flight was purely an aerodynamic test of the airframe modifications, and the reheat system was not used in flight until later in the month. Extensions on the end of the standard engine nacelles housed the reheat units, which had variable nozzles projecting beyond the outer skinning, and the rear fuselage adjacent to the jet outlets was strengthened locally. Test-flying was interrupted in September when Rolls-Royce displayed RA435 at the SBAC Farnborough show – and we heard the sound of reheat for the first time, as the system was selected on the climb-out from the operational runway.

The company's assistant chief test pilot, Jim Heyworth, carried out most of the flying in the twelve-month Derwent reheat programme; in this time, asymmetric handling trials were conducted with the port side unit switched off, and altogether more than sixty test-flying hours were logged. The last flight with the system was made in July 1950, after which Hucknall restored RA435 to standard condition. It then saw time with No. 209 AFS at Weston Zoyland and No. 215 AFS, Finningley, before becoming an instructional airframe with the number 7131M, at No. 2 School of Technical Training (STT) in July 1954. On 30 June 1955 the aircraft was transferred to No. 4 SST, and after this its history disappears.

G.41G Meteor F.4, RA490

RA490 was from the final batch of Gloster's first F.4 contract, and it enjoyed a rather chequered existence. First of all, it was one of several airframes in the batch that were fitted with specially modified centre-sections, in preparation for their use as flying testbeds. Prior to commencing this role, the manufacturers retained the aircraft in order for it to participate, during November 1947, in tests to determine the definite strength of the centre-section and undercarriage, as a complete unit. A custom-designed rig was fabricated, and the aircraft was raised to a maximum height of 36in (91.4cm) by a pair of telescopic jacks; it was then harnessed in two F-type bomb release gears, sited over special compound loading platforms which could simulate side loads as well as vertical drag. Measurements from a variety of points on the airframe were registered by dynamic recording equipment, supplemented by slow-motion cine film. At that time, these tests were considered to be the most comprehensive made on any airframe, and the US Navy expressed great interest in the company's approach to the subject, as well as the results, which cleared the Meteor for landing 1,000lb (453.5kg) heavier than the 15,000lb (6,802.5kg) design figure. On completion of these tests RA490 was divested of its armament and its camouflage, and was resprayed in the soon-to-become-standard overall silver finish before embarking on its considerable engine testbed career.

Test-flying of Metropolitan-Vickers' F2 axial-flow engine had started in the rear fuselage of the first Lancaster prototype, BT308, with Lancaster BII LL735 taking over when BT308's airframe hours expired. The third prototype F.9/40 had been powered by a pair of F2 engines when it first flew on 13 November 1943, these engines being underslung, as the airframe was then not capable of taking the longer engines within the wing structure. This Metrovick engine finally became the F2/4, developing 3,850lb (1,746kg) thrust, and was given the name Beryl; it was installed in the Saro SR.A/1 flying-boat fighter, and RA390 joined the Metrovick test-flying team, also to be fitted with a pair of Beryl engines. Its modified centre-section incorporated inverted U-sections in both the front and rear spars, in order to accept various engines, while allowing adequate ground clearance.

With the Beryls installed, RA490 participated in the 1948 SBAC Display, which was the first year that the then-annual event had been staged at Farnborough, after three post-war years at Handley Page's Radlett airfield. On 13 January 1949 it was announced that an altitude of 40,000ft (12,192m) had been attained in 7.5 minutes, which was 4 minutes quicker to the same altitude than the standard Meteor F.4. Later in the same year, the

F.4 RA435 shows the early Roll-Royce reheat trial installation on its Derwent 5 engines. Author's collection.

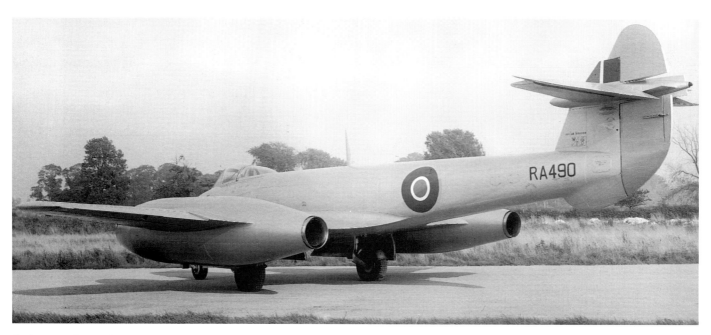

The large nacelles required to house the Metropolitan Vickers F.2 are clearly shown here when F.4 RA490 flew as the engine's testbed. Author's collection.

aircraft suffered a hydraulic failure while being flown by Bill Waterton and he had to make an emergency wheels-up landing. Metropolitan-Vickers requirements for the Meteor had reduced, and although Waterton had made a good forced-landing, in which only limited damage was suffered by the airframe, the engine company declared that they did not consider they had any further use for it.

Experiments to try and reduce the high approach speeds of naval aircraft generated a revival of interest in schemes to reduce the stalling speeds of jet aircraft by deflecting their exhaust efflux downwards, and at an angle to the line of flight. The National Gas Turbine Establishment (NGTE) and the RAE, both based at Farnborough, set up a joint discussion group to evaluate various methods of applying such a system. It was agreed that a suitable aircraft should be modified to incorporate jet-deflection, though without impairing its general flying qualities, and the RAE considered that the Meteor, with its twin-engined layout, was the best airframe for such an adaption. With RA490 no longer being required by Metro-Vickers following the wheels-up incident, it was selected as the testbed airframe for a jet-deflection flight programme.

Early in 1954 the aircraft was delivered to Westland Aircraft at Yeovil, who had been commissioned to make the con-

siderable modifications that were necessary. The design and construction of the jet-deflector units was to be the responsibility of the NGTE, and they started by setting the angle of deflection at 70

degrees. Later it was found that 60 degrees was preferable; also from the four different duct sections that had been proposed, a circular section was manufactured. A pair of special Rolls-Royce Nene engines, each

Westland's conversion of RA490, to accept the Nenes and their jet-deflection system, is clearly illustrated in this photograph taken at Yeovil. Author's collection.

producing a little over 5,000lb (2,267.5kg) thrust, were selected as the power source, to be installed ahead of the arched front wing-spar in order for the thrust line to pass close to the aircraft's centre of gravity. Condensed exhaust cones connected the engines to the deflector units, via flexible joints.

The positioning of the Nenes necessitated abnormally broad and long nacelles; these projected over 8ft (2.4m) ahead of the wing leading-edge. Although the armament and standard nose-ballast had been removed, the aircraft was still extremely nose-heavy and ballast had to be installed in the rear fuselage, to restore the c.g. position. It was considered that the vast nacelles, plus the increased side area, would produce lateral instability, so the original rear fuselage was removed and a Meteor F.8 assembly fitted, together with two small end-plate fins on the tail-plane, as had been installed on EE227, the Meteor Trent testbed.

Lateral control in the event of engine failure was predicted to be critical, so to maximize control, standard long-span wings were fitted, these being taken off the Meteor PR.10 production line. With the larger nacelle diameters, in its new configuration RA490 was assured of having the greatest Meteor wingspan, at 44ft 4in (13.51m); and while the original main-

wheels were retained, a nose-wheel unit of increased strength was fitted, this from Baginton's NF.11 production line. Manufacture and assembly were achieved in a remarkably short time, with the aircraft making its first flight in the middle of May 1954; the pilot for the occasion was Sqn Ldr Leo de Vigne DSO, DFC, AFC, Westland's chief test pilot. After three months of manufacturer's trials at Yeovil, the jet-deflection Meteor was delivered to RAE Farnborough, in August 1954.

When RA490 was flown as a conventional aeroplane, its low speed and stalling manner were very similar to a standard production Meteor. The approach was made at a speed of 138mph (222km/h), and the jet efflux was deflected at a height of 200ft (60.9m); this reduced the forward speed, and as it decreased further, power was reapplied, so that a balance of forward speed/deflected power was maintained until touch-down. With the jet deflection in operation, the lowest indicated air speed achieved was 75mph (120.6km/h) on full power, over 11mph (17.7km/h) below the normal figure. The NGTE deflection units gave trouble-free service, and when they were inspected after twenty-five flying hours, they were found to be in perfect condition; they were reinstalled for another seventy-five hours of operations, before again being dismantled.

Because weight was one of several limiting factors, the jet-deflection principle was not adopted for service use. RA490 was transferred to the recently completed RAE airfield at Bedford, which had absorbed the World War II Eighth US Army Air Force base at Thurleigh; from here the 306th Bomb Group was in continuous action over a longer period than any other group in the 8th AF, flying 9,614 sorties for the loss in action of 171 aircraft. The Meteor arrived on 27 April 1955 and was placed on the inventory of Aero Flight, with Flt Lt Colin Mitchell being the Flight's first pilot to experience jet deflection. Lt Cdr W. Noble, R.N., Aero Flight's commanding officer, flew a total of sixteen sorties in RA490, the first being on 20 June 1960. The aircraft was not used very much, and it appeared in public only once, at the RAE Jubilee held at Farnborough on 7 and 9 July 1955. Any further information on its movements seem to have been deflected into the mists of time.

G.41G Meteor F.4, RA491

Coming from the same portion of the batch that produced RA490, RA491 was also fitted with the modified and strengthened centre-section in order that it could participate in engine-flying testbed programmes. Like RA490, it came off the Hucclecote line with a 32ft 2in (11.3m) short-span wing, but it retained this length throughout its working life. Unlike other production F.4s, it was devoid of armament and engines, the powerless airframe being transported by road direct to Rolls-Royce at Hucknall, where it arrived on 18 November 1948.

Rolls-Royce's first axial-flow turbojet, the AJ.65 Avon, had been test-running for nearly two years, producing 6,500lb (2,947.7kg) thrust, and on 15 August 1948 two RA.2s, installed in outboard nacelles on Avro Lancastrian C.2 VM732, became airborne for the first time. This Lancastrian was originally registered as a civil aircraft with the marking G-AGPK, but it is not believed to have flown in this form, and later it was joined by another ex-RAF C.2 VL970. Together the two Lancastrians provided a large part of the Avon's development flying, VL970 being successively fitted with RA.3s, RA.7s, RA.9s, and finally RA.14s; it was RA.14s that were being tested when the aircraft crashed on 29 March 1955, due to

RA490 photographed in its jet-deflection configuration at the RAE Jubilee, Farnborough. Author's collection.

asymmetric power on take-off. The Avon RA.3 was also test-flown in VM732, this aircraft finishing involvement with Rolls-Royce in the autumn of 1950.

The Avon's potential had become fully recognized, and the next generation of interceptors for the RAF, the Swift and Hunter, were being designed around it, as well as the beautiful twin-engined bomber taking shape in English Electric's factory, which would be named Canberra. The forthcoming four-engined bombers were also scheduled to be powered by the axial-flow engine, at least at the prototype stage, and, because some problems were being encountered with the engine's compressors, great pressure was being placed on Rolls-Royce to resolve these. It was because of the Avon's importance that RA491 was brought into the test programme, and its contribution to the engine's development cannot be over-emphasized.

Hucknall fabricated a pair of nacelles over 25 per cent larger than the standard ones, in order to fit two Avon RA.2 engines in the Meteor; external oil-cooler intakes were positioned on the nacelle undersides; and a slab-sided anti-spin parachute housing, reminiscent of the Trent Meteor, was fitted at the rear of the tailplane/fin intersection bullet fairing – and the whole installation was completed in April 1949. On 29 April, Bill Waterton was at the controls for the maiden flight: when he lifted off from Hucknall's runway he was flying the first aircraft powered solely by Avons. The maiden flight terminated at Moreton Valence, and here and at Bitteswell, a total of thirty-six test flights were carried out before the aircraft returned to Hucknall.

A pair of Avons giving a combined thrust of over 13,000lb (5,895.5kg) made RA491 a much more potent aircraft than any previous Meteors. New parameters in handling this amount of power had to be established, such as retracting the undercarriage on take-off before the airfield boundary was crossed, otherwise the 'undercarriage down' speed would be exceeded. The rate of climb was an entirely new experience, 40,000ft (12,192m) being attained in just under 4 minutes.

When RA491 returned to Rolls-Royce's Flight Development Establishment at Hucknall, a heavy landing on 15 July 1949 grounded it for nearly five weeks while the airframe was being stress-checked, and it was 22 August before it went back to

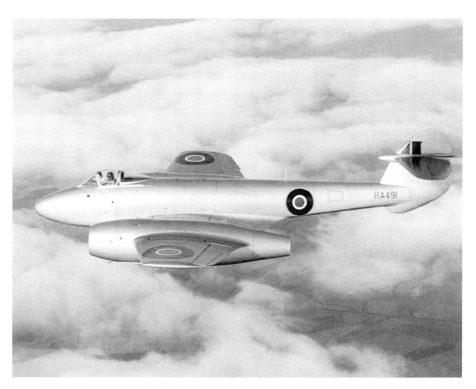

F.4 RA491 flying as the Rolls-Royce Avon RA3 testbed. Author's collection.

Moreton Valence to resume test-flying. This was just in time for it to participate in the flying programme at the 1949 SBAC Display, where it was flown with RA435, the Derwent reheat test aircraft. After Farnborough, more RA.2 testing carried on until 22 November, when the engine's programme was completed, after over forty hours flying. RA491 then returned to Hucknall, and RA.3s replaced the RA.2s, the nacelles being slightly recontoured, and the oil-cooler intakes deleted. On 28 April 1950 it once more departed from Hucknall, to embark on another six-month testbed programme, during which it showed off the RA.3s at the 1950

The later conversion of RA491, to test-fly the French SNECMA Atar turbojet. Author's collection.

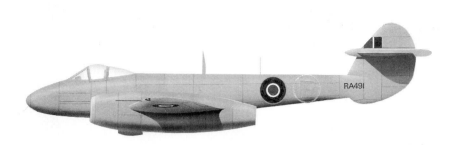

The difference in side profiles made to RA491 when fitted with Avon engines and later, Atars. Author's artwork.

SBAC show. By 26 October, when the aircraft made its last RA.3 sortie, over forty-five hours' testing of the RA.3 variant had been accumulated. The Avons were removed by Rolls-Royce, and the engine-less airframe was taken for storage at No. 60 MU, with the Instructional Airframe number 6879M, ready for an anticipated transfer to Cranwell. But RA491's test-flying days were not over.

Air Service Training (AST) at Hamble, near Southampton Water, had been converting existing airframes to act as test vehicles for many years, with a succession of Lancasters, Lancastrians and Lincolns passing through their works. So when RA491 was sold to France for a SNECMA engine testbed programme, it was AST who collected the airframe from No. 60 MU on 28 September 1951 and proceeded to modify it to take the first French indige-nous turbojet. At the end of 1945, four French engineering companies had amal-gamated to form the *Société Nationale d'Étude et de Construction de Moteurs d'Aviation*, now internationally known as SNECMA. Their first large engine design was an axial-flow turbojet which they named 'Atar', and this engine was destined to be the propulsive source for a large part of France's military aircraft production for many years.

Major changes were made to RA491 by AST before it became the Atar testbed, the most obvious being the fitting of a Meteor F.8 front fuselage and cockpit in place of the production F.4. SNECMA engineers wanted the aircraft to be equipped with an ejector seat in view of what they thought would be lateral control problems, with the Atar giving 33 per cent more thrust than the standard Derwents – in this they seemed to have been oblivious to the fact that RA491 had flown with Avons for over eighteen months, and these were giving over 100 per cent more thrust than the Derwents! The French aircraft company supplied AST with two Atar 101 B-21 engines, numbered 1125 and 1126, for installing in the Meteor. Rather unusual, in view of the fact that France owned the aircraft, was the retention of RAF roundels and markings, including the yellow proto-type 'P'. With its new engines and front fuselage, RA491 made its third 'maiden' flight in March 1952; it then left Hamble on 27 March and was flown by a British pilot to join SNECMA's flight test centre at Melun-Villaroche. The company's test pilot Marel put in about eight hours flying between March and December – hardly excessive testing – and he reported having encountered heavy lateral control prob-lems. By the beginning of 1953, Dassault Ouragan and Mystere airframes were avail-able: could Monsieur Marel have been just 'going through the motions', awaiting their arrival? Anyway, the French aircraft were used for further Atar development, and RA491 became no more than a source of

The later Rolls-Royce Derwent reheat system, tested on F.4 VT196. Author's collection.

spares for other Meteors operating in France, until it was eventually scrapped.

G.41G Meteor F.4, VT196

VT196 was in the second batch of thirty-two aircraft of Gloster's second F.4 production contract; this Meteor never saw RAF service of any kind, being used solely by a variety of different experimental establishments.

The Telecommunications Flying Unit (TFU) at Defford had employed examples of just about every type of aircraft produced in Britain during the war, plus some post-war types, as well as many from across the Atlantic Ocean, and VT196 joined the unit on 15 June 1948. However, its stay at Defford was very short, for in the first week of July it left and flew to Hucknall to commence several years' testing of various Rolls-Royce engine developments. Fitted with the standard 3,500lb (1,587kg) thrust Derwent 5s, it was used for trials of the many ancillary equipment modifications evolved for that variant of the engine. Over a timespan of eighteen months, 210 flying hours were devoted to this work, before it went into the shops for its first real conversion.

Early reheat trials had already been flown on RA435, and modifications made to the system required testing separately from that aircraft. VT196 was selected for these trials, and its conversion was completed by the end of March 1950, with a different variable nozzle arrangement from the one installed on RA435. Following ground-running tests, VT196 made its first flight, with reheat fitted but not operative, early in April 1950, and on 17 April, a ten-month test programme was started.

Meanwhile the Derwent 8 was going into production at Rolls-Royce's Derby works, and a reheat system was fabricated for testing. VT196 went back into the Hucknall workshops for a Derwent 8, with reheat, to be installed as a replacement for the Derwent 5 unit in the starboard nacelle, and comparative trials of the two different engines began on 4 April 1951. Over 100 hours of flying were logged in these trials before the two engines were removed, and at the end of June 1953 the aircraft was restored to its original production standard before being flown to No. 47 MU at Sealand, the packing depot for No. 43 Maintenance Group. From there,

Side and plan elevations of VT196, showing the great difference made to its appearance when fitted with the Canadian reheat installation. Author's artwork.

VT196 was transported by sea to Canada, for a four-month series of cold-weather trials, in the winter of 1953.

Following these, VT196 was loaned to Canada's National Aeronautical Establishment (NAE) for yet another reheat conversion: during World War II, Victory Aircraft Limited of Malton, Ontario, had built over 1,000 aircraft for A.V. Roe, and on 1 December 1945, Avro bought the Canadian company to form A.V. Roe Canada Limited. They designed and built the CF-100 Canuck, the CF-102 Jetliner and the magnificent CF-105

Arrow all-weather fighter. The company's Gas Turbine Division, later to be renamed Orenda Engines, produced Canada's first indigenous turbojet engine, the Iroquois, delivering over 6,000lb (2,721kg) thrust.

A reheat system was designed for the Iroquois, and NAE requested that VT196 could test-fly it. The installation added over 450lb (204kg) to the aircraft's weight, and was fitted in massive nacelle extensions that put a 50in (127cm) increase on the standard nacelle length. Flight-testing started on 14 January 1954 and the results were very encouraging, with the standard

Derwent 5's 3,500lb (1,587kg) thrust being increased to nearly 4,400lb (1,995kg). The climb performance was also greatly improved, 20,000ft (6,096m) being reached in 3.1 minutes, compared with the standard F.4's 4.9 minutes. The reheat system was planned for engines to be installed in production versions of the twin-engined Arrow, the prototypes having been powered by Pratt and Whitney J75s; but, like the TSR.2 in Britain, the CF-105 became a political football, so only one production aircraft was completed and this was never flown. With a pair of Iroquois, each giving 26,000lb (11,791kg) dry thrust, the Arrow was potentially a very fast aeroplane, but although an engine was test-flown in a starboard rear fuselage location on Boeing B-47B 51-2057, the Iroquois was never put into production.

When VT196's Canadian test-flying was completed at the end of 1954, it was once more restored to its original configuration and returned to Britain, by sea, in the summer of 1955. On 11 June 1958 the aircraft was damaged in a wheels-up landing at No. 20 MU Aston Down, and was transferred in its damaged state to FRL at Tarrant Rushton for conversion to a U.15. Resplendent in its scarlet-and-yellow target drone finish, it still continued to get into the records book as on 9 February 1963, VT196 made the last flight of any U.15.

G.41K Meteor F.8, WA820

Contract No. 6/ACFT/2983/CB7(b) for 210 F.8s was divided between Gloster and Armstrong Whitworth, and when WA820, the eighth aircraft from Gloster's first batch, rolled out onto the Hucclecote tarmac, no one could have known that it would become the most powerful of all Meteors.

Retained as a manufacturers' aircraft, it was loaned to Armstrong Siddeley to further that company's engine-testing requirements. Armstrong Siddeley's first entry in the turbojet field was their ASX, which was test-flown in a bomb-bay installation on Lancaster ND784, a Mark III that had been modified to Mark IV standard. When Metropolitan-Vickers made their exit from aircraft turbojet design and manufacture, they had a big axial-flow engine on the drawing board, which Armstrong Siddeley amalgamated with their existing developments, to produce the Sapphire – an engine which Rolls-Royce admitted had superior pressure/flow characteristics to their own Avon. Licence agreements with Curtiss-Wright in the United States produced that company's version of the engine, designated the J65, which powered the Republic F-84F and Martin B-57B (itself a licence-built product of British design, the Canberra).

Lancastrian C.2 VM733 was used by Rolls-Royce, Rotol and de Havilland for a variety of testing, and was then put into storage; but at this time the Armstrong Siddeley Sapphire had just commenced bench-running, and so in January 1948, VM733 re-emerged and was sent to AST at Hamble to be engineered for accepting two Sa1 Sapphires, each producing 7,200lb (3,265kg) static thrust, in the outer nacelle positions. Two years later, on 18 January

F.8 WA820, fitted with a pair of Armstrong Siddeley Sapphire Sa2 engines. Author's collection.

1950, it took the Sapphire into the air for the first time.

WA820's role in the development of the Sapphire was to provide a more representative test platform for the engine. The original variant first flown in the Lancastrian was being superseded by the Sa2, developing 7,600lb (3,446.6kg) thrust, and in order for the Meteor to be a successful testbed for a pair of engines in this power category, the airframe required considerable strengthening. The Sapphire's physical dimensions determined that the front spars had to arch over the engines, and this in turn necessitated major reinforcement of a large percentage of the wing structure. In the summer of 1951, WA820 appeared with an E.1/44-type tail assembly, all signs of armament removed, a much enlarged tail bumper, and a fuselage sitting between two enormous nacelles. The whole aircraft exuded power, and flight-testing confirmed that this was a very quick variant in which higher speeds were registered than had ever been possible in any previous Meteor.

Gloster test pilot Jan Zurakowski flew the aircraft to London's Heathrow Airport on 30 August 1950 for a demonstration – following its removal from the 'secret list' – and the next month he displayed it at the 1950 SBAC Show. There followed a year of intensive testing conducted from Bitteswell and Moreton Valence, during which the Sapphire fully confirmed its design potential. An appearance at the 1951 SBAC Display was prefaced in the evening of Friday 31 August by the establishing of four time-to-height records. To achieve this, Armstrong Siddeley test pilot, Flt Lt R.B. 'Tom' Prickett, flew the aircraft from Moreton Valence: following take-off, he held WA820 down to about 200ft (61m) for 2.5 miles (4km), letting the speed build up to an indicated 540mph (869km/h). He then lifted the nose from an initial 17 degree angle, to about 45 degrees by the time 40,000ft (12,192m) had been cleared. The four records, promulgated by the Royal Aero Club on behalf of the *Fédération Aeronautique Internationale* (FAI), were time-to-height from rest to 3,000m, 6,000m, 9,000m and 12,000m, and the times taken for the four heights were 1min 16sec, 1min 50sec, 2min 25sec and 3min 7sec respectively. In the course of the ascent, the average rate-of-climb from 10,000ft to 40,000ft (3,048m to 12,192m) was approximately 16,000ft/min (4,876.8m/min).

Not unexpectedly, resplendent with prominent Hawker Siddeley Group logos on either side of the nose, WA820 attracted much attention at the SBAC display, and it was amazing to see the speed along Farnborough's main runway being attained by a basic design constructed when thrusts in the order of 2,000lb (907kg) were considered spectacular. But that was about as far as the Meteor could be expected to go in the development of the Sapphire. Sa6 and Sa7 variants had been produced, and these had been type-tested at 8,500lb (3,854.75kg) thrust and 10,500lb (4,761.75kg) thrust respectively. This sort of power was beyond even a much-strengthened Meteor, and further Sapphire testing was taken over by the Canberra.

WA820 went to the Central Fighter Establishment (CFE) at West Raynham with the Sa2 engines still *in situ*; here it was operated by the Air Fighting Development Squadron (AFDS), which at that time was commanded by Wg Cdr 'Bobby' Oxspring. This man had been CO of No. 54 Squadron when on 14 July 1948 they flew their Vampires to make the first jet crossing of the Atlantic. It has been stated that the aircraft rarely flew twice in one day, because it took so long to recharge the air starter's compressed air bottles. At the 1952 summer CFE Fighter Convention, WA820 was demonstrated by Flt Lt

'Jimmy' Shaw, while another of its regular pilots was Sqn Ldr Peter Vaughan-Fowler; the latter had made a name for himself flying Lysanders in World War II, servicing secret agents in German-occupied France. On 31 March 1954, WA820 went from West Raynham to No. 1 School of Technical Training (STT) at Halton, where it acquired the instructional airframe number 7141M.

G.41K Meteor F.8, WA982

Covered by the same split-contract as WA820, WA982 was built by Armstrong Whitworth Aircraft at Baginton and first served with No. 56 Squadron, based at Waterbeach. However, the squadron only held it for a short time, as RAE Farnborough needed it to participate in a test programme that they were conducting – but again, that stay was brief.

On 2 November 1952, after a total of only fifty hours flying, WA982 went the way of so many engine testbed Meteors, to Hucknall, where it was to be modified to fulfil Rolls-Royce's requirement to test an entirely new engine. The previous year, Winston Churchill had started the premiership of a newly-elected Conservative government, while relations between the NATO powers and the Soviet bloc were verging on conflict. The new

Flt Lt R.B. 'Tom' Prickett in the cockpit of WA820 prior to his record flight. Derek N. James.

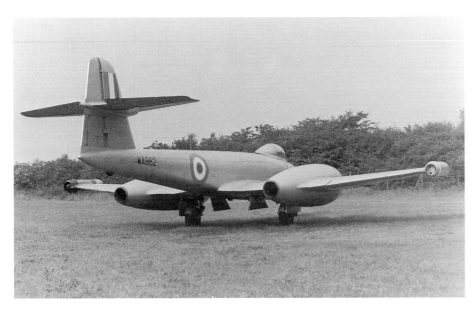

F.8 WA982, fitted with a Soar RSr.2 on the port wingtip and a ballasted engine casing on the starboard side. Author's collection.

government carried out a reassessment of the Services and, as getting a new bomber into service within a couple of years was quite out of the question, interest arose in the designing of a flying-bomb type of offensive aircraft. These thoughts were put into a more tangible context with the issuing, in April 1951, of Specification UB.109T, codenamed Blue Rapier, in which both Vickers-Armstrongs and Bristol Aircraft were interested enough to submit designs. The Bristol proposal was its Type 182, a single-engined aircraft constructed in Durestos and powered by the company's own BE.17 expendable turbojet.

Vickers-Armstrongs at Weybridge came up with an entirely different design, based on using three of the new Rolls-Royce RB.82 short-life/expendable engines, named after a tributary of the River Trent, the Soar. As so often happened, official thoughts changed direction and Specification UB.109T was cancelled, but the encouraging thrust/weight ratio, together with a superior thrust/frontal area ratio to any other existing gas turbine, convinced Rolls-Royce that the Soar should not be abandoned. The single axial compressor, with an annular high-intensity combustion chamber, fitted within an overall length of under 60in (152.4cm) and a diameter of 15.8in (40.1cm). Furthermore, an engine with a dry weight of 275lb (124.7kg), producing 1,810lb (821.8kg) thrust, was worth developing,

even though it was only made for a life of ten hours and further applications were optimistically considered highly likely. In fact, in 1957 Operational Requirement (OR) 1149 was raised, covering the design of a cruise missile to supersede the Blue Steel Mk 1 stand-off bomb. A 1,000 mile (1,609km) range was called for, and Avro, the Blue Steel's manufacturer, submitted a

design powered by two Soars – but again the requirement was cancelled.

Returning to November 1952, when WA982 arrived at Hucknall, plans were put in hand for the aircraft to be modified to carry two Soar RSr.2 engines, one at each wing-tip, which entailed more than just a reworking of the tips; an entirely new pressure fuel system had to be installed within the mainplanes, and it was the end of March 1953 before this was completed. However, this was well ahead of a flight-cleared Soar's availability, so the aircraft was operated by Hucknall on general Derwent 8 testing for the rest of the year.

One Soar RSr.2 was ready for flight-testing early in 1954, its installation on WA982's port wing-tip commencing on 21 February, with a ballasted engine casing being fixed to the starboard side. Four days later, all systems had been tested and the short-life engine became airborne for the first time, in a twenty-four minute maiden flight during which it was successfully run. Further flight-testing continued over the next six months, after which it went back into Hucknall's works, to be prepared for the 1954 SBAC Display and become a four-engined Meteor for the first time, although this lasted only a few days.

Nearly every photograph published of this testbed has referred to it as being four-engined, but unless the picture was taken

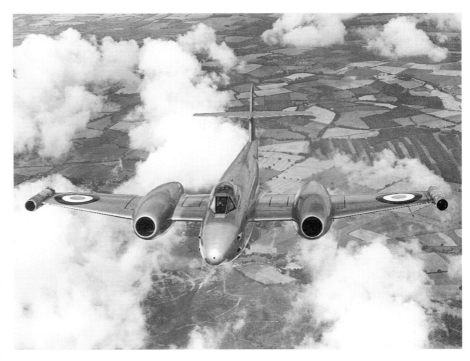

During the only week that WA982 had two working Soar engines, it is seen en route to the 1954 SBAC display. Author's collection.

at that year's Farnborough, or when it was *en route*, this is incorrect. At the end of August 1954, Hucknall's fitters removed the ballasted engine casing from the starboard tip and replaced it with a new, fully working Soar just for the show. Bad weather restricted flying that year, also the organizers had one 'civil aircraft only' day, so that the actual number of flights made with both engines operating were very few. After the display, on the last day, 12 September, WA982 departed from Farnborough and went back to Hucknall, where both engines were removed for returning to Rolls-Royce for overhauling. When they came back, the new engine which had been installed on the starboard side for Farnborough, was refitted on the port side, and the ballasted engine casing was returned to the starboard side, ready for flight-testing to be resumed. However, no production application for the Soar materialized, so the programme was gradually run down and the last Soar sortie was made on 22 March 1956.

Hucknall restored WA982 to standard – although whether the additional pressure fuel system was removed, has not been recorded – and then it spent time at both Boscombe Down and Little Rissington, before going to Tarrant Rushton, where FRL converted it into another U.16 that ended up at Llanbedr.

sion was the delta Type 720, with a 27ft 3in (8.32m) spanning wing, that was to carry D.H. Firestreak missiles, and the Ministry of Supply's Specification 137D covered the production of a prototype with the serial XD696. Interception was to be made on the power of one Armstrong Siddeley Screamer rocket motor, after which the aircraft returned to base on the thrust of an ASV.8 Viper 101 turbojet, made by the same engine manufacturer.

Meteor VZ517 joined Armstrong Siddeley at Bitteswell to fulfil their requirement for a Screamer flying testbed. The rocket motor was a single-chamber, pump-fed unit which ran on LOX, a highly volatile mixture of 60 per cent liquid oxygen, 23 per cent kerosene and 17 per cent water. The thrust of the motor could be varied between 1,000lb and 8,000lb (453.5kg and 3,628kg) at low level, increasing to over 9,000lb at 40,000ft (4,081.5kg at 12,192m). The Screamer was sited in the rear of a strengthened, restressed ventral tank which also housed the liquid oxygen tank, and its outlet was tilted 10 degrees downwards in order to keep the flame clear of the fuselage when ground-running. As an additional safety measure a stainless-steel protective plate was attached to the fuselage underside, aft of the rocket motor's orifice, and the

kerosene tank was housed in the aircraft's ammunition bay.

Flight clearance for the Screamer was given in December 1955, but by this time the RAF had gone off the idea of LOX as a rocket motor fuel, not only for its volatile aspect, but because of the operational limitations that it imposed – all mechanical systems would have to be maintained at a high temperature in order not to freeze solid, and a LOX-fuelled aircraft could not remain on alert without a system of continual topping-up, again operationally quite unacceptable. The Service opted for the high-test peroxide (HTP) system employed in the de Havilland Spectre. The Avro 720 was cancelled in 1956 – officially on the grounds of national economy, but the abandoning of LOX was the more obvious one – and the Saunders Roe SR.53 submission to OR301, powered by a Spectre, went as far as two prototypes, plus a mock-up of the definitive SR.177, before the whole project was cancelled in 1958. Incidentally, this aircraft's cancellation took with it the DH Spectre rocket motor, which gave that the distinction of being, at £5.75 million, the most expensive of all British engine projects that failed to go into operational service.

The Screamer, a culmination of ten

G.41K Meteor F.8, VZ517

The first contract for building the Meteor F.8 was split between Hucclecote and Baginton, with VZ517 being the last Gloster-built aircraft in the order. From 16 June 1950 to 17 September 1953 it was used at Hucknall for a series of tests conducted by Rolls-Royce, to perfect a cure for the engine surge problem that was sometimes encountered with their Derwent 8. These trials were very extensive, with over 300 hours of flying being accrued over the three years. The aircraft was then transferred to another engine manufacturer, for a different type of power source.

In the early 1950s, Britain went through a phase of considering mixed-power interceptors for the main defence of the United Kingdom against high-speed, high-altitude bombers. Operational Requirement (OR) 301 was issued for the design of such an aircraft, to which Saunders-Roe and Avro submitted proposals. The latter's submis-

Armstrong-Siddeley's Screamer rocket motor, installed in a re-stressed ventral fuel tank on F.8 VZ517. Author's collection.

years' rocket motor development by Armstrong Siddeley, just disappeared, and VZ517 was transferred to No.1 SST at Halton on 12 April 1956, with the Instructional Airframe number 7322M.

G.41L Meteor FR.9, VZ608

Only six of the 126 FR.9s built never saw operational service, and one of them was VZ608: it came off the Hucclecote line early in 1951, and on 15 March, with a total of thirty-five minutes flying time on the clock, was delivered to Hucknall where it was to operate for the best part of the next fourteen years.

Fitted with Derwent 8 engines nos. 6891 and 6202, it spent several days on nacelle temperature checking before going into the test establishment's works, on 28 March, to have its Derwents converted to take yet another new reheat system that Rolls-Royce had fabricated. This was a much neater installation than the previous units tested, first on RA435 and then VT196. When VZ608 came out of the shops seven months later, it looked virtually the same as when it went in, for the new reheat units were contained within the nacelles, the tail-cones being very slightly more tapered, over an 18in (54.7cm) extension – very different from the earlier conversions. Several days of ground-running trials were followed by a successful maiden flight on 19 October 1951. Subsequently the aircraft was used

VZ608 being used for thrust-reversal trials, with a rather crude attachment to the port engine jet pipe, for ground-running only. Author's collection.

for over twelve months on the testing programme, which by the end of 1951 had occupied nearly 100 flying hours. No Derwent went into production with a reheat system, but the data gathered was embodied in later Rolls-Royce engines and VZ608 was scheduled for use on another project altogether.

The engine company's design department had been working throughout the early 1950s on a system whereby an engine's efflux could be reversed, to act as a deceleration force. With VZ608 having completed the reheat trials, it went back into the works in May 1954 to be fitted with a very elementary thrust reverser that had been made up for ground-running only. It was installed on the port engine's jet pipe, the rear nacelle cowling having been removed, and with the front nacelle cowling also discarded, a nine weeks' test programme was run until July 10. The unit was then removed, and the earlier 18in (45.7cm) longer nacelles were restored before the aircraft was wheeled back into the works for another – and final – conversion, the work entailed being its most extensive.

Rolls-Royce had also been busy in the 1950s, giving thought to the principle of getting an aircraft other than a helicopter off the ground in a vertical trajectory – and back down the same way. The RAE had co-operated with them, and in 1954 two thrust-measuring rigs (TMRs) were manufactured. Euphemistically called the 'Flying Bedstead', the device was a collection of scaffolding built around two Nene engines with their jet pipes turned through

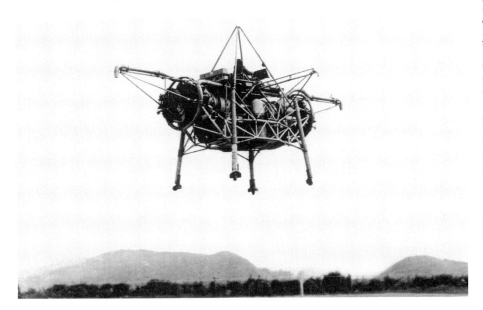

Where vertical take-off and landing (VTOL) trials in the United Kingdom originated: Rolls-Royce's thrust-measuring rig XJ314, the 'flying bedstead'. Author's collection.

ninety degrees, in order to direct the thrust straight downwards. After many tethered hovers, the first free flight was made on 3 August 1954, with Captain Ronald Shepherd at the controls. He was the founder member of the Rolls-Royce Flight Test Establishment in 1933, and as the company's first pilot, was responsible for the flying of all the piston and jet engines on their first flights, with very few exceptions and following each phase of development. He was a most respected manager within Rolls-Royce and the aircraft industry as a whole. Parallel with the TMRs, Rolls-Royce's chief scientist Dr A.A. Griffiths (who wrote the report in 1926 considering the gas turbine as a propulsive system) had proposed that design studies for a custom-built vertical-lift turbojet should be made, his provisional calculations estimating that a thrust/weight ratio between 8:1 and 9:1 would be necessary.

The Soar was a product of these proposals, but it was designed purely as a short-life engine. The MoS agreed to guarantee financially the engine company's concept, which contended that multiple installations of small, high-thrust-ratio engines was the way to go for vertical take-off and landing aircraft. Specification ER.143 was raised for the production of two research airframes, the contract being awarded to Short Brothers in Belfast, who

The dorsal intake for the RB.108 engine is well shown here, as is one of the booster pump housings under the fixed underwing tanks. Author's collection.

designed and built its SC.1, the first of which, XG900, was completed in November 1956. In order to provide Short Brothers with a tried and tested power-plant, Meteor VZ608 was allocated to be the testbed for the 2,130lb (966kg) thrust Rolls-Royce RB.108, an axial-flow turbojet development from the Soar.

Once again, because Gloster Aircraft's design office and experimental shops were

fully occupied, VZ608's conversion had to be placed with another company, F.G. Miles Ltd at Shoreham being selected. Established at Redhill in Sussex by Frederick George Miles, after the collapse of Miles Aircraft on 19 November 1947, the company moved to Shoreham, also in Sussex, and this is where the FR.9 arrived in June 1955. It was to be modified to accept a single RB.108 installed vertically behind the cockpit, on the line of the c.g., where the main fuel tank was normally positioned. Provision was made in the design of the mounting for the engine to swing up to fifteen degrees on either side of the vertical, and F.G. Miles liaised closely with Short Brothers in order to ensure that the dorsal intake, which had a grille flush with the fuselage top surface, was capable of supplying a proportionate volumn of air to that required in the SC.1. The Meteor's ventral fuel tank was removed so that a hole could be cut where the RB.108 would exhaust, and because some compensation needed to be made for the weight of the test engine, all armament was taken off the aircraft.

As the main fuel tank, plus the ventral tank, had been removed, the sole fuel carriers were the two 100-gallon (455-litre) underwing tanks, which were made permanent. This meant that, whereas before conversion VZ608 had provision for 795 gallons (3,617 litres), it now had only 200 gallons (910 litres) and an extra engine to feed! The maximum

The RB.108 aboard VZ608, being utilized to test various ground surfaces, prior to Harrier operations. Derek N. James.

endurance of thirty minutes was not a lot of time to test-fly an engine. Small booster pumps in housings on the underside of each engine nacelle transferred fuel into a collector tank in the nose for distribution to all three engines. Several RB.108s had been bench-run prior to the assembly of flight engines, and unit No. 22 was transported to Sussex for flight-testing in the FR.9. Modifications were completed by the end of April 1956, with the RB.108 installed, but as Shoreham was an all-grass airfield, systems checking and engine running was not practical, so an alternative site had to be arranged. Just over 20 miles (32 km) to the west lay Tangmere, with acres of tarmac runways, so early in May 1956, VZ608 was transported from Shoreham to the operational fighter station, and two weeks later, on 18 May, the aircraft took an RB.108 into the air for the first time, although it was not started up. Further systems checks occupied the next five days, and then on 23 May, VZ608 departed from Sussex and returned to the engine makers' experimental facility at Hucknall.

Sqn Ldr Brian Hegworth, who undertook a lot of the flying, had many frustrating sorties because of the engine's reluctance to start in flight, but on 23 October 1956 his patience was rewarded and the RB.108 started in the air for the first time. Test-flying progressed through the rest of 1956 and all 1957, during which it was found that the lift-engine could maintain the aircraft's weight with the Derwents at mid-power. Short Brothers had flown the first SC.1 from Boscombe Down in a conventional mode, and the second prototype XG905 made its first hovering trials on 23 May 1958.

RB.108 test-flying in VZ608 continued until 1962, and a small nose-mounted probe had been installed to register the angles of incidence assumed by the aircraft when the engine was run at high power settings. By June 1962, the company had finished with the Meteor as an RB.108 testbed, but looking to the future and the forthcoming Harrier operations, VZ608 was employed to investigate ground-erosion of various surfaces likely to be encountered. These continued over a period of two years until eventually, on 29 September 1965, the aircraft was struck off charge. VZ608 is at the Newark Air Museum in Nottinghamshire where it has been fully restored and is now on display. Its RB.108 vertical lift engine was displayed at the Royal Air Force Museum, Hendon, for many years, but they have loaned it to Newark for inclusion with VZ608.

CHAPTER THIRTEEN

Trials and Research Meteors

Had the seeds of jet propulsion and radar been cultivated in a climate of international stability, there is no doubt that their growth would not have been so prolific. However they were, and in Britain the Gloster Meteor became one of the principal airborne laboratories to further their proliferation. The realms of increasing operational radii, boundary-layer suction, prone piloting, emergency evacuation and missile armaments were all advanced or disproved through trials conducted with Meteors over the years, some of the following aircraft being actively engaged in the researches.

G.41C Meteor F.3

EE246. Having served with No. 616 Squadron as YQ-A, this aircraft went to Malcolm Lobell (ML Aviation) as a trials aircraft during the company's brief excursion into ejector-seat design, which was operated in conjunction with RAE Farnborough during the early part of 1946

EE348. This aircraft too served with No. 616 Squadron, and it was then delivered to the Central Radar Establishment (CRE) at Defford on 21 September 1945, where it became the first British turbojet-powered aircraft to be fitted with AI radar. The unit was the well established wartime podded American AN/APS-4 'ASH' system, carrying the British designation AI Mk15, which had been used extensively as an attachment on Royal Navy/Fleet Air Arm Avengers, Barracudas and Fireflys in the final years of the conflict. David Henderson, the Chief Designer at the CRE, used the Meteor's strong nose-wheel frame structure to install a fabricated interface platform on which the AI Mk15 pod was mounted. A new nose cowling was tailored, with the front fairing being a transparent second window of appropriate

radar wavelength section, which was the accepted technology of that era, and the armament was removed, with the cannon ports faired over.

The CFE at West Raynham was eager to assess the potential of radar in terms of combat range measurement. Head-up glass reflector Gyro gunsights (GM-II) were standard on all front-line fighters, which equally measured the correct range for weapon firing relative to the gun's harmonization point, provided the target's wingspan was set on the graticule selector switch. EE348's 'one-off' programme was not concerned with the AI role as, being a single-seat aircraft, no operator was present to vector the pilot for a visual contact. The trials with the experimental

installation were to establish that it would provide a quick-reference facility of a target ahead in marginal weather conditions and supply range information for weapon firing, thereby eliminating the time-consuming manual setting of the graticule selector switch. Several pilots with experience on the de Havilland Sea Hornet NF.21, fitted with AN/APS-4, flew EE348, and the aircraft was later joined by another F.3, EE350, which came to Defford from Boscombe Down, but this is not believed to have been equipped with the same instrumentation as EE348.

At the beginning of October 1951, an experimental homing head for guided-weapon research was installed in EE348, using the original interface design but with

Flight Refuelling Limited's combination of Lancaster BIII G-33-2 and Meteor F.3 EE397, during their early trials. *Aeroplane Monthly.*

only one non-transparent radome, faired to the same profile. Later the aircraft was transferred to No. 4 STT at St Athan, with the instructional airframe number 6975M.

EE397. Flight Refuelling Limited (FRL) had been formed on 29 October 1934, and their founder Alan (later Sir Alan) Cobham's concept of aerial refuelling had slowly advanced over the years. With the turbojet engine's prodigious thirst, the company considered that keeping a jet-powered fighter airborne for a longer patrol period would be just as advantageous as extending its strategic range. They used two ex-RAF Lancaster B.IIIs registered in FRL's 'B-condition' markings, former ND648 being G-33-1 and PB972, G-33-2, both aircraft perfecting the probe/drogue system to a point where the use of a jet fighter as a receiver was the next logical step.

Through perseverance, FRL was loaned Meteor F.3 EE397 by the Air Ministry, and the aircraft arrived at Tarrent Rushton early in 1949. A receiver probe was fitted on the extreme nose, and the associated internal plumbing modifications expedited as quickly as possible, so the aircraft would be ready to make a flying demonstration which was to be attended by General Carroll of the USAF on 6 April 1949. Two days before the scheduled visit, FRL's pilot Pat Horridge took off in EE397 to rendezvous with tanker G-33-2, flown by another company pilot, Tom Marks. Good dry contacts were made throughout the day. The official demonstration on 6 April was also very successful: flown at 140mph (225.3km/h) at a height of 2,000ft (609.6m), seven fuel transfers were accomplished before an array of dignitaries flown in a Vickers Viking alongside the Lancaster/Meteor duo. Sir Alan did emphasize that his system could transfer at 600 gallons (2,730 litres) per minute, while flying at 450mph and 35,000ft (724km/h and 10,668m). Since the service ceiling of the Lancaster B.III *without* bomb-load was only 24,500ft (7,467.6m), this claim was somewhat academic, but later in the year FRL received Lincoln RA657, together with Meteor F.4 VZ389, in order to expand the trials envelope.

FRL knew the publicity value of attempting a 'world first', and they felt that their probe-and-drogue system could do nothing but benefit from securing an endurance record for jet aircraft. So the team of Tom Marks, Pat Horridge, G-33-2

Side elevation of F.3 EE416 as originally converted for the first live ejection, and an understandably apprehensive-looking 'Benny' Lynch. Author's artwork and collection.

and EE397 took to the air again on 7 August 1949, and a continuous orbit by Horridge in the Meteor, ranging over Dungeness, Devon and Bristol, with ten refuelling link-ups to the Lancaster in the Isle of Wight area, gave EE397 a 12hr 3min record. G-33-2 made only one return to Tarrent Rushton halfway through the attempt, to top up the tanks, and the next link-up with the Meteor was spot on schedule.

The arrival of the F.4 VZ389 marked the end of EE397's contribution to FRL's early probe-and-drogue trials. Having proved the principle, the aircraft became Instructional Airframe 7168M at No. 1 STT, Halton.

EE416. It can possibly be said that this aircraft made one of the greatest contributions to the history of military aviation. As the operational speeds of aircraft increased, the question of pilot evacuation in an emergency was assuming increasing proportions, and in the early summer of 1944 Wg Cdr John Jewell was sent by Fighter Command to meet James Martin at his Martin-Baker Aircraft Limited works in Denham. Martin had already given the problem serious thoughts, with one idea being a dorsal-mounted swinging arm that could be adapted to be installed on current fighters; however, the Air Ministry decided that pilot ejection would only be incorporated in jet aircraft. Martin was commissioned by the Ministry of Aircraft Production (MAP) to design an ejection seat, and this led to trials in which ballast was fired up a 16ft (4.87m) steel ramp; he was able to extend these much further when, in December 1944, Boulton Paul Defiant DR944 arrived, an aircraft that had previously been used by the USAAF in Britain as a target tug. Five months were spent modifying the Defiant, and then at Wittering on 11 May 1945, before an assembly of high-ranking officials, Rotol's chief test pilot Brian Greensted took off to give the first airborne display of ejecting a dummy.

By autumn the Defiant had reached the limit of its practical contribution to the programme, and James Martin applied for the use of a Meteor in order to test his seat at current operational speeds. F.3 EE416 was delivered to Denham on 6 November 1945, and the extensive conversion of the single-seater to accept an ejection seat, plus a second crew member, was begun. The seat was to be positioned in place of the ammunition bay behind the pilot, and the principal alterations centred around the replacing of the original seat bulkhead with a new one further aft, which was inclined at a steeper angle; these were carried out in full liaison with Gloster's stress department. Floor beams were strengthened to cater for the loads imposed by the ejection forces, and a new canopy was fabricated for the pilot – an open aperture was faired in behind it to facilitate the ejection seat's upward trajectory. The work was completed in seven months, which is highly commendable considering it was the first encounter with a Meteor by Martin-Baker's engineering department. The modified aircraft was transported to the company's airfield at Chalgrove, an ex-30th photographic-reconnaissance squadron wartime base operating with a mixture of P-38 Lightning variants, 10 miles (16km) south-east of Oxford. On 8 June 1946, the aircraft was jacked up and the first ejection from a Meteor was successfully accomplished, with the dummy landing in a catch-net.

Two weeks later, on 24 June, EE416 made its maiden flight for Martin-Baker, and a series of dummy ejections was commenced – with depressing results. The parachute burst at the seams, to become entangled with the seat so that dummy and seat could not separate before they both crashed to earth. However, over the next four weeks, thirteen more trial ejections

with dummies took place and results were excellent, and this convinced everyone, including a company fitter, that the system lived up to its promise. This fitter, known as Bernard 'Benny' Lynch, volunteered to be the 'guinea pig' for a first live ejection, placing his stocky frame in the test seat behind Martin-Baker's test pilot John 'Scotty' Scott, an ex-Imperial Airways captain who had been seconded from the National Gas Turbine Establishment (NGTE). EE416 took off to formate on another Meteor, piloted by Squadron Leader 'Johnny' Booth, who was to photograph the event. Both aircraft approached and flew over Chalgrove prior to commencing a very wide circuit, which led into a long straight-in approach to land without an ejection. On reaching the dispersal, it was seen that Lynch was sitting in the test seat, with the blind that was pulled down to trigger the seat firing mechanism still covering his face! The ground crew frantically, but very carefully, replaced the firing pin to make the seat safe, before helping Lynch to climb out and report a malfunction in the sequence. Everyone became fully aware that at any time during the aircraft's descent and landing, Benny could have been shot out. The problem was quickly identified and rectified by the company's mechanics, but James Martin proposed postponing the test

until the following day. Benny Lynch, however, was adamant that he wanted no further delay, so the Managing Director relented, allowing both aircraft to be refuelled and take off again. The two Meteors approached the airfield in echelon at a height of 8,000ft (2,438.4m), flying at 320mph (514.9km/h), and Lynch carried out Britain's first live ejection from an aircraft in flight. A 16g thrust cleared him from the Meteor and eight seconds later he manually unfastened the straps holding him in the seat that was descending on its parachute and threw himself clear to deploy his own canopy. The whole sequence was a complete success and both parachutes landed on the airfield almost simultaneously. The 'guinea pig' suffered nothing more serious than a ripped sleeve to his fleece-lined leather jacket, plus the loss of a lens from his two-piece goggles. This test, on 24 July 1946 was the harbinger of, although far removed from, today's fully automatic procedure.

A total of over 400 more live ejections were made from EE416, which in the course of the programme was stripped of its camouflage and resprayed overall silver. Benny Lynch made a further thirty ejections and received the British Empire Medal (BEM) for his pioneering work. Another Martin-Baker fitter, former Army paratrooper Peter Page, joined Lynch, and

EE416 in the half-way condition, with all except the wings resprayed silver. Author's collection.

on 14 August 1946 he made his second ejection, which was being conducted at 400mph (643.7km/h), the highest speed yet attempted. Unfortunately, the jolt of the seat canopy's opening dragged Page's personal parachute ripcord from its housing and, unable to separate from the seat, he fell to the ground with it – and his luck continued to desert him, for the seat landed on the runway, instead of the grass. The ex-paratrooper broke his neck and was fortunate not to have been killed. As a result of the accident, modifications were incorporated in the personal parachute ripcord housing. Two weeks later, Lynch ejected from EE416 as it flew at 505mph (812.6km/h), to set a new world record for high-speed ejection.

At the end of 1951 the Mk2 automatic seat with leg-restraining straps had been tested, and as far as Martin-Baker was concerned, with the completion of these tests EE416 had come to the end of its useful life; the company was now requesting a Meteor T.7 to replace it. On 30 January 1952, T.7 WA634 arrived at Chalgrove, and EE416's front section, together with Benny Lynch's first ejection seat, were donated to the Science Museum in London. During EE416's time at Denham, as well as at Chalgrove, it was joined by two Meteor F.3s, EE338 and EE415, both being allocated for air-to-air photographic recording, although the results obtained were not as good as had been expected. A further F.3, EE479, together with F.4 EE519, also joined the Martin-Baker trials programmes, but their stays were of short duration and they departed to be used at other establishments.

EE445. Professor A.A. Griffith comes into the history of the Meteor once again. EE445, a Hucclecote-built aircraft, arrived at Armstrong Whitworth's Bitteswell airfield in December 1945, loaned to the company to further Professor Griffith's researches into laminar-flow wing sections. Since March 23 of the same year, Hawker Hurricane Mk IIB Z3687 had been flying with laminar-flow mainwing panels, designed and manufactured by Armstrong Whitworth. The company's chief test pilot Charles Turner-Hughs had made the maiden flight, with his assistant F.R. Midgley and the RAE's Lt Cdr Eric 'Winkle' Brown also participating in the test-flying programme. The results were rather disappointing, because of the

The port wing of F.3 EE445 fitted with the 'Griffith's wing', showing the thicker-than-standard section required to house the system. Also very noticeable is the concave section of the elevator's top surface. Author's collection.

difficulty of keeping the wing surfaces constantly smooth and free from undulations or foreign bodies.

EE445 was allocated to help expand the programme, and in particular so that a new aerofoil could be evaluated: designed by Professor Griffith, it differed from the Hurricane's test wing in so far as boundary-layer suction was employed to maintain a clean flow over the whole surface. This was only possible because of the Meteor's turbine power source, and Rolls-Royce's Barnoldswick experimental department received an order from AWA for a pair of engines to be prepared for delivery by February 1946. The engine would be the basic Derwent 1, but incorporating modifications such that air could be drawn off the proposed wing section via a series of ports. The new engine was designated Derwent 3 and three units were manufactured, two being supplied to Bitteswell, while one was retained at Barnoldswick for future allocation, although it is not thought ever to have been despatched to AWA.

The new wings for EE445 were thicker than standard, this being necessary to accommodate the piping from the continuous-suction ports at the gap between the wing surface and the ailerons. These were the length of almost the whole span of the new outer-wing section, which was attached to the airframe outboard of the

engine nacelles. The modifications were completed by the end of 1946, and on 21 January 1947, Sqn Ldr Eric Franklin took off from Bitteswell to give the Meteor a maiden flight with the Griffith wing. Evaluation of the wing by Franklin occupied many months, following which EE445 was transferred to RAE Farnborough in August 1948, for their assessment.

Lt Cdr Brown was the designated pilot; his first flight was on 25 August 1948, and he found that the gain in lift was less than expected. Modifications were made by sealing over the underside aileron slots with rubber strips, and Brown made a second flight on 1 October. He described this flight to me thus:

In flight the rubber blew out on the starboard side, and this set up a violent aileron oscillation and overbalance of the controls so that the ailerons themselves could only be seen as a blurred mass, and the wings were flexing alarmingly. At the same time the aeroplane was rolling violently from side to side and sometimes going over the vertical. I was unable to alleviate this situation, so announced to Farnborough ATC my intention of baling out. They responded by saying another aircraft in my vicinity was being homed onto me by radar to monitor the bale-out. Within seconds another Meteor appeared, flown by one of my own pilots from Aero Flight. He observed that as my aircraft rolled into the near-inverted position, the rubber seal was beginning to peel off the port wing – so I stuck with the situation until the rubber actually came adrift, and the rolling stopped. I then returned to base.

Eric Brown summarized the whole experience by remarking 'The Griffith suction wing was not a great success story, but it contributed to our knowledge of boundary-layer suction.' The resulting data was incorporated into the Armstrong Whitworth AW.52 flying wing research aircraft – but EE445 had served its purpose and was restored to standard; whether the Derwent 3s were removed has not been recorded. The aircraft is believed to have been transferred to No. 49 MU, but is known to have been struck off charge on 30 June 1950.

G.41G Meteor F.4

EE573. Originally built at Hucclecote as a single-seat fighter, EE573 was allocated for service with the Telecommunications Flying Unit (TFU) at Defford. Their work required a two-seat layout, so the aircraft was converted to T.7 airframe standard.

During World War II, German research into night-fighter target identification centred on infra-red wavelengths, with the 20-degree cone-of-scan *Kiel Gerät* system. Being infra-red, it was passive and therefore never matched British centrimetric equipment, and Germany recognized this discrepancy to the point of developing the *Lichtenstein Gerät* system. Towards the end of the war, Junkers Ju88G, *Werk nr.* 622960 and equipped with *Kiel Gerät*, was captured on the island of Sylt; it was made ready to be flown from Sylt to Defford, for the Telecommunications Research Establishment (TRE) scientists to evaluate. Unfortunately the aircraft crashed at Heston; however, the *Kiel Gerät* was undamaged and was removed at the crash-site, to be transported by road to Defford. It was tested in the establishment's Avro Tudor 7 VX199, the objective being to investigate the radar's passive nature as a research basis for future guidance of projectile weapons.

From these researches, 'Homing Eye' evolved in the early 1950s, and EE573 was commissioned as the carrier aircraft for the system. Defford had a very significant engineering facility, and modifications to the Meteor's nose were implemented in order for the TRE equipment to be fitted; this would be in a manner similar to the installation incorporated several years earlier in F.3 EE348, although this time the radome was reprofiled and the nose-cap was opaque. Airborne testing of Homing Eye (which had a parallel code title of 'Bay Window') continued throughout 1953, and during this period EE573 received equipment relative to other branches of TRE/TFU research. Investigations had been conducted into systems of aircraft tail-warning against attacks from the rear, these programmes being related to the defence of aircraft in the forthcoming V-bomber force.

These TRE-developed tail-warning devices dated back to the latter years of the 1939–45 conflict, when Lancaster JB675 had been engaged in 'Boozer' warning equipment trials: 'Boozer' Mk1 picked up signals from *Lichtenstein* AI-equipped interceptors, Boozer Mk2 detected *Wurzburg* ground surveillance radars, while the Mk3 version detected anti-aircraft gun-laying radar. EE573 received a wave-guide tail horn installation to detect centrimetric AI transmissions; this took the form of a rectangular bell-mouth located at the rear end of the fin/tail-plane bullet fairing, replacing the rear identification lamp.

Later Marks of Meteor were operated at Defford, and eventually EE573 was surplus to TRE requirements. It was used by Fairey Aviation for a while on their extensive missile projects, then transferred to RAE Farnborough. With its useful flying days finished, EE573 was scrapped on 6 May 1958, having furthered British research into airborne electronics for over a decade.

VW790. The penultimate F.4 built at Hucclecote to Contract No. 6/ACFT/1389/CB7(b), signed on 2 August 1947, VW790 went from the manufacturer to its MU for storage, only to be withdrawn within a very short time and flown to RAE Farnborough. Although it was quite a late production aircraft, both the F.3 tail assembly and long-span wings were fitted.

VW790 was operated by both the RAE and A&AEE Boscombe Down as a Ministry of Supply (MoS) aircraft, to assist Vickers-Armstrong's guided weapons division; the latter was heavily involved in the development of a large, active-homing, all-weather missile code-named 'Red Dean' and designed to meet Specification 1105. In fact the whole of the British guided missile industry was so surrounded by security that very little came to light regarding systems that did not reach production stage; Red Dean was no

Close-up of the reconfigured 'Homing Eye' nose-cone on EE573. Author's collection.

exception, and VW790's role in the programme has not been revealed. One photograph taken at the RAE in June 1949 shows that the Hispano cannon armament had been removed, together with the gun-ports.

Reports have indicated that the aircraft was used at Boscombe Down in a programme of canopy modification trials, and it is known to have been transferred on 6 February 1953 to RAF Hornchurch – where No. 19 Squadron were operating Meteor F.8s – with the Instructional Airframe number 7012M. Some years later the airframe was donated to Benfleet's Air Training Corps squadron on Canvey Island, in the Thames estuary. In 1968 VW790/7012M made its last move, going to the Cotswold airfield at Little Rissington, where it was scrapped.

VZ389. This aircraft was the fourth F.4 off Armstrong Whitworth's production line at Baginton, and four months after FRL had taken delivery of F.3 EE397 early in 1949, VZ389 joined it at Tarrant Rushton, to assist in the company's probe-and-drogue in-flight refuelling research. By the end of 1949 the aircraft was fully equipped with FRL's system, and dry couplings with the company's Lancaster G-33-2 were started in March 1950, with the first fuel transference taking place on 2 April. However, the Lancaster was unable to operate above 20,000ft (6,096m) and this restricted these trials, so Lincoln RA657, which could operate fuel transfers at higher altitudes, was loaned to FRL to be converted into a tanker, for working in conjunction with VZ389. The first public demonstration by the combination took place at the 1950 SBAC Display – although well below their usual operating altitude! Post-display trials continued for another year, during which de Havilland considered incorporating in-flight refuelling facilities in their Comet jet airliner; the company's Chief Test Pilot John Cunningham went to Tarrant Rushton, where he flew several sorties in VZ389, engaging with RA657.

But nothing materialized from Cunningham's visit, and the Meteor left FRL to have short spells operating with Fairey Aviation and Percival Aircraft, although the reasons for them do not appear to have been recorded. On 24 July 1954, VZ389 returned to Tarrant Rushton, but to the other side of the airfield where it was converted to U.15 drone standard; it was then shipped to the

F.4 VW790, which was used for the Red Dean missile trials, showing the absence of cannon armament. Derek N. James.

Australian Weapons Research Establishment (WRE) at Woomera.

G.43 Meteor T.7

VW411. The second production T.7, VW411 had a chequered career as a Ministry of Supply (MoS) aircraft, spending a large proportion of its life at nearly all the major experimental research establishments at some time. Much of its work was undertaken for the MoS, assisting in the early days of FRL's drone conversion programme, in which Farnborough, Bedford and Boscombe Down all had vested interests. It was also employed in a series of trials under the auspices of the A&AEE: these concerned

an automatic airbrake system which limited the maximum airspeed achievable in a dive, thereby relieving the pilot of at least one operation during weapons delivery in a dive-bombing situation.

In the course of its life VW411 became something of a hybrid, being fitted with a production F.8 rear fuselage, complete with tail assembly and a PR.10 nose on which the glazed side windows were painted over, leaving just the forward-facing camera window operative. In 1963, while being an element of RAE Bedford's Experimental Flying Wing, the aircraft was painted an overall pale blue and sported a large ace of diamonds playing-card motif on its nose. Three years later, VW411 was repainted yet again in an overall royal blue finish, while serving with the Proof and

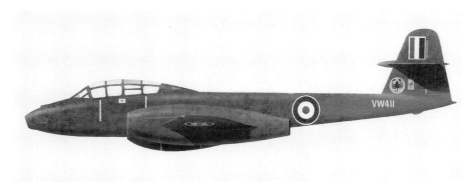

T.7 VW411 became something of a hybrid, being fitted with the later F.8 rear fuselage and a PR.10 nose section. Author's artwork.

Experimental Establishment (PEE) at Foulness. During its PEE operations, the aircraft spent time at the Royal Netherlands Air Force (RNethAF) base at Soesterberg and was adorned with a graphic scorpion logo on its lower fin. As the main role of the PEE was the testing of contemporary armaments against existing airframes and the resilience of materials to those armaments, it is quite possible that once its flying days for the establishment were over, VW411 became a target; but this has not been confirmed.

VW443. Constructed in the same batch as VW411, this was the thirty-seventh T.7 built, and it was another two-seat Meteor that never reached RAF squadron service. De Havilland Propellers at Hatfield had started developing its first air-to-air guided missile in 1951 under the code-name 'Blue Jay', and the company was allocated several Meteors to assist in the project – which must have gone against the grain a little, considering that their parent company produced an 'in-house' two-seater, the Vampire T.11.

VW443 was employed as a photographic aircraft for the air-firing tests, and its nose was modified by having a large, forward-facing glazed panel to facilitate this role. The Meteor remained throughout the Blue Jay trials, until the missile went into production as the 'Firestreak', Britain's first guided missile cleared for service. This marked the end of VW443's usefulness to the Hatfield

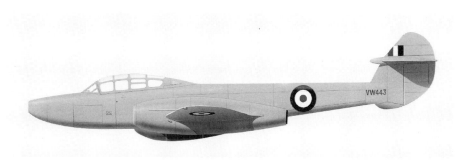

The revised nose fitted to T.7 VW443 when it was engaged in photographic work with Blue Jay missile tests can be seen in this side elevation. Author's artwork.

company, and it was seconded to the NGTE at Pyestock, who shared Farnborough's flying facilities with the RAE. There, VW443 operated in the Establishment's researches relative to experimental radio acceptance programmes; these extended into the U.15 electronic guidance equipment trials that the RAE was conducting. As far as can be ascertained, this was the last of the research programmes for which the aircraft was used, and it is believed to have been scrapped at Farnborough.

VW470. The first aircraft from Hucclecote's second T.7 production batch, VW470's first posting was to the Telecommunications Flying Unit (TFU) at Defford, where it was fitted out as a radar trials aircraft for the Unit. The Radar Research Establishment (RRE) at Malvern

was engaged on a specially developed radar ranging instrumentation, directed for use by the forthcoming Hunter and Swift interceptors, to provide them with ranging-to-target information. Initially started on Meteor F.3 EE348, VW470 was instrumental in the testing of later variants of the equipment, which continued until the end of 1952.

In the last week of January 1953 the aircraft left Defford and was flown up to Turnhouse, outside Edinburgh, from where the Ferranti Flying Unit (FFU) operated. There it was to participate in a series of tests associated with gunsight tracking with autostabilization, the Meteor in general being noted for its suffering as a gun-platform, because of 'snaking'. VW470 went down to Airwork Limited at Blackbushe, where it was re-engineered for the FFU trials. On returning to Turnhouse in July 1954, because it had been fitted with an F.8 tail assembly that carried the autostabilizer, it was dubbed a 'Meteor Mk7 1/2' by the FFU, and this appellation stuck with it throughout its service with the Unit. The objective of the trials was to establish suitable damping factors in a new gunsight, and the programme produced some of the FFU's most harrowing moments: on occasions, when the selected damping factor matched the natural oscillating frequency of the aircraft, the autostabilization system's overriding switch had to be hit pretty quickly in order to keep VW470 in one piece!

The Ferranti trials continued for over two years, but by October 1956 the programme had been completed and FFU pilot John Field flew the 'Meteor 7 1/2' to No. 20 MU at Aston Down for storage. As no further use was found for the aircraft, on 22 July 1958 it was broken up for scrap.

Martin Baker later constructed a new canopy for WA634 when they started testing their Mk4 rocket-powered seat, which is shown in the side-view and the close-up. A test seat had not been installed at the time these photographs were taken. Author's collection.

WA634. Coming from the first batch of Gloster's third T.7 production contract, WA634 was fitted with the E.1/44-type tail assembly right from the start, and did not go into squadron service but started life on charge to the A&AEE. Martin-Baker Aircraft had requested a replacement aircraft for the F.3 EE416, which had outlived its usefulness, and they particularly wanted a T.7 which they could adapt to test their new Mk3 ejection seat. So WA634 left Boscombe Down for Denham, where it arrived on 30 January 1952.

Modifications to meet Martin-Baker's requirements included the removal of all flying controls from the rear cockpit and the strengthening of its floor-pan. The bulkhead between the two cockpits was replaced by a much stronger structure, while the hood framing and glazing of the standard canopy's rear portion was cut away. A test Mk3 seat was installed in the modified rear cockpit area, and a production Mk2 seat was mounted up front, making WA634 the first T.7 to have an ejector seat for the pilot – in fact it was the only Meteor to have ejector seats for both crew members. The structural changes were completed in the late summer of 1953, and on 31 August the aircraft had its maiden flight in the new configuration. The following year, however, the company had to turn its attention to an urgent RAF and RN service requirement.

Air-crew fatalities were occurring due to engine failure on take-off, but the current ejector seats were not capable of supplying safe ejection and parachute recovery from such low-altitude emergencies. Design and fabrication were therefore put in hand to supply a seat with the capability of safely ejecting a pilot at runway level. Based on the current Mk3, the new seat was equipped with a telescopic ejection gun that generated an 80ft per second (24.3m per second) force, and a drogue parachute capable of being deployed less than two seconds after ejection. Known as a 'zero-feet' seat, it was successfully tested with dummies during the summer of 1955, and the first live ejection was planned. On 3 September 1955, Captain John 'Scotty' Scott took up the pilot's station in WA634, with Sqn Ldr John Fifield – who later succeeded Scott as the company's Chief Test Pilot – installed in the test seat. Opening up the throttles, the aircraft moved down the runway and the pilot was on the point of lift-off at a speed of 120mph (193km/h) when John Fifield made the

The first Martin-Baker conversion to T.7 WA634, with the modified standard trainer canopy. Author's collection.

ejection, followed by an excellent parachute deployment that enabled him to make a perfect descent; this completed a successful maiden test, which was gratifying to service pilots.

At the other end of the operating spectrum, high-altitude test firings were made during trials, some of them being at 41,000ft (12,496.8m), with a barostat-operated delay that released the recovery parachute 30,000ft (9,144m) lower, the whole sequence operating with very few problems. Further service requests were received for the company to investigate a means of reducing the time required to jettison aircraft hoods, a problem which was jeopardizing the operational introduction of the zero-level seat. Martin-Baker produced an explosive bolt system for removing the canopy, and it was installed as the first phase of the seat-ejection cycle.

The next programme for the company was the development of the lightweight Mk4 seat, for which WA634 was again to be the test aircraft; these trials lasted over a year. Meanwhile the design department was drawing up plans for a rocket-powered seat to facilitate successful ejection at the higher end of the current operational performance envelope, and WA634 was taken back into the company workshops

for the further modifications required to test this type of seat. Internal and external reinforcements were made to the rear cockpit structure, and the whole canopy was redesigned, the original heavily framed T.7 hood being discarded. A new one-piece hood covered the pilot, and the open rear cockpit had high side-fairings fitted.

Trials of the rocket-propelled seat started with dummies, as had all previous test programmes, and these demonstrated that the installation was reliable enough for a first live ejection to be arranged. On 13 March 1962, the Institute of Aviation Medicine (IAM) at Farnborough supplied Sqn Ldr Peter Howard to make the maiden trial, performed at 250ft (76.2m) above Chalgrove airfield, with the pilot, John Fifield, holding the aircraft at 290mph (466.6km/h). Sqn Ldr Howard cleared the aircraft, successfully separated himself from the seat and descended by parachute, to prove that the rocket-powered seat was a viable proposition.

That was nearly the end of WA634's services to Martin-Baker Aircraft. It was decommissioned in April 1962, when WA638, a later T.7, arrived to take over; but the value of WA634's contribution to military air-crew safety has been recognized, and today it is the pivot of a special display at the Aerospace Museum, Cosford, devoted to Martin-Baker's history, as the founders of British ejector seats.

WF877. Having served with both Nos. 11 and 96 Squadrons, this aircraft is reported to have been modified at some time, by having a PR.10 nose installed. It was also used as a trials aircraft, in a programme that Folland Aircraft conducted in the 1950s, on an ejector seat designed for their Midge/Gnat aircraft with Sqn Ldr Jake McLoughlin participating in the live ejections.

WL419. Several RAF units took this aircraft on charge, including No. 233 OCU at Pembrey, No. 11 Group Communications Flight (GCF) at Ouston, and No. 13 GCF at Martlesham Heath. No. 85 Squadron at Binbrook, which operated the Canberra T.11, also used it, before the aircraft was taken over by the Ministry of Aviation (MoA) in August 1963. At Martin-Baker's, T.7 WA634's successor, another T.7, WA638, was operating as the company's seat-trials aircraft, and the MoA gave them WL419 to be a source of spares for their test aircraft. However, in 1979 the situation was transposed and WL419 was rebuilt to take over from WA638.

By 1980 the conversion work was completed, and since then, right up to the present day, WL419 has been the test vehicle for every aspect of Martin-Baker's ejection seat research. In a conversation made with a representative of the company at the time of writing, this is a situation which will prevail for many years to come. Understandably, airframe hours have to be monitored, therefore the aircraft is not often seen on the European airshow circuit, but it did appear at Abingdon early in the decade, and it also attended the 'Classic Jet and Fighter Display' held at Duxford in 1996. This is because WL419 is a most valuable piece of test equipment, which cannot be made available just for the gratification of the aircraft enthusiast – which is fully understandable.

G.41K Meteor F.8

WA775. A product of Armstrong Whitworth's first batch of F.8s, WA775 flew from Baginton to its holding MU prior to squadron allocation. However, the

WL419 as currently used by Martin-Baker, with scorch-marks made by the operation of the rocket-powered seat. Author's collection.

A&AEE needed its services, following which it was transferred to the TRE and became one of a host of Meteors of various Marks held during the Establishment's very busy days of research in the early 1950s.

The de Havilland Blue Jay programme was in full flow, and the air-to-air missile was being considered as a part of the Hawker Hunter's armament. The TRE was in the primary stages of refining a nose radar for WA775, the equipment having initially been tested in the establishment's Tudor 7 VX199. The Meteor's role was to continue the trials of the Blue Jay electronics in a more representative installation, and it was converted at Defford for the task. Testing was undertaken for some considerable time during 1955 and it was found to perform well. The proposed Hunter requirement was abandoned, but the production 'Firestreak'

F.8 WA935 comes in to land at Baginton, possibly after its maiden flight, and certainly before the respray was finished. Philip Jarrett.

became operational with the Sea Vixen and Javelin FAW.7, both of which carried four, while the early Lightnings were armed with two. That the missile's electronics were successful was due in no small measure to the trials conducted in TRE Meteors, which included WA775.

From Defford the aircraft flew to FRL at Tarrant Rushton, where it was modified to become the prototype U.16 target drone; its first flight in this form was made on 22 October 1956. The drone was flown to Llanbedr for service on their ranges, but while it was there it suffered a control failure and crashed – a rather ignominious end, considering the value of its research flying.

WK935. This was the last F.8 built by Armstrong Whitworth and physically it became the largest Meteor ever produced – and ironically the one that has received an inordinate share of publicity.

The notion of a pilot operating from a prone location had been considered in relation to a number of projects in the British aircraft industry – which no doubt remembered that the Wright brothers had flown in the same position. In 1947, the RAE at Farnborough employed two German designers, Drs Multhropp and Winter, who produced a project for a Mach 1.2 swept-wing aircraft, powered by a Rolls-Royce AJ.65 engine, in which the pilot was prone in a capsule, situated within the intake. Although the idea did not leave the drawing-board, an investigation of the problems that might be encountered in such a position was made in a modified Reid and Sigrest RS.3 Desford, originally on the civil register as G-AGOS, but given the military serial VZ728 and renamed the RS.4 'Bobsleigh' in this modified form.

In 1952, the prone-pilot concept was brought back into the spotlight by Bristol Aircraft, who submitted their Type 185 design for a projected rocket-powered interceptor, powered by a D.H. Spectre and piloted from a prone position so that the increased 'g' forces could be withstood. This sufficiently moved the IAM at Farnborough to call for an aircraft to analyse the concept thoroughly. Armstrong Whitworth was given the contract to design and produce a conversion in order to test-fly a prone-pilot position, and with WK935 being built at Baginton, the whole metamorphosis became an 'in-house' project.

Close-ups of the prone-pilot's cockpit, with and without pilot. Sqn Ldr R.S. Wambeek DFC, of Farnborough's Institute of Aviation Medicine, shows that there was not an abundance of space for the pilot. *Aeroplane Monthly.*

Right from the beginning it was agreed that the standard cockpit would be retained and manned during all flights. Not only did this provide a safety factor, but it meant that engine starting and fuel control did not have to be duplicated in the prone cockpit, which by its very nature would have to be ahead of the Meteor's nose-wheel frame structure bulkhead. The new cylindrical nose, as long as aerodynamic requirements allowed, had a beautiful blown canopy cover with a separate windscreen, installed just behind the pointed nose-cone. The standard F.8 fuselage length of 44ft 7in (11.3m) was increased to 52ft 5in (15.9m), and an NF.12 tail assembly was fitted to maintain stability.

The prone pilot lay on a custom-built, leather-covered foam-rubber couch, inclined at nearly 30 degrees from chest to hips, with an additional 5-degree section to support the upper thighs. Arm-rests for the forearms and a V-sectioned chin-rest were also fashioned in leather-coated foam. A redesigned control column was offset to the starboard side, while rudder control could be achieved by ankle movements via suspended pedals with cupped ends to retain the feet. All controls were interconnected to the standard cockpit, with flight instruments grouped on three panels set round the prone-pilot's field of vision. As Martin-Baker had not considered an ejection seat for horizontal pilots, emergency escape had to be through the underside of the extended nose. This involved disconnecting and lifting the rudder pedals, jettisoning the ventral fuel tank, as well as retracting the nose-wheel, should it be down at the time of emergency, before actually activating the escape panel in the floor – so it was probably a good thing that the requirement never arose. With James Martin's track record, he would most likely have relished the challenge, had he been approached to perfect an ejection system.

The design and engineering to convert WK935 occupied nearly two years, so it was 10 February 1954 before Eric Franklin took the unique aircraft into the air for the first time. Considering there was such major alteration to a standard F.8 airframe, the fact that only small adjustments were required after the maiden flight speaks well for AWA's design department. Six months of manufacturers' flight trials were completed, and on 31 August 1954 the first – and to date the only – British jet-powered prone-pilot aircraft was delivered to its customer, the IAM at Farnborough.

Ninety-nine test sorties were made over the following eleven months, in a total of fifty-five flying hours. Four IAM pilots, including Wg Cdr Allan Crawford and Sqn Ldr R.S.Wambeek, as well as a couple of RAE pilots, made flights in the unorthodox aircraft, while several test pilots from the aircraft industry were also invited to give their opinions on its handling. *Flight* magazine's editor at that time, Mark Lambert – with 380 Meteor-flying hours to his credit – was given the chance to fly it, and found that the unconventional control positions could be mastered quite quickly, but he also found that the close proximity to the runway on take-off was a little unnerving. The aircraft was surprisingly manoeuvrable, although over-sensitive power-boosted ailerons made the control centre position rather difficult to locate, and the high rate of roll was something to which he could not get accustomed.

Bristol's Type 185 project was cancelled, and on 31 July 1955, WK935 made its final sortie for the institute. Three weeks prior

WA935 as displayed at the RAE Jubilee, alongside RA490, the jet-deflection Meteor. Author's collection.

to this, the prone-pilot Meteor was presented to the public for the first time, as a static exhibit at the RAE Jubilee. The data it supplied during the IAM testing programme confirmed that a prone-pilot control system was feasible, but whether it was practical in an operational environment is debatable. In August 1955 the aircraft was placed in cocooned storage at No. 12 MU, Kirkbride, following which it had spells at Wroughton and Colerne, where it became Instructional Airframe 7869M. St Athan housed the aircraft for a while, but it is now on permanent display at the Aerospace Museum, Cosford, restored to the original WK935 standard.

The modified underwing tank, housing a rearward-facing high-intensity searchlight, can be seen in this profile of WD687. Author's artwork.

G.47 Meteor NF.11

WD585. The first production NF.11 came off Baginton's lines to start RAF service with the Central Fighter Establishment (CFE) at West Raynham. In November 1952 it was transferred to the newly re-formed No. 256 Squadron at Ahlhorn in West Germany, which operated NF.11s until it was disbanded and renumbered No. 11 Squadron – which was rather appropriate, considering the aircraft that it flew! WD585 did not linger at Ahlhorn however, as the TRE at Defford received it, together with the four succeeding aircraft on the AWA production line, WD586, WD587, WD588 and WD589. It is known that WD586 was struck off charge on 5 October 1957, and WD589 followed suit five months later, on 31 March 1958. WD585 was required for radar trials, for which the Defford engineering department gave it a more pointed nose-cone; a similar conversion was applied to WD587.

In 1957 the Royal Navy approached Armstrong Whitworth to supply twenty TT.20s by conversion of NF.11s; by this time WD585 had fulfilled its functions at the TRE, so it was recalled to Baginton for modification to target-tug standard. It saw service at several RN land bases before going to the Fleet Requirement Unit (FRU) at Hurn, where it was scrapped on 7 November 1966.

WD670. This aircraft came from the second batch of Armstrong Whitworth's first contract, and was used at the A&AEE to explore the problems being encountered in the night-fighter variant's fin and rudder area; these were eventually rectified by the

additional fin area introduced on the NF.12. The trials were taken over by WD687, and WD670 flew up to Turnhouse at the beginning of April 1954, to join the Ferranti Flying Unit (FFU), with whom it operated for the next nine years.

The unit's requirements for the aircraft entailed structural modifications centred round a re-profiled nose, which in turn necessitated the incorporating of an NF.12-type tail assembly. This work was contracted by Ferranti to Airwork Limited at Blackbushe, but the aircraft's flight down to the Hampshire-based company took an unexpected twelve days, the original cause being a faulty radio which required an unscheduled landing *en route*. The FFU's Dakota, TS423, was sent to collect the instruments and return them to Turnhouse for repair, and when this had been done, it took them back to the stranded Meteor, over a week later. With the repaired radio installed, WD670 continued its flight to Blackbushe, although a refuelling stop was necessary at Scampton since the aircraft was not fitted with long-range tanks at that time.

The newly configured WD670 returned to Turnhouse in the middle of July 1954 – where the FFU referred to it as the Meteor 11/12 because of its non-standard tail unit – and the trials of Ferranti's air-to-surface radar ranging equipment were started. An updated Strike Sight and Radar Range (SSRR) Mk4 was installed in the aircraft during 1956, and the following year the FFU became involved in the evaluation of the 'Red Brick' target-illuminating radar, destined for the new Bristol Bloodhound surface-to-air guided missile, for which, on this programme, WD670 was flown as the co-operative airborne target. Red Brick testing lasted up to the end of 1959 and in

1960 the Meteor 11/12 was fitted with the naval SSRR destined for installation in a new high-speed, low-level strike aircraft being built by Blackburn Aircraft Limited to Admiralty Specification N.A.39, which would go into production as the Buccaneer. Blackburn received an order for twenty pre-production N.A.39s, and one of them, WK525, was transferred to Turnhouse for *in situ* trials of the system.

By the end of the winter of 1963 WD670 had exceeded its fatigue life, and on 7 April the aircraft was struck off charge, to be rather ignominiously consigned to the Turnhouse Fire Department, who used it as a practice airframe.

WD687. The MoS directed this second-batch NF.11 to take over the Boscombe Down fin and rudder trials previously conducted with WD670. When these had been completed, WD687 became another Defford-operated aircraft, its specific task to act as an illuminated airborne target aircraft, for night operations being administered by the Royal Radar Establishment (RRE).

So that the tracking station situated at RRE Malvern could maintain both radar and visual reference for high-speed, low-level targets, one of WD687's underwing fuel tanks had a small rear-facing, high-intensity searchlight incorporated in its aft tip. For this programme, the aircraft was joined by a stable-mate NF.11, WD791, which had a similar searchlight mounted at the port wing-tip. The aircraft were operated both as a pair and singly for these nocturnal trials, and on very clear nights this produced an unexpected reaction from the public, who reported to the police the sighting of UFOs in the vicinity of the Malvern Hills!

Towards the end of 1952, WD687

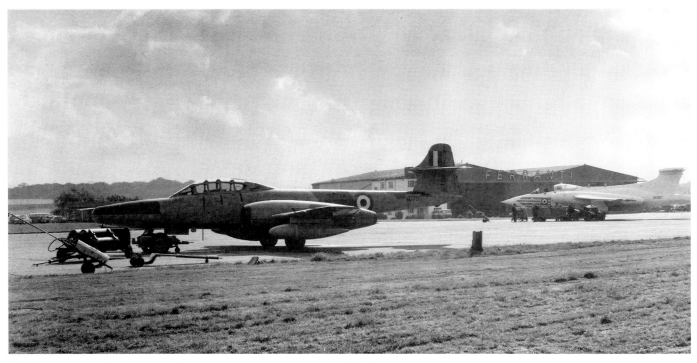

WD790 seen at Ferranti's Turnhouse airfield, with a revised nose-cone housing AIRPASS equipment.
Author's collection.

returned to Armstrong Whitworth to become one of the NF.11s used to develop the succeeding NF.12. Its Derwent 8 engines were replaced by 3,800lb (1,723kg) thrust Derwent 9s, and the nose was extended to accept the American APS 21 AI radar. It was operated by several Ministry establishments in this form, until finally being consigned for scrap at Stansted.

WD790. This aircraft was destined to have the longest allocation to radar research of all Meteors, and possibly of any aircraft in Britain's Research and Development (R&D) activities.

Early in 1952 the TRE at Malvern – which was renamed the Radar Reseach Establishment (RRE) the following year – had its flying unit based at Defford. When WD790 joined, the unit was engaged on programmes concerning electronic countermeasures (ECM), and Defford's engineering department prepared the aircraft to take part in the evaluations. Tail-warning radar, code-named 'Orange Putter', that had evolved from the wartime 'Boozer' system, was destined for use in the Canberra, and WD790 contributed to its development. This was followed by the trials of 'Red Garter', the ECM projected for the V-bomber force,

which gave the pilot and the Air Electronics Office (AEO) visual identity, as well as aural warning to all crew members. After Red Garter, the aircraft was adapted to serve as an Orange Yeoman test vehicle for ground radar system targeting; then for Blue Joker trials, which involved an experimental early warning system suspended from a tethered balloon at 5,000ft (1,524m), to detect very low-flying aircraft – WD790 acted as the target

for this programme.

Indicative of the many applications for which the TFU prepared the aircraft that were held on charge, WD790 went back into the works in 1953 to receive another nose-cone, this one to assist in experimental guided-weapon radar head trials. This was an ongoing programme over several years, during which WD790 was fitted with nearly every component associated with the system. Once the trials were

When photographed at the Finningly 'Battle of Britain' display, WD790 was being operated by RRE Pershore and had another revised nose section. *Aeroplane Monthly.*

completed, the aircraft was available for a new application, at a new base.

In 1956 the MoS had contracted Ferranti, through RRE at Malvern, to provide the future AI Mk23 radar system for the English Electric Lightning, and the Scottish company expanded their flying unit at Turnhouse in readiness for the forthcoming flight trials. WD790 left Defford on 22 May 1958 to fly up to the company's base and be prepared for taking the new system, known as AIRPASS. The Meteor worked in conjunction with a Canberra B(I).8 WT327 that the FFU held on loan, together with the company's own Dakota TS423, and these two, both carrying whole AIRPASS units, undertook more of the active trials programme than the Meteor. In view of this, when WD790 was not engaged on AIRPASS, it was used as a fast, high-flying target for Ferranti's portion of the Red Brick programme; the latter was to be renamed 'Indigo Corkscrew' in 1960, when the electronics were extended to the 'Thunderbird' ground-to-air guided missile.

Ferranti's Deputy Chief Test Pilot, John Pascoe Watson, did much of the WD790 flying, assisted by John Cockburn and an ex-ETPS examiner, Colin Curtis. On 19 October 1958 the aircraft was taken out of service to be adapted to carry a Decca flight log, which had previously been installed in the company's Dove and had proved to be very difficult to operate. Two years of testing in WD790 convinced Ferranti to change the roller-map method of staying on track, in favour of an easier system of lattice co-ordinates displayed on dials. The Indigo Corksrew testing was continued in parallel with the flight log programme, and maximum-duration sorties were flown during both of them. WD790 carried fuel for a total of 2hr 5min, including take-off and approach abort, and on at least one occasion John Cockburn claimed 2hr 5min *flying* time, with the touch-down on fumes! In short, the aircraft was being utilized at the limit of its endurance in an attempt to extend the operating range of the ground-based radar section of the system. Later trials required two targets flying in close proximity to each other, to evaluate the radar's powers of discrimination, and Canberra B.2 WD953, from the RAE's stock, joined the programme on 30 October 1961.

Because of the necessary heavy flying schedules, Pat Reeve joined the FFU from the Weapons Flight at RAE Farnborough,

Wearing the 'raspberry-ripple' colours of RAE Bedford, WD790 is pictured just before it went to RAF Leeming for dismantling. *Aeroplane Monthly.*

flying his first sortie in WD790 on 9 September 1963, and later to help perfect Indigo Corkscrew until November 1964. After the end of the trials, the Meteor flew thirty-one air tests connected with its own condition, and project test-flying was not resumed until 16 February 1965. These were associated with the Forward-Looking Radar (FLR) terrain-following system being developed by Ferranti, and continued until 19 October 1965, when the aircraft went to Scottish Aviation at Prestwick for a repaint that lasted three weeks. The next year, John Cockburn flew it as a taxi to Warton on 22 March 1966, and this was its final service for the FFU. On 12 April, the Canberra B(I).8 WT327 left Turnhouse to return to the RRE and two months later, on 23 May, WD790 followed it, with its nose restored to NF.11 standard. By this time the initials RRE stood for 'Royal Radar Establishment', following its royal recognition, and the organization had moved their flying activities, now designated the Radar Research Flying Unit (RRFU) a few miles from Defford, to Pershore. Ferranti had a scientific enclave at Pershore, and the development of the terrain-following low-level radars continued, with the AI.23/AIRPASS conical radome on Canberra WT327 being transferred to WD790 during 1966/67.

Owing to the dangerous aspects of very low flying, the RRFU cannibalized an ex-A&AEE Meteor T.7 in order to transfer its rear cockpit controls, less trimmers and throttles, onto WD790: in this arrangement the rear pilot was able to fly very low on the experimental cockpit displays,

while the front pilot was in a position to override quickly, should the outside world get too close. To everyone's relief, the system worked. As an aside, it is worth recording that, over the years, WD790 with the AIRPASS installation has been referred to as having a TSR.2 nose. AI.23 was indeed intended to be incorporated in the TSR.2, but as it was cancelled on 6 April 1965, over two years before WD790's conversion, the description is not strictly accurate. Despite TSR.2's cancellation, work to perfect AI.23 continued, but it took a long time to bring it up to operational standard and it was still being developed in 1974 when the RRFU's commandant was instructed to transfer the system from WD790 to Buccaneer XN975, which was on charge to Pershore – after which the Meteor was to be scrapped. Luckily the RRFU's CO saw further than officialdom and realized that, if WD790 was scrapped, the programme faced dire consequences should anything happen to the Buccaneer.

The often-derided 'old boy' network was brought into play. The commandant of the RAE at Llanbedr was a long-standing friend of Pershore's leader, and he made out a case to accept WD790 on its charge and to keep it intact. This was an unofficial arrangement, but it proved well worthwhile because XN975 crashed on 13 June 1978 and WD790 was transferred to RAE Bedford, to where Pershore's flying unit had been relocated in 1976 when all R&D activities were centralized. Its new owners gave WD790 a new livery – the establishment's 'raspberry ripple' colour scheme – and it resumed its test-flying career until November 1981 when, after thirty years operations on radar research, it went to RAF Leeming for dismantling. This was done in a strictly controlled manner, the various elements going into storage to provide spares for the Meteor half of the Vintage Pair, which finished so disastrously at the 1986 Mildenhall Air Fete.

WM180. Armstrong Whitworth's second NF.11 contract had been for the aircraft to be built in three batches, the first producing fifty aircraft, with WM180 being among them. The TRE was one of those establishments into which aircraft virtually 'disappeared', so security-conscious was everything and everyone connected with it. I have been fortunate enough to correspond with a senior engineer responsible for much of the establishment's work, and he readily concedes that: 'the Government's radar establishment had no interest whatsoever in aircraft other than as airborne platform facilities (they were accepted like a set of tools in a tool box)...' Some 1,000 aircraft involving over 100 types (excluding Marks of types) passed through the unit, and of these, thirty-five were Meteors. Equipments required by the scientific fraternity to fly were installed in the most suitable aircraft selected by the Aircraft Department senior engineer, who took a very broad view on requirement and flight operation; thus hardware could be interchanged between various types of carry vehicle...it was in effect a factory capable of operating world-wide trials and not an aerodrome maintenance organization capable of fitting 'black boxes'.

With this knowledge, it is easier to understand why the history of some aircraft is so difficult to compile. WM180 is known to have been involved in the 'Homing Eye' infra-red project in February 1956, which it shared with Meteor F.4 EE573, the equipment having initially been tested in TRE's Tudor Mk7 VX199. It was also a constituent in the tests to develop warning devices to counter rear-end air attacks for the V-bomber force, and it too was fitted with an experimental tail-horn, this one being on the rear fuselage tail-cone. WM180's time at RRE was shorter than many other aircraft, and it was scrapped on 16 June 1958.

WM262. In company with WM265, this Meteor came out from Baginton incorporating nose radome modifications, Decca

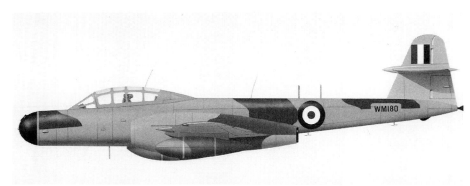

NF.11 WM180 showing the shorter TRE nose-cone associated with the Homing Eye project and the tail-warning trial fitment, together with a close-up of the latter. Author's collection.

Navigator electronics and a Sperry Gyroscope Company-developed autostabilizer.

A consortium of Vickers-Armstrong and EMI had produced a TV-guided air-to-surface missile design as a private venture. It was subsequently adopted by the MoS to meet their Operational Requirement (OR) 1059, code-named Blue Boar, capable of carrying a 5,000lb (2,268kg) kiloton-range nuclear warhead. The modifications to WM262 and WM295 were to enable them both capable of executing the electronic trials associated with the missile. As many projects in the 1950s, the Blue Boar project was cancelled in June 1954, after £3.1 million had been

expended on it, the RAF deciding that they would prefer to operate an all-weather stand-off bomb. Two years later, OR1132 was issued in March 1956, and the outcome was the Avro Blue Steel weapon; this was initially issued to No. 617 Squadron in the 1960s, for them to nestle in their Vulcan's bomb-bays at Scampton.

WM295 stayed with Vickers, to be employed on later missile programmes conducted by the company; some reports have mentioned it ending in France. WM262's location after Blue Boar was in Australia, where it became A77-3 in the Royal Australian Air Force, working in conjunction with the WRE at Woomera,

A close-up of the Blue Boar electronics fitted into the modified nose-cone of WM262. Author's collection.

A close-up of the nose-cone of NF.11 WM372, showing the small radome with the two recording-camera windows above. Author's collection.

before it was eventually scrapped.

WM372. The Fairey Aviation Company commenced work on the first British air-to-air guided missile in 1949, under the code-name 'Blue Sky'. It featured an unusual layout, in that the missile was propelled by two solid-fuel boost motors, one above and one below its body, which were jettisoned after burn-out. Armstrong Whitworth considered Blue Sky could become an operational weapon for the Meteor night-fighter, and with this in view, airframes WD743, WD744 and WD745 were adapted during their production to become trials aircraft for the missile. Fairey's Guided Weapons Division at Heston worked in close liaison with AWA from 1952, so that the three Meteors were adapted to carry two missiles, in either under-wing or wing-tip locations, the latter being found to be the more acceptable.

In 1953 three additional aircraft – WM372, WM373 and WM374 – were built, these incorporating modifications developed from the results of the trials with the earlier aircraft; also revisions made to the electronics required that a small additional radome was added on the tip of the original nose profile, beneath a pair of recording-camera windows. The three new aircraft joined the original trio at Heston, and eighteen months of testing were carried out at both Boscombe Down and the Aberporth missile range in the Cardigan Bay area of central Wales, before the programme ended. The idea of arming NF Meteors with Blue Sky was abandoned, but the No.6 Joint Services Trials Unit (JSTU) was formed at Valley, to make the missile, produced as the 'Fireflash', an operational weapon.

While three of the Blue Sky trials aircraft became a part of No.6 JSTU, WM372, WM373 and one other of the sextet were delivered to Woomera, WM372 arriving on 29 November 1954. In Australia, all three aircraft were divested of their night-fighter camouflage and resprayed an overall white, with various areas of red being introduced at a later date. Their length of operations or tenure at Woomera is uncertain, but it is fairly safe to assume that all three were either destroyed or scrapped there at some time.

G.47 Meteor NF.14.

WM261. Originally produced in the second batch of AWA's last NF.11 contract, WM261 was retained by the company for the trials of a new clear-view, sliding canopy to replace the heavily framed, side-hinging structure fitted on all production two-seat Meteors. An additional longer nose, together with its associated increased fin area, made the aircraft the aerodynamic prototype for the NF.14, and following the company type trials it was transferred to the FFU at Turnhouse.

Its originally projected use in the Red Garter electronic countermeasures trials

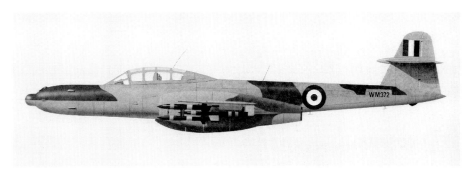

Profiles of WM372 with the 'Fireflash' missile fitted and its partner in the trials, WM374, as painted when later operating on the Woomera range. Author's artwork.

Mr. D.M. McCallum, general manager of Ferranti, presents the logbook of G-ARCX to Mr Tebble of the Royal Scottish Museum. Author's collection.

programme did not last long, as Ferranti needed a high-speed company communications aircraft, their trusty old Dakota, TS423, having seen service with the RAF Heavy Glider Service Unit and No. 436 Squadron RCAF before arriving at Turnhouse, simply unable to meet all FFU needs in the time required. Therefore, in 1963 the company entered into an agreement with the MoS to purchase WM261 and it was placed on the civil aircraft register as G-ARCX, which had the additional benefit of making the aircraft available for private-venture equipment trials. The Dakota was pensioned off and used in the Yorkshire Television series *Airline*, as well as being displayed at Duxford before passing into the ownership of Aces High, to whom it still belongs.

Circumstances at Ferranti changed rather quickly and economics restricted G-ARCX's flying to the effect that it was not used at all in the last quarter of 1964. By June 1965 the Meteor became a little more active, but the FFU had to be reduced in 1967 as, for the first time in fifteen years, Ferranti had no new equipment ready for flight trials. The unit was down to two pilots and two aircraft, the lack of flying time requiring G-ARCX to be tested for a new certificate of airworthiness (CofA) on 15 February 1968. Turnhouse hosted an air display on 22 June of the same year, and the aircraft flew a ten-minute slot, but insurance conditions dictated that there could be no aerobatics.

The air display proved to be G-ARCX's last flight, with the aircraft going into one of the Turnhouse hangars for an indeterminate period a few days later. Ferranti received an offer from an arms dealer, but when it was discovered that the aircraft's destination was the war in Biafra, the sale was called off. On 14 August 1973, with 364 hours flying time in its logbook, WM261/G-ARCX was presented by Ferranti's General Manager, Mr McCallum, to Mr Tebble of the Royal Scottish Museum of Flight. The aircraft was transported to the museum's home at East Lothian airfield and it is still there, displayed as possibly one of the freshest Meteors that exists.

CHAPTER FOURTEEN

Meteors in Foreign Markings

The successful mass-production of aeroplanes requires large areas of floor space, large numbers of skilled or semi-skilled workers and large amounts of money. When World War II ended on 15 August 1945, both the United States of America and the Soviet Union had an abundance of all three, and as a result had the two biggest air forces in the world. By comparison Britain was tiny, and after almost six years of war was virtually bankrupt – but in technical expertise and performance she was more advanced. She had four operational squadrons using Meteors, and they could out-perform the vast numbers of propeller-driven aircraft, in nearly every sphere.

War-surplus piston-engined aircraft were being handed out to overseas air forces like jellies at a birthday party while America was building F-80s and F-84s to modernize the USAAF; this was because political pressures within the country obstructed their sales abroad, so that piston-engined fighters were all the United States had to offer. But foreign arms' buyers were clamouring for turbojet fighters, and Gloster Aircraft's Sales Division recognized that there was a very profitable market-place out there for the Meteor. In terms of speed of production they might not be able to match the United States, but if they got in there first, good profits could be made. So the company took the initiative and arranged overseas tours for their carmine-red demonstration aircraft G-AIDC and G-AKPK, and organized a huge publicity campaign.

Fourteen overseas customers received various Marks of Meteors, some of which had been used or ordered by the RAF, others built new to meet specific orders; in addition, some 360 or more were constructed under licence by Avions Fairey and Fokker Aircraft in the Low Countries, a small number of which went to third-party customers. Due to periodic arms embargoes, sometimes in place and sometimes not, confusion has arisen over the precise number of Meteors delivered to some countries, but the following is as accurate an account as exhaustive research can produce.

Argentina

The Argentinian administration of Juan Peron had been inclined to be pro-Nazi during World War II, although it did meet its own exporting requirements by supplying a major percentage of the United Kingdom's beef during the conflict. An unofficial post-war agreement between America and the newly elected British Labour Government to refrain from selling arms to the South American country because of its wartime leanings was weighed against Gloster's first export order for Meteors – 100 F.4s for Argentina – and economics overruled principles.

The order was signed on 5 May 1947, and the *Fuerza Aérea Argentina*/Argentine Air Force (AAF) prepared to operate two *Escuadrons* at Moron, near the River Plate estuary. A unit price of £32,800 per aircraft was quoted, with the total including the training of a dozen Argentinian pilots and some groundcrews at Moreton Valence.

Six of the ordered aircraft were retained in Gloucestershire for this tuition, with three production F.3s ordered by the RAF – EE367, EE460 and EE470 – also being allocated for the courses. So that the order could be fulfilled as soon as possible, fifty of the aircraft were diverted from existing RAF contracts, while the rest were new-build F.4s, specifically for the customer. The order was delivered by sea, as component assemblies, and it began at the end of May 1947.

Gloster sent a team to assemble and test-fly the aircraft in Argentina, under the leadership of their CTP 'Bill' Waterton. The last aircraft arrived on 20 September 1948 and the whole consignment was fully operational by January 1949. Six years later, the anti-Peron uprising started, and during the short conflict, a government repair workshop at Cordoba, complete with three Meteors, was overrun by rebel forces. The aircraft were hastily repaired, to be pressed into operational service by their captors who, finding no accessible jet fuel, promptly filled the tanks with petrol. Technical recommendations by Rolls-Royce that petrol could be used in an emergency but only if diluted with lubricating oil, carried very little weight with Latin-American rebels in the heat of battle

C-009 of the Argentine Air Force, which was built as F.4 RA392. Mike Hooks.

– and within three days, one of the aircraft, on a ground-strafing sortie, disintegrated through engine overheating.

A year after the cessation of hostilities the Meteors continued in service, although this had not in fact been the Argentine government's intention: their plans to purchase Canadair Sabre Mk6s from Canada in 1956 had had to be postponed due to lack of finance. Some of the Gloster aircraft were still flying in the early 1970s, when F-86s started to be received by the AAF – this time from the United States.

Australia

The Meteor's participation in the Korean War is recorded in Chapter 8. No. 77 Squadron RAAF, the aircraft's operator, remained on stand-by in Korea and Iwakuni in Japan for eighteen months following the cease-fire of 27 July 1953. They had departed from Australia in June 1950, a Mustang-operating squadron, so their return in December 1954 with Meteors made them the only twin-engined fighter squadron in the country, as the de Havilland Aircraft Pty Ltd was equipping the service with Vampire FB.30s and the CA-27 Sabre was going into production at the Commonwealth Aircraft Corporation Pty Ltd. Apart from two F.3s – EE427, which had been shipped to the country in the late 1940s, and EE395, loaned to New Zealand in 1950 and finishing in the Auckland Museum – these were the first Meteors in Australasia. The squadron is confirmed as bringing forty-five aircraft with them from Korea, seven being T.7s and thirty-eight F.8s. During the war, a total of one T.7 and forty-nine F.8s had been lost in operational service. Three additional F.8s – WE905 (A77-207), WF750 (A77-422) and WH251 (A77-510) – are known to have been in Korea, but their history remains largely unknown.

Back in Australia, the squadron celebrated their return by flying a sixteen-aircraft formation over Sydney, forming '77' viewed from below. Much of the squadron operated from Williamstown, with Nos. 75 and 76 Squadrons, both equipped with Vampire FB.30s, together forming No. 78 Wing. Gradually, as the CAC-built Sabres were introduced into squadron service, Meteors were transferred to training duties, while the Citizen Air Force's (CAF) Nos. 22 and 23 Squadrons also used quite a few. All of

them had been retrofitted with the all-clear canopies. No. 75 Squadron was their final service operator; amongst other duties they formed an aerobatic team named the 'Meteorites' with A77-882, A77-875 and A77-870, and took part in air-shows for a short while.

Australian skies had not seen the last of the Meteor, because the Weapons Research Establishment (WRE) at Woomera in the state of South Australia operated dozens as U.15, U.16 and U.21 target drones. Although most of the conversions to drone standard were made by FRL at Tarrant Rushton, several ex-RAAF aircraft were converted by Fairey Australasia Pty Ltd, using modification kits supplied by FRL.

Belgium

Belgium's French-speaking *Force Aérienne Belge* and her Flemish *Belgisch Luchtmacht*/Belgian Air Force (BAF) operated Spitfires of various Marks until their first order to Gloster Aircraft for Meteors. Signed on 12 March 1949, it was for forty-eight F.4s at a unit price of £29,400, with delivery scheduled by the end of

Built as T.7 WA732, A77-702 is currently on display at Point Cook. Derek N. James.

November. All were new-build aircraft, and the whole consignment, built at Hucclecote, was completed by September 1949. With BAF serials EF-1 to EF-48 inclusive, the aircraft were operated by Nos. 349 and 350 Squadrons of No. 1 Wing based at Beauvechain, south-east of Brussels, which had been Advanced Landing Ground (ALG) B68 during the Allied advance through the European mainland.

Two-seat T.7s were also bought in a succession of small orders, the first being for three new-build aircraft at a unit cost of £31,000; these were given the serials ED-1, ED-2 and ED-3, the trio arriving with the BAF four months before the F.4s. A follow-up order for twenty ex-RAF aircraft – numbered ED-4 to ED-12 and ED-33 to ED-43 inclusive – was received, after which a further twenty trainers were contracted. This was fulfilled by the conversion of surplus BAF F.4s into T.7s by Avions Fairey SA at Gosselies, using two-seat component assemblies supplied by Hucclecote. The BAF operated the T.7s with No. 1 Fighter Wing (FW) at Beauvechain, No. 7 FW at Chievres and No. 13 FW at Brustem, plus a number at the Belgian Fighter School, their equivalent of the RAF's CFE. Avions Fairey later modified several aircraft to receive E.1/44-type tail assemblies, and others to become target-tugs.

In releasing F.4s for T.7 conversion, the

Back to 'Oz'

The following aircraft returned from Korea and Japan with No. 77 Squadron, RAAF:

Meteor T.7

VW410(A77-2),	WA680(A77-705),
WA731(A77-701),	WA732(A77-702),
WF843(A77-706),	WG974(A77-703),
WH118(A77-707).	

Meteor F.8

WA783(A77-446),	WA786(A77-744),
WA952(A77-368),	WA964(A77-17),
WA998(A77-802),	WE889(A77-157),
WE896(A77-397),	WE903(A77-31),
WE907(A77-734),	WE969(A77-193),
WH252(A77-793),	WH254(A77-258),
WH405(A77-865),	WH418(A77-861),
WK650(A77-854),	WK674(A77-868),
WK683(A77-851),	WK685(A77-867),
WK727(A77-869),	WK728(A77-855),
WK730(A77-863),	WK748(A77-870),
WK791(A77-871),	WK792(A77-872),
WK796(A77-873),	WK798(A77-875),
WK800(A77-876),	WK821(A77-879),
WK907(A77-878),	WK909(A77-874),
WK910(A77-880),	WK912(A77-883),
WK913(A77-877),	WK931(A77-884),
WK937(A77-882),	WK938(A77-886),
WK944(A77-881),	WK973(A77-885).

To their credit, Australia has preserved over a dozen Meteors, with the following aircraft being confirmed:

Meteor T.7

WA732(A77-702) and WA680(A77-705) are both displayed at the RAAF Museum, Point Cook, while WH118(A77-707) is on show at the Australian Aircraft Restoration Group's museum at Moorabbin.

Meteor F.8

WK685(A77-867), converted into a U.16, is also at Moorabbin, while Point Cook holds WK748(A77-870), and WA952(A77-368) is at the Canberra War Museum. RAAF Wagga Wagga is greedy, with WK791(A77-871) and WK909(A77-874) both as gate guardians. RAAF Williamstown has WK798(A77-875) on their gate; RAAF Villawood in Sydney holds WK907(A77-878); and the Camden Museum of Aviation displays WK674(A77-868). The Warbirds Museum at Mildura has the front section of WK683(A77-851). Meteor F(TT).8 WA880, which was sold to Singapore as an instructional airframe, is now believed to be at the Queensland Museum, together with WD647, a TT.20 previously used at WRE Woomera; neither of them received RAAF markings.

New-build F.4s in service with No.1 Wing of the BAF. Author's collection.

BAF recognized that the Mark was becoming obsolescent, so in the late autumn of 1949 an order was placed with Gloster for twenty-three F.8s, all being ex-RAF aircraft and given the numbers EG-201 to EG-223 inclusive. A licence-production agreement had been drawn up between Gloster Aircraft and Avions Fairey SA, for the Belgian company to build F.8s, but the order for 150 Meteors of this Mark was placed with N.V. *Koninklijke Nederlandse Vliegtuigenfabriek Fokker* in the Netherlands, Avions Fairey fabricating sub-assemblies for Fokker. BAF serials EG-1 to EG-150 inclusive were applied to these aircraft, and yet another order, for thirty F.8s – to be built by Avions Fairey manufacturing with assemblies supplied by Fokker – were given the numbers EG-151 to EG-180 inclusive. Later still, an additional thirty-seven aircraft were assembled from sets of components supplied by Hucclecote, the serials EG-224 to EG-260 inclusive being applied to them.

Fleming and Walloon Meteors

Research has been unable to produce a complete list, but the following ex-RAF aircraft are known to have been supplied to the Belgian Air Force:

Meteor T.7

WA684(ED-40),	WA688(ED-38),
WF814(ED-43),	WF817(ED-4),
WF818(ED-6),	WF827(ED-5),
WG970(ED-42),	WH114(ED-39),
WH117(ED-41),	WH171(ED-11),
WH174(ED-12),	WL399(ED-7),
WL415(ED-10),	WL427(ED-9),
WL428(ED-8),	WL486(ED-33),
WN320(ED-34),	WS140(ED-35),
WS141(ED-36),	XF273(ED-37).

Meteor F.8 (assembled from Fokker components)

WF691(EG-148),	WF692(EG-146),
WF693(EG-147),	WF701(EG-149),
WH448(EG-150).	

Meteor F.8

VZ450(EG-201),	VZ457(EG-205),
VZ459(EG-206),	VZ499(EG-207),
VZ553(EG-211),	VZ562(EG-204),
VZ566(EG-217),	WA755(EG-220),
WA870(EG-208),	WA876(EG-210),
WA878(EG-209),	WA881(EG-202),
WA883(EG-213),	WA884(EG-203),
WA887(EG-214),	WA888(EG-215),

WA889(EG-216),	WA892(EG-212),
WA895(EG-220),	WA898(EG-219),
WA900(EG-221),	WA901(EG-222),
WA902(EG-223)	

Meteor NF.11

WD590(EN-19),	WD594(EN-16),
WD596(EN-20),	WD602(EN-13),
WD622(EN-15),	WD661(EN-18),
WD724(EN-14),	WD726(EN-1),
WD727(EN-7),	WD728(EN-4),
WD729(EN-5),	WD730(EN-6),
WD731(EN-8),	WD732(EN-9),
WD733(EN-10),	WD735(EN-11),

WD736(EN-12),	WD741(EN-21),
WD760(EN-17),	WD763(EN-22),
WD775(EN-2),	WD777(EN-3),
WM221(EN-23),	WM263(EN-24).

Belgium has retained one F.4 EG-18 as a gate-guardian at Chievres. F.8 EG-79 is also a gate-guardian, as Brustem and F.8 EG-162 is at Duiant Citadel. *The Musee Royal de l'Armee* in Brussels displays EG-224, and an NF.11, believed to be WD777 (EN-3) is also in Brussels. F.8 EG-247 is displayed at the Kbely Museum in Czechoslovakia.

WD590, an ex-RAF Flying College No. 1551 Squadron NF.11; this aircraft went to the Belgian AF as EN-19, after which it became OO-ARZ for COGEA. George Pennick.

New licence-built F.8s for the BAF, ready for delivery outside KNV Fokker's assembly shops. Author's collection.

Meteor F.8s were distributed to all thirteen fighter squadrons of the BAF. These flew in four wings: No. 1 Wing was based at Beauvechain, having Nos. 4, 10, 11, 344 and 350 Squadrons; No. 7 Wing at Chievres operated with Nos. 7, 8 and 9 Squadrons; while the Bierset-based No. 9 Wing contained Nos. 22 and 26 Squadrons. No. 13 Wing at Brustem used Nos. 25, 29 and 33 Squadrons, and two Target-Towing Flights also used a few. Single-seat Meteors remained in service with the BAF until the arrival of Hawker Hunters in 1956.

The Belgian Air Force night-fighter requirements were met by the de Havilland Mosquito NF.30 equipped with American AI Mk10 radar, plus one Mosquito NF.XVII and an NF.XIX. In the early 1950s, the BAF started to consider turbojet replacements for the 'Mossies',

Avions Fairey-built F.8s EG-117 and EG-118, produced from assemblies manufactured by KNV Fokker. Author's collection.

and as the Armstrong Whitworth-built Meteor NF.11 was the only jet night-fighter in the export market, it was a case of 'Hobson's choice', although this had the advantage of some components being common with other Meteors that they flew. Two orders were placed with AWA, each for twelve aircraft, the first batch – numbered EN1 to EN12 inclusive – being delivered to the BAF between August 1952 and February 1953. By this time the Mosquitoes had deteriorated to the point where, in October 1956, only one was airworthy, so before the second NF.11 order arrived, a few T.7s and F.8s were taken over by the two BAF night-fighter units, Nos. 10 and 11 Squadrons.

Between January and March 1956, NF.11s of order number two were delivered, their serials running from EN13 to EN24 inclusive. All twenty-four were refurbished ex-RAF aircraft, and were unusual in that they carried BAF serials on the rear fuselage, while retaining their original RAF serials under the wings. The BAF had mixed feelings about the NF.11, with half of them being lost during the five years that they were in service. The reasons for the losses varied between mechanical faults, insufficient crew training and, in at least two cases, adulterated fuel. Belgium started looking for a replacement in 1956, and at the end of the following year, Avro Canada CF-100 Canuck all-weather

fighters began to arrive. Ten of the remaining NF.11s were purchased by the civil operator COGEA, who used them on target-towing duties for the Belgian Ministry of Defence until 1959, their serials changing to NF11-1 to NF11-10 inclusive.

Brazil

The second South American country to order Meteors was Brazil – the largest country in the continent and the fifth-largest in the world. The negotiations were unusual in that they

were conducted on a barter-basis, as the country had very little convertible currency and Britain needed to export. Ten T.7s at a unit price of £40,310, and sixty F.8s costing £42,810 each, were traded in exchange for 15,000 tonnes of raw cotton. The contracts were signed on 28 October 1952 and delivery was scheduled to be completed within twelve months and, as with the Argentinian agreement, the training of *Fôrca Aérea Braziliera* (FAB) pilots, together with groundcrews, was included in the package.

The ten T.7s, serialled 4300 to 4309 inclusive, were aircraft built to an un-delivered RAF contract, while all sixty F.8s, numbered 4400 to 4459 inclusive, were new-build aircraft. An FAB contingent arrived at Moreton Valence in the spring of 1953 for type-conversion, together with technicians to be trained in the aircraft's ground-handling requirements. Delivery to Brazil began with the arrival of four T.7s in April 1953, and by October, Gloster aircraft had completely replaced the P-47 Thunderbolts which had been received from the United States after the war; these were operated by No. 1 *Grupo de Aviacão* de Caca at Santa Cruz. All seventy aircraft were in operational service by the beginning of 1955 and, although the FAB received F-80Cs and T-33s from Lockheed Aircraft in the late 1950s, Meteors remained active into the 1970s. Each FAB F.8 was fitted with a radio compass, as were some T.7s, all being dorsal installations similar to the RAAF Korean F.8s, and whip aerials replaced the rigid posts. The Brazilian T.7s also differed from standard by being fitted with Derwent 8 engines.

Meteors for Gossypium

Brazil's T.7 order was supplied by ten aircraft serialled for the RAF, but not delivered.

Meteor T.7

WS142(4300),	WS143(4301),
WS144(4302),	WS145(4303),
WS146(4304),	WS147(4305),
WS148(4306),	WS149(4307)
WS150(4308),	WS151(4309).

All Brazil's F.8s were new-build aircraft, a few of them originally being ordered by Egypt but transferred to the FAB following a then-current arms-embargo to Middle East countries.

Brazil has retained T.7 WS150(4308) at Campo Grande, Manaus, while no less than ten F.8s are held in the country. *Museu de AFA* at the Pirassununga (Air Force Academy) has 4413, the *Museu Aeroespacial* holds 4460, and Bebeduoro's Museum shows the oldest FAB F.8, 4409 plus 4442. The airbase at Cauoas holds 4439 and 4448, while 4441 is at Santa Cruz. Galaleo airbase shows 4438 as a gate guardian, mounted on a very imposing plynth, and 4452 is held at Curtiba.

Canada

The Royal Canadian Air Force (RCAF) was never a Meteor operator, preferring the de Havilland Vampire F.3. However, the RCAF did purchase Meteor F.3 EE311, from Gloster's second production contract, on 28 September 1945, to be used by the Test and Development Flight of the Turbo Research Company at Rockcliffe, Ontario. Transported by sea, it arrived to partake in a programme of winterization trials in the intense Canadian winter of 1945/46, but it ran out of fuel during a flight on 29 June 1946 and the pilot had to ditch into Helen Bay Lake, Ontario. The aircraft was recovered in August but was too badly damaged to warrant repair, so it was written off and scrapped.

Several other Meteors were assigned tasks by the RCAF and various Canadian establishments, but they were always under the ownership of the Air Ministry and returned to Britain once their respective trials had been completed.

A flight of three of the ten T.7s ordered by the Brazilian Air Force, prior to delivery. Derek N. James.

Denmark

The *Kongelige Danske Flyvevben*/Danish Air Force (DAF) was formed by an amalgamation of the country's army and naval air components on 1 October 1950. Over a year prior to this, on 21 May 1949, the Danish government had ordered twenty Meteor F.4s for the forthcoming Air Force at a unit price of £29,500, once again the contract covering the training of DAF personnel at Moreton Valence. The aircraft were given serials 461 to 480 inclusive, and their delivery to the newly formed Naval Air Arm's 3rd Air Flotilla at Karup started on 6 October 1949. After the formation of the DAF, *eskadrilles* (squadrons) were formed, and on 8 January 1951 the flotilla was retitled *Esk.723*; *Esk.724* was formed later, and this was also equipped with Meteor F.4s.

Nine T.7s were also ordered in April 1950, numbered 261 to 269 inclusive, while in the same month, still before the birth of the DAF, a contract for twenty F.8s, numbered 481 to 500 inclusive, was signed, both orders being fulfilled between January and June 1951. This was the first time the F.8 had been exported, and a cost of £31,500 per new-build aircraft was negotiated. Several *eskadrilles* received the

aircraft, and the F.8 remained on the DAF's inventory until the Hawker Hunter F.51 joined the Service in 1956. The Meteors were gradually relegated to communications and target-tug duties, some operating into the 1960s.

On 28 November 1952 *Esk.723* started to re-equip as a night-fighter unit with Meteor NF.11s, the DAF having ordered twenty of the Mark earlier in the year. The batch was allocated Danish serials 501 to 520 inclusive, the aircraft having been given RAF serials prior to production and re-allocation to the DAF, who received them as new-build airframes. The order made Denmark the first overseas customer for Armstrong Whitworth's night-fighter and they produced them quickly, so that the last aircraft was with the DAF by March 1953. NF.11s were in service with the Danish Air Force until the summer of 1958, when examples of the F-86D variant of the Sabre started to reach *Esk.723*. When the full complement had been received from North American, nearly all the Meteors were scrapped; however, at least six were returned to Baginton early in 1959 for TT.20 conversion and later flew

Denmark's nocturnal Meteors

The following aircraft, originally built for the RAF but not delivered, served with the DAF ESK.723:

Meteor NF.11

WM384(501),	WM385(502),
WM386(503),	WM387(504),
WM388(505),	WM389(506),
WM390(507),	WM391(508),
WM392(509),	WM393(510),
WM394(511),	WM395(512),
WM396(513),	WM397(514),
WM398(515),	WM399(516),
WM400(517),	WM401(518),
WM402(519),	WM404(520).

Denmark has preserved two F.4s, one T.7, two F.8s and one NF.11 in museums. F.4s 461 and 469 are both at the *Danmarks Flyvemuseum* at Billund, as is NF.11 WH387(504). T.7 265 is held at the *Flyvevabnets Historiske*, Samling. F.8 491 is retained at the Karup museum, and F.8 499 can be seen at the *Nordsjaellands Flyvemuseum* in Slangerup.

with the Station Flight at Karup. In 1966, two were refurbished by Swedair Ltd in Sweden, returned to Denmark and sold to West Germany in 1969.

Ecuador

The third South American country to purchase Gloster Meteors was Ecuador, twelve FR.9s being ordered in May 1954, for service with the *Fuerza Aérea Ecuatoriana* (FAE). All were ex-RAF aircraft, refurbished by Flight Refuelling Limited (FRL) and numbered 701 to 712 inclusive. They were delivered in numerical order, 701 going on 9 July 1954 and 712 completing the order on 19 November of the same year, all of them serving with Ecuador's No. 21 Squadron, based at Taura. Some of them were still in service at the beginning of 1970.

South American cameramen

The twelve ex-RAF aircraft supplied to Ecuador were:

VW366(703),	VZ597(701),
VZ610(705),	WH136(704),
WH540(706),	WH543(707),
WH547(702),	WH549(708),
WH550(709),	WH553(710),
WH554(711),	WH555(712).

One FR.9 held by the *Museu Aereo de la FAE* at Quito is numbered FF-123, but which of the original twelve it is remains unknown.

Egypt

Of the three Middle East countries to fly Meteors, Egypt was the first, placing an order for two F.4s on 8 August 1948 at a unit price of £30,000. They were given the Egyptian Air Force (EAF) serials 1401 and 1402, but were withheld until 27 October 1949 due to the British government's embargo on all war materials to the area. 1401 was delivered on that date, followed by 1402 on 16 January 1950. A T.7 – numbered 1400 – was also ordered in August 1948 at a cost of £31,200; its delivery was made in October 1949 by 'Bill' Waterton, and the CTP remained in Egypt for three weeks to train EAF pilots. In January 1949 a second F.4 order was placed, this time for three aircraft at the

Brazilian F.8 4420, believed to have been displayed in Sao Paulo when photographed. Derek N. James.

Denmark's fourth F.4, serialled 464, ready for collection. Derek N. James.

A nice tight formation of five F.8s being delivered to the DAF in June 1951, the original caption quoting an altitude of 30,000ft (9,144m). Author's collection.

712, the last of the FR.9s ordered by the Ecuadorian Air Force, was built as WH555 before it was diverted.
Derek N. James.

Meteors over the Nile

While earlier Egyptian contracts were met by new-build aircraft specific to the orders, the following are confirmed as refurbished ex-RAF operational aircraft, or new-build RAF aircraft diverted to the EAF before RAF allocation.

Meteor F.4

VZ420(1406),	VZ421(1407),
VZ422(1408),	VZ423(1409),
VZ424(1410),	VZ425(1411),
VZ426(1412)	

Meteor T.7

VW435(1439),	WA730(1440),
WG994(1441)	

Meteor F.8

WH350(1415),	WH371(1420),
WL183(1423),	WL185(1424),
WL187(1425),	WL186(1421),
WL188(1419),	WL191(1426).

Meteor NF.13

WM325(1427),	WM326(1428),
WM328(1429),	WM338(1430),
WM340(1431),	WM362(1432).

In view of the losses during *Musketeer* and the lack of cordiality prevailing at the time, it is perhaps understandable that no Egyptian Meteors were retained for preservation.

same unit price as before; these were delivered in the first two months of 1950, and the numbers 1403, 1404 and 1405 applied as they arrived. Egypt's third and final order for F.4s was made in October 1949; this was for seven aircraft, numbered 1406 to 1412 inclusive, and the EAF received these between March and May 1950.

A contract for two additional T.7s was signed on 26 October 1949, serials 1413 and 1414 being allocated to the new-build aircraft; 1413 arrived in Egypt on 17 February 1950, and its partner three months later, on 22 May. In September, an order for three more T.7s was received at Hucclecote, and it was planned to meet it with ex-RAF WL485 and WL486, together with WS149 yet to be built. However, the arms ban was reintroduced

and in August 1953 the order was placed in abeyance; it was eventually cancelled, and WL485 was delivered to France, WL486 went to Belgium to become ED-33, and WS149 was completed as 4307 for Brazil. Two years later, three well used ex-RAF T.7s were handed over to the EAF as 1439, 1440 and 1441, but whether these were on the reinstated original order or not, cannot be verified.

Two orders for F.8s were received in 1949. The first was in October for nineteen aircraft, followed in December by the second for another five, but both orders came up against the government ban and were cancelled. Ten of the aircraft were transferred to the Danish F.8 order, and the remaining fourteen were eventually delivered to the RAF. Three years later, in

December 1952, the embargo was again lifted and Egypt contracted for twelve F.8s. Ex-RAF aircraft were refurbished to meet the order, the EAF numbers 1415 to 1416 inclusive being allocated to them. Four of the twelve – 1416, 1417, 1418 and 1422 – were delivered in February 1953, with 'Bill' Waterton once again flying one; but before the balance of the order could be fulfilled, the arms embargo was once again restored. The remaining eight F.8s were diverted to other contracts in hand at Hucclecote, six going to Brazil and two to Israel. When the dust had settled once more in the Middle East, eight ex-RAF F.8s were refurbished to complete the contract; the original outstanding EAF numbers were applied, and delivery was made to Egypt in 1955.

When Egypt decided to set up a night-fighter unit, they turned to Armstrong Whitworth and six aircraft were ordered in 1954. Meteor NF.13s – basically tropicalized NF.11s on order for the RAF – were diverted as new-build aircraft for the EAF, with the numbers 1427 to 1432 inclusive; delivery was made between June and August 1955. On 31 October 1956 the Suez Crisis arose, and Operation *Musketeer* was precipitated into action. Air attacks on EAF bases destroyed 85 per cent of their Meteors on the ground, but at least one RAF Vickers Valiant had an encounter with an Egyptian NF.13 during the seven-day campaign; it took evasive action, however, and was undamaged. By the end of the decade, all EAF Meteors had been replaced, with the Soviet Union becoming the service's principal supplier.

France

The *Armée de l'Air*/French Air Force (FAF) was not a great Meteor operator and in fact never flew single-seaters. Two F.4s were purchased by France, both being used as trials aircraft. The first, EE523, bought for £12,500, was registered F-WEPQ and disappeared into the mystic world of French research – no doubt the Gallic equivalent of the British TRE! The only other F.4 was the ex-Rolls-Royce Avon testbed RA491, which SNECMA used to further their Atar turbojet engine's development; it kept its British markings.

A pair of T.7s was ordered on 30 September 1950 at a unit price of £31,540 each. Due to the arms embargo on some

The serial 1409 on the nearest aircraft would indicate that these are from Egypt's third F.4 order. Derek N. James.

Middle East deliveries, two Syrian-ordered aircraft that were new-builds on an RAF contract were diverted to meet the French order. Registered 91 and 92, they were delivered to the *Centre d'Essais en Vol* (CEV) at Bretigny, the French opposite to RAE Farnborough, on 7 February 1951, retaining the Syrian registrations. Another former RAF aircraft, that had been in

No.1689 Flight at Benson, was refurbished by FRL and handed over as F-BEAR to Melun on 6 April 1955. Seven ex-RAF T.7s were purchased by the FAF for delivery between 23 June and 25 August 1953, with the serial range F5 to F11 inclusive; No. 30 Squadron was to concentrate on using them as training aircraft for the unit's future role as a night-fighter

squadron. Two further redundant RAF aircraft have been recorded as going to France between September 1955 and June 1956, but their destinations are unknown.

France's main Meteor associations are with AWA's night-fighters. They contracted for twenty-five new-build NF.11s numbered NF11-1 to NF11-25 inclusive, the order supplied by diverting aircraft in production for the RAF, their ownership being changed to the FAF prior to completion. Delivery was made between January and May 1953, the newly converted No.30 *Escadre de Chasse Tour Temps*/All-weather Fighter Wing at Tours-St Symphorien being the recipients. The following year an additional order for sixteen NF.11s was received, and this was fulfilled by the refurbishing of former Royal Air Force aircraft. The first was flown from Baginton to No.30 Wing on 17 September 1954 and the order was completed on 21 April 1955. By 1957, the indigenous Sud-Aviation SO-4050 Vautour IIN started to be accepted for operational service, and several NF.11s were transferred to research establishments, five going to the *Centre du Tir et de Bombardement* (CTB) at Cazaux, while a similar number went to the CEV at Bretigny. At the CEV, a variety of trials programmes made use of the aircraft, including radar and missile development flying, while one became a SNECMA S-600 ramjet testbed, with an example under each wing. Another CEV Meteor, NF11-6,

1400, the first T.7 for the Egyptian Air Force. Author's collection.

Meteors *aux Francais*

The following are either RAF-allocated aircraft diverted to French orders during construction, or ex-squadron service aircraft refurbished for export to France:

Meteor F.4
EE523(F-WEPQ), RA491(RAF serial retained).

Meteor T.7
WA607(F-BEAR), WH136(92), WG997(91)
WF832,   WH168,   WL425,
WL471,   WL476,   WL485,
WN312 (given French registrations F5 to F11 but individual aircraft allocations are unknown).

WF776, WH228 (recorded as delivered to France but registrations unknown).

Meteor NF.11
Ex-RAF squadron aircraft delivered in 1953 but individual French registrations unknown:
WD619,   WD628,   WD631,   WD655,
WD669,   WD674,   WD683,   WD698,
WD701,   WD756,   WD783,   WM153,
WM164,   WM235,   WM243,   WM265.

RAF-allocated aircraft diverted to French orders during production:
WM296,   WM297,   WM298,   WM299,
WM300,   WM301,   WM302,   WM303,
WM304,   WM305,   WM306,   WM307,
WM368,   WM369,   WM370,   WM371,
WM375,   WM376,   WM377,   WM378,
WM379,   WM380,   WM381,   WM382,
WM383.

Meteor NF.13
WM364(NF-F364), WM365(NF-F365).

Meteor NF.14
WS747(NF14-747), WS796(NF14-796).

Meteor TT.20
Each aircraft given the French Ferry Serial F-ZABD. WD649, WD652, WD780, WM242, WM255, WM293.

French preservation of the Meteor has been very good, with no less than twelve held for display. The *Ailes Anciennes* at Toulouse/Blagnac holds T.7s 91 and 92, while another T.7 with the registration F6 is in the *Association des Amis du Musée du Château* at Savigny-les-Beaune, as are TT.20s SE-DCF and SE-DCH from Germany. The *Museé de l'Air et de l'Espace* at Le Bourget have NF.11s registered NF11-5 and NF11-24, as well as an NF.13 with the serial NF13-365 and an NF.14 numbered NF14-747. NF11-1 in the *Musée Aeronautique des Champagne* is the first French NF.11 and another, NF11-8 is in the *Ailes Anciennes* at Toulouse/Blagnac. One more NF.11 is on display in France, NF11-9 at the *Musée Aeronautique de Nancy* at Nancy/Essey, while the French NF11-14 is held in the *Wehrtechnische Studiensammlung* at Koblenz in Germany.

French government and transported to No. 5 MU at Kemble for furbishment to airworthy condition. They were delivered in pairs on 28 November, and 3 and 11 December 1974, each aircraft being given the ferry serial F-ZABD for their flights to Bretigny. Their planned utilization as target tugs did not materialize, however, and the six became 'hangar queens' for the CEV's assortment of trials Meteors.

Israel

The *Heyl Ha'Avir*/Israeli Air Force (IAF) came into being with the founding of the state of Israel in 1948. They had operated a humdrum collection of ex-World War II piston-engined types, but following the precarious truce made with Egypt at the beginning of 1949, they felt that they needed to modernize their equipment. With Egypt receiving Meteors in October 1949, Israel was anxious for parity to be established and they signed a contract on 10 February 1953 for eleven F.8s, priced at £36,250 each, plus four T.7s at a unit price of £34,250. The T.7s were to be modified for target-towing duties, with special lugs attached to the ventral tank supports, while the F.8s would be equipped with the later Martin-Baker Mk2E seat. Israel would supply all cannon armaments, and the underwing structure required modifications to carry rails for a total of eight American HVAR rocket projectiles.

The T.7s were numbered 2162 to 2165, while the F.8s carried serials 2166 to 2169

flew as the chase plane during Concorde 001's early flights.

In June 1956 a couple of Meteor NF.13s – NF13-364 and NF13-365 – were received at Bretigny for research flying, both being former RAF aircraft. Among the myriad of trials undertaken, it is known that NF13-165 was employed, with an 'Exocet' nose grafted onto its radome, as part of the missile's development programme. France also purchased two Meteor NF.14s in 1955, for use at the CEV for various experimental trials; these had also served as RAF operational aircraft. Given the French serials NF14-747 and NF14-796, they put in many years of flying at the centre, with NF14-747 recorded as still being in service as late as 1983.

In 1974, six Meteor TT.20s that had been in storage were purchased by the

T.7 serialled F1, being prepared for delivery to the French Air Force. Derek N. James.

NF.14 WS747 served with No. 264 Squadron before being sold to France, where it became NF14-747 serving with CEV, Bretigny. M. Hiscock/NBS Aviation.

and 2172 to 2178, all inclusive. Delivery of the four trainers began in June 1953, and F.8s started arriving on 21 August of the same year, with the final aircraft being flown in on 17 January 1954. The last three F.8s – 2176, 2177 and 2178 – were in fact originally built as Egyptian aircraft, but were withheld awaiting the lifting of the arms ban. I am sure that the irony of them becoming *Heyl Ha'Avir* aircraft was not

lost on the Israeli defence hierarchy! Two additional T.7s, acquired later – both fitted with E.1/44-type tail assemblies – were supplied by Avions Fairey in Belgium.

The grumbling appendix of the Sinai Peninsula became more inflamed in the autumn of 1956, and once again British aircraft exports were ranged against each other. Israeli Meteor F.8s engaged Egyptian Vampire FB.5s on several occa-

sions, and at least three de Havilland aircraft were brought down by the products from Gloster. But engagements a few months later, by which time Egypt had started operating MiG-15s, proved to Israel that the Meteor needed replacing, and Dassault Mysteres were purchased for the country's first line of defence, leaving the F.8s to provide top cover.

The *Heyl Ha'Avir* received seven FR.9s, all ex-RAF aircraft refurbished by FRL at Tarrant Rushton. With Israeli serials 211 to 217 inclusive, they were delivered between 1955 and 1956, by which time six NF.13s had also been ordered. Again, refurbished former RAF aircraft fulfilled the contract. In fact Operation *Musketeer* was launched during their delivery, so that only three were received in 1956, the balance being delivered in the spring of 1958. IAF serials 4X-FNA to 4X-FNF inclusive were allocated to the night-fighters, but again their obsolescence became apparent within a couple of years, and they were replaced by Mirages.

Malaya

One ex-RAF aircraft, PR.10 WB165, which had first served with No. 13 Squadron in the Middle East, then No. 81 Squadron in the Far East, was sold to the

2165, the third new-build T.7 delivered to the Israeli Air Force, arrives on 6 July 1953. Author's collection.

Israeli Air Force F.8 with HVAR rocket projectiles. Derek N. James.

Royal Malaysian Air Force as a ground instructional airframe in November 1963.

The Netherlands

The *Koninklijke Luchtmacht*/Royal Netherland Air Force (RNethAF) was the biggest Meteor operator outside the United Kingdom. They were ordered from Gloster as new-build and ex-RAF aircraft, as well as a licence-build production line contracted between the company and *N.V.Koninklijke Nederlandse Vliegtuigenfabriek Fokker* (Fokker Aircraft).

The first RNethAF order was for thirty-eight F.4s, and was arranged as four contracts. The first was signed on 27 June 1947 for five aircraft at £15,000 each, numbered I-21 to I-25 inclusive, and they were delivered between June and October 1948. Contract two came into being on 31 August 1948, again for five aircraft, with a unit price of £16,000; they flew to Holland between 30 July and 1 October 1948 carrying the serials I-26 to I-30 inclusive. Twenty-four F.4s formed the third contract, signed on 30 April 1949, the price £18,950 per aircraft and their numbers I-31 to I-54 inclusive; these were despatched between 17 January and 17 June 1949, followed in 1950 by the remaining four, serialled I-55 to I-58 inclusive. I-50 crashed at Thorney Island en

route, but whether it was replaced has not been recorded. It will be noticed that deliveries often commenced *before* the respective contracts were signed, indicating a mutual trust between supplier and customer which nowadays is sometimes sadly lacking.

RNethAF squadrons Nos. 322 and 327 at Soersterburge shared distribution of the F.4s with Nos. 323 and 326 at Leerwarden, both bases being supplied by the Fighter School at Twenthe, who first received the aircraft from Britain. A later order was placed for twenty-seven ex-RAF F.4s, given the serial range I-54 to I-85 inclusive. British records give three additional ex-RAF F.4s as also being delivered to the RNethAF, but their Dutch serials are unknown.

As the RNethAF had previously only operated with piston-engined wartime-vintage aircraft, the acquisition of F.4s was a step that required assistance, so Meteor T.7s were ordered from Gloster Aircraft at a unit price of £29,975. The total of thirty-nine trainers was made up by the private-venture demonstrator/prototype G-AKPK, plus thirty-eight former RAF service aircraft of various ages. Delivery was in several batches, spread over five years – and it started off badly, as G-APKP was written off in a landing accident very shortly after its arrival in 1948. Late in their lives, several T.7s saw service for a few years with the *Marineluchtvaartdienst*/ Netherlands Fleet Air Arm.

At the end of the decade, the RNethAF looked at several different types, with a view to replacing the F.4. The performance of the Meteor F.8, plus an agreement nego-

RNethAF F.4s stand at Evere, sharing the base with an assortment of F-80s, C-47s, Beechcraft 18 and an Anson. Author's collection.

tiated with Gloster whereby Fokker Aircraft would build the aircraft under licence, convinced the Dutch Air Ministry that this would be their next front-line interceptor. Fokker, as the main contractor, received Gloster-produced components while placing the work for sub-items with Avialanda and De Schelde, then undertook the final assembly. Construction started in the autumn of 1950, and the first home-produced F.8 was handed over to the RNethAF on 12 January 1951. Also in 1951, five undelivered aircraft built to an RAF contract, were flown to join the Fokker-built F.8s; these had the serials I-90 to I-94 inclusive.

Fokker's agreement for building F.8s under licence was a good move by the company. A total of 155 aircraft was built for the RNethAF, the serials running from I-101 to I-255 inclusive, and delivery was made in five batches from January 1951 to

NVK Fokker's tarmac is well covered with home-built F.8s and F.4 for the RNethAF, with six additional F.8s ready for Belgium. Author's collection.

Meteors from and to Amsterdam

All RNethAF Meteor F.4s were Gloster-produced aircraft, the first thirty-eight being new-builds constructed to contract. A follow-up order for an additional twenty-seven was supplied by the following ex-RAF aircraft:

VT333(I-76), VW263(I-77), VW264(I-72), VW286(I-66), VW288(I-71), VW291(I-73), VW295(I-79), VW296(I-80), VW309(I-65), VW310(I-74), VW313(I-75), VW315(I-81), VZ387(I-60), VZ388(I-62), VZ390(I-63), VZ391(I-55), VZ393(I-56), VZ394(I-78), VZ395(I-57), VZ396(I-58), VZ397(I-59), VZ398(I-67), VZ399(I-64), VZ400(I-61), VZ402(I-68), VZ408(I-70), VZ409(I-69)

VW305, VW306 and VW307 are also recorded

as being delivered to the RNethAF, but their Dutch numbers have not been given.

Meteor T.7
The RNethAF have been quoted as receiving forty-three T.7s, all ex-RAF apart from the first, which was a Gloster-owned aircraft. Only thirty-nine have been confirmed and these are given here, the RNethAF serial system changing during the delivery timespan:

G-AKPK(I-1), VW417(I-320), WA592(I-322), WA623(I-18), WA626(I-9), WA633(I-10), WA674(I-319), WF856(I-323), WG998(I-304), WH125(I-305), WH135(I-316), WH165(I-11), WH177(I-325), WH179(I-16),

WH193(I-13), WH196(I-14), WH199(I-15), WH202(I-17), WH203(I-12), WH207(I-301), WH222(I-322), WH233(I-19), WH237(I-308), WH245(I-310), WH247(I-324), WL412(I-309), WL426(I-306), WL469(I-18), WL477(I-309), WL482(I-20), WL487(I-303), WN315(I-307), XF275(I-317), XF276(I-315), XF277(I-311), XF278(I-314), XF279(I-313).

VW475 and WA594 were also delivered, but their RNethAF serials have not been recorded.

Meteor F.8
All F.8s in RNethAF service were licence-built by Fokker, except for the following five ex-RAF aircraft:
WF694(I-93), WF696(I-94), WF697(I-90), WF698(I-91), WF699(I-92)

The Netherlands have preserved five Meteors for display. The only F.4 VZ387(I-60) is in the *Militaire Luchvaart Museum* at Kamp van Zeist, Soesterberg, as is F.8 I-189, and F.8 I-187 is also at that base as a memorial. Two T.7s are displayed, WH233(I-19) in the *Zuidkamp Museum* at Twenthe, and VW417(I-320) at Leeuwarden.

F.8 I-187 on display at Soesterberg. Mike Hooks.

F.3 EE395, which went to New Zealand to become NZ6001, and then instructional airframe 147. Derek N. James.

November 1945 and fifty-six RNAF pilots, as well as the dedicated pilot Squadron Leader McKay, flew it until 15 March 1950, when it was struck off charge, to become instructional airframe 147. Today it is displayed in the RNZAF Museum at Auckland, with the serial NZ6001.

Singapore

When Meteor T.7 VW487 finished its RAF service with No. 1574 Target Towing Flight at Seletar, it was given to the Singapore Air Force on 12 January 1971 as an instructional airframe. F.8 WA880 had also arrived with No. 1574 Flight and it was struck off charge earlier than the trainer, on 4 November 1969. It was then sold to Singapore as an instructional airframe for the SAF and is now in the Sentosa Museum.

South Africa

One Meteor F.3, EE429, was loaned by Gloster Aircraft to the South African Air Force on 23 March 1946, and they operated it for three years. However, due to the country's internal political situation, no order ensued and the aircraft was returned on 11 June 1949. It was soon allotted the

February 1954. They also built 150 for the Belgian Air Force, and delivered another thirty via the Belgian company Avions Fairey. RNethAF Meteor F.8s served with Nos. 322, 327 and 328 Squadrons at Soesterburg, while the four Leeuwarden-based Nos. 323, 324, 325 and 326 Squadrons were also operators, both airfields being base to the type from 1951 to 1956. By that time, Hawker Hunters had supplanted Meteors in the RAF, and the RNethAF followed suit – with Fokker Aircraft again getting in on the act. Several Meteors were employed in a target-towing role for a while, but by 1958 they had all been struck off charge.

New Zealand

This country's association with the Meteor was singular. A brand-new F.3, EE395, went to New Zealand by sea in

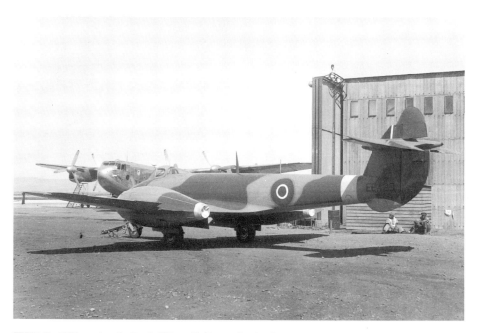

EE429, the F.3 loaned to the South African Air Force, shortly after arriving at Palmeitfontein in March 1946. Author's collection.

The former G-ANSO, fitted with a standard T.7 rear fuselage and outer wings, being prepared for painting in Swedair's overall yellow, with the serial SE-DCC, in 1959. Derek N. James.

The two TT.20s, SE-DCF on the right and SE-DCH on the left, outside SFAB's hangar. Derek N. James.

instructional airframe number 6684M, and transferred to RAF Henlow.

Sweden

Although Gloster demonstrated their private venture F.4 G-AIDC, in the country during 1947, no orders were forthcoming and the *Kungl. Svenska*

Flygvapnet/Royal Swedish Air Force (RSAF) opted for the de Havilland Vampire.

Eight years later, on 29 July 1955, the Swedish company *Svensk Flygtjanst AB*/Swedair Ltd. in Stockholm, whose aircraft were painted overall yellow, purchased an ex-RAF No. 607 Squadron T.7 that had been refurbished by FLR at Tarrant Rushton as a target tug. Swedair

Ltd. had been contracted by the RSAF to supply target-towing services and they used the T.7, registered SE-CAS, for four years. It was joined by a former No. 205 Advanced Flying School aircraft, which again went through FLR, in September 1955, with the civil registration SE-CAT. This aircraft crashed when approaching Visby on 21 January 1959 and was destroyed.

A third aircraft was supplied on 11 August 1959, after a Gloster-produced metamorphosis. Originally built in 1950 as the single-seat, private venture, ground-attack prototype Reaper, first registered G-AMCJ and then given the 'B' classification G-7-1, in 1954 it became the second T.7 to have a two-seat front fuselage grafted on and be re-registered G-ANSO. Four years later, in November 1958, Swedair Ltd. purchased the aircraft, requesting original production T.7 tail assembly and outer wings to be fitted, G-ANSO having retained the Reaper tip tanks. Conversion was completed in July 1959 and the aircraft was delivered as SE-DCC, on 11 August 1959.

Svensk-Flygtjanst AB replaced their two

Buttercup Meteors

All seven Swedish Meteors were civil registered and employed in a target-towing role by Svensk-Flygtjanst AB.

Meteor T.7
G-AMCJ/G-7-1/G-ANSO(SE-DCC), WF833(SE-CAS), WH128(SE-CAT).

Meteor TT.20
Four ex-RAF/DAF aircraft operated to meet a Danish Air Force contract:
WM391/508(SE-DCH),
WM396/512(SE-DCF),
WM400/517(SE-DCG),
WM402/519(SE-DCI).

Only two Meteors have been preserved in Sweden, both T.7s: WF833(SE-CAS) is in the *Flygvapenmuseum* at Malmslatt, Linkoping and the seemingly-everlasting G-AMCJ/G-7-1/G-ANSO(SE-DCC) in Ugglarp's *Svedinos Bil Och Flygmuseum.*

A flight of three Syrian Air Force F.8s. Author's collection.

T.7s with four former Danish TT.20s that had operated from Karup. In November 1964 the company was contracted by the Danish Air Force to provide target-towing services, and SE-DCF, SE-DCG, SE-DCH and SE-DCI were used for these duties. SE-DCF finished operations in November 1965, and in the following March, the others did the same. Both SE-DCG and SE-DCI were reduced to scrap in 1966, while SE-DCF and SE-DCH were returned to Denmark.

Syria

At about the same time as Egypt up-dated her Meteors, Syria placed an order with Gloster Aircraft to supply two T.7s for the *Al Quwwat al-Jawwiya al Arabia as-Suriya*/Syrian Air Force (SAF) at a unit price of £31,200, and they were accepted on behalf of the SAF at Moreton Valence on 10 June 1950. However, the ever-recurring arms ban was again in force, so

Desert Meteors

Although the two T.7s numbered 91 and 92, delivered in November 1952, were ex-RAF aircraft, their identity has been referred to by so many different British serials over the years, that their true identities are unconfirmed so far as this author is concerned and they are therefore excluded from this list. Syria's first twelve F.8s, numbered 101 to 112 inclusive are also unconfirmed as to their true identity.

Meteor F.8
Seven additional ex-RAF machines ordered:
WA785(413), WE965(418),
WH260(419), WH503(417),
WK868(415), WK984(416),
WL174(414).

Meteor FR.9
WB133(480), WX972(481).

Meteor NF.13
WM330(473), WM332(471),
WM333(476), WM336(472),
WM337(474), WM341(475).

So far as is known, no Meteors have been preserved by Syria.

WD592, the NF.11 that went to the United States as N94749, is dwarfed by a Douglas C-133 Cargomaster at Mojave. Author's collection.

The Meteor and Javelin are nearly at the stall as they overtake the Gladiator, giving Russell Adams a unique photograph that encompasses over thirty years of Gloster Aircraft. Although the NF.14 is an Armstrong Whitworth product, it stems from Hucclecote's basic design. Derek N. James.

while they could not be delivered, the aircraft were used to train Syrian pilots at the Gloster airfield. When the pilots were type-cleared, the two T.7s were transferred to France, and in November 1952, with the embargo lifted, a pair of former RAF aircraft was delivered to fulfil the contract, carrying the originally allocated serials 91 and 92.

A contract for twelve Meteor F.8s was drawn up in January 1950, priced at £31,700 each, but at the time of their completion at Hucclecote the arms ban stalled delivery and the aircraft were moved onto an RAF order. Two years later the contract was restored to activity and delivery of the aircraft, numbered 101 to 112 inclusive, began at the end of 1952. A subsequent order for an additional seven F.8s was served by the supplying of ex-RAF aircraft between March and June 1956, carrying the SAF numbers 413 to 419

inclusive. A pair of ordered FR.9s was also delivered in the summer of 1956, these too being former Royal Air Force aircraft, allocated the serials 480 and 481, to be used for ground-attacks in conjunction with the F.8s.

Syria had also requested six NF.13s back in the beginning of 1954, and this was also met by refurbished RAF aircraft, which were given the SAF serials 471 to 476 inclusive. All six were supplied in May 1954, to form the sole Syrian night-fighter unit. Long before Meteors became time-expired, SAF requirements for new aircraft were being met by the Soviet Union.

United States of America

DG210/G, the first production Meteor F.1, was loaned to the USAAF for evaluation at Muroc Lake, on 18 February 1944,

wearing 'star-and-bar' markings. It was returned to Gloster Aircraft on 24 April 1945, and after RAE service, became instructional airframe 5837M at Malksham.

WD592, an NF.11 converted to TT.20 standard, was purchased by American preservers Al Letcher and Associates at Mojave, in June 1975. During its time with Al Letcher it was used in at least one film being flown by well-known film pilot Paul Mantz. It was subsequently sold to Al Hansen, also of Mojave, who in turn passed it to the Edwards Air Base museum as part of a complex deal. During its active life in the U.S. it received the palindromic registration N94749.

CHAPTER FIFTEEN

Epilogue

When Wilfred George Carter was given the task of designing an operational fighter around Frank Whittle's turbojet engine, he stuck to what he knew. It was enough to be dealing with a new engine – in fact more than that, a new type of engine – without thinking along the lines of trying anything aerodynamically unconventional. One thing at a time, and an operationally untried method of propulsion was enough to be getting on with. Actually, by proposing a nose-wheel undercarriage, he was giving service squadrons two innovations.

Therefore his first jet-powered fighter, which was also his first production monoplane, was of conventional design and construction. And after years of considering Whittle's idea as fanciful (if they thought of it at all), the Air Ministry was suddenly anxious to utilize this new propulsive power. But Carter was well aware that his company was churning out Typhoons, under licence, on the other side of Gloster's airfield, which were capable of much higher performances than he could provide with a Whittle W2B. He would have to use two engines to produce anything like the demands of Specification F.9/40, and squadron performances in the event of engine failure, with its asymmetrical results, was not the happiest of reading.

There were no computors or wind-tunnels in that corner of Gloucestershire, and some learned bodies had forecast that jet-blast would be problematic around the tail end. These prophecies proved quite false, and in fact the undercarriage brakes gave far more trouble than the turbojets – as did finding an airfield from which the preliminary test-flying could be conducted. So the fact that Carter's design was in squadron service within fifteen months of its maiden flight, says a great deal about his orthodox approach to the demands. The basic aeroplane required progressive strengthening as more power was supplied, and increased operational demands were made by the Air Ministry. Stability was a problem right from the start, and while it was greatly reduced over the years – especially with the introduction of a longer fuselage, coupled with the E.1/44-type tail assembly – it was never completely eradicated.

Unknown to Britain at the time, Germany was having even more troubles with their first operational turbojet, the Me262. Reliable engines were so unavailable that the first prototype flew with a piston engine in its nose; tricycle undercarriages arrived later in the aircraft's development. The German engines were nearly always a source of unreliability, and their output per pounds' weight was greatly inferior to Whittle's. Although aerodynamically Willy Messerschmitt's design was well ahead of Carter's, the Meteor was the better operational aeroplane for its day; and in terms of powerplant, Whittle's centrifugal compressors were far more reliable than the axial layouts being used by Junkers. The fact that axial-flow engines are now the 'norm' has come via years of development and testing, undertaken without the pressure of wartime conditions. There is no doubt that the Meteor would not have met the same time-scale, had the engines not started off being better engineered and tested. Germany's introduction of superior armament could have swung the balance, if the war had continued for another year, but that was no reflection on the Gloster/Rolls-Royce combination.

Training pilots on the T.7 was rather like teaching learner-drivers on heavy goods vehicles, when all their qualified driving would incur taking the family around in a 1.5 litre saloon. The T.7 required heavy footloads on the rudder pedals, and was not happy when taken to the limit of control, as there was not a large margin for error. When the student became a pilot, he flew the later F.8 and night-fighters which, with the new tail assemblies, were feather-like by comparison. Furthermore, they were not as draughty as the trainer.

A perusal through the preceding chapters will have conveyed the enormous variety of applications, powerplants and adaptations that the airframe endured throughout its life, a variety that would not have been maintained by a more sophisticated and, most likely, more temperamental, design. As recounted earlier, it was due to the association between Frank Whittle and Whitehall's overseer at Hucclecote, Sqn Ldr McC. Reynolds, that the engine pioneer was introduced to George Carter. Also to the fact that Gloster's project office was not exactly overloaded with work, so they were available to get Whittle's engine into the air; and having proved their prowess in flying the E.28/39 within fifteen months of starting the project, the company was chosen by the Air Ministry to design the fighter. It could have gone to one of several other manufacturers, and who can say what difference that would have made – judging by Hawker's and Supermarine's problems with their respective Meteor successors, it would not necessarily have been any easier or quicker.

In retrospect – which can make experts of anyone – the fact that George Carter's designs provided genuine service flying and not just pretty demonstrations at air shows, for well over four decades, says that he got it right.

Technical Data

Role

Mark 1, 3, 4 and 8. Single-seat day fighter.
Mark 7. Two-seat operational trainer.
Mark 9. Single-seat photographic-reconnaissance fighter.
Mark 10. Single-seat photographic reconnaissance aircraft.
Mark 11, 12, 13 and 14. Two-seat night fighter.
Mark 15, 16 and 21. Single-seat radio-controlled target check aircraft and unmanned target drone.
Mark 20. Two-seat target tug.

Dimensions

Wingspan: *Mark 1, 3, 4 early aircraft, 10, 11, 12, 13, 14 and 20,* 43ft 0in (13.1m); *Mark 4, 7, 8, 9, 15 and 16,* 37ft 2in (11.3).
Overall length: *Mark 1 and 3,* 41ft 3in (12.5m); *Mark 4 and 15,* 41ft 0in (12.49); *Mark 7,* 43ft 6in (13.2m); *Mark 8 and 9,* 44ft 7in (13.5in); *Mark 10,* 44ft 3in (13.1m); *Mark 11, 13, 16 and 20,* 48ft 6in (14.7m); *Mark 12,* 49ft 11in (15.2m); *Mark 14,* 51ft 4in (15.5m).
Overall Height: *Mark 1, 3, 4, 7, 8, 9, 10, 15, 16, 20 and 21,* 13ft 0in (3.9m); *Mark 11, 12, 13, 14,* 13ft 11in (4.2m).
Wing area: *Mark 1, 3, 4 early aircraft, 10, 11, 12, 13, 14, 20 and 21,* 374sq ft (34.7sq m); *Mark 4, 7, 8, 9, 15 and 16,* 350 sq ft (32.5sq m).

Weight, Empty

Mark 1, 8,140lb (3,737kg); *Mark 2 and 4 early aircraft,* 10,519lb (4,771kg); *Mark 4,* 11,217lb (5,088kg); *Mark 7,* 10,645lb (4,929kg); *Mark 8,* 10,684lb (4,846kg); *Mark 9,* 10,790lb (4,894kg); *Mark 10,* 10,993lb (4,986kg); *Mark 11,* 12,019lb (5,451kg); *Mark 12,* 12,292lb (5,575kg); *Mark 13,* 12,347lb (5,600kg); *Mark 14,* 12,620lb (5,724kg); *Mark 15, 16, 20 and 21* weights varied dependent on sortie equipment and therefore are not included.

Powerplants

Mark 1 and 3 early aircraft: two 1,700lb (771kg) static thrust Rolls-Royce Welland 1; *Mark 3 later aircraft:* two 2,000lb (907kg) static thrust Rolls-Royce Derwent 5; *Mark 4 and 15:* two 3,500lb (1,587kg) static thrust Rolls-Royce Derwent 5; *Mark 5, 7, 8, 9, 10, 11, 13, 14, 16, 20 and 21:* two 3,500lb (1,587kg) static thrust Rolls-Royce Derwent 8; *Mark 12:* two 3,800lb (1,723kg) static thrust Rolls-Royce Derwent 9.

Performance, Clean

Mark 1 and 3: 415mph at 10,000ft (675km/h at 3,048m); *Mark 4 early aircraft:* 575mph at 10,000ft (925km/h at 3,048m); *Mark 4:* 580mph at 10,000ft (933km/h at 3,048m); *Mark 7:* 590mph at 10,000ft (949 km/h at 3,048m); *Mark 8 and 9:* 598mph at 10,000ft (962km/h at 3,048m); *Mark 10:* 575mph at 10,000ft (925km/h at 3,048m); *Mark 11 and 12:* 580mph at 10,000ft (933km/h at 3,048m); *Mark 13 and 14,* 585mph at 10,000ft (940km/h at 3,048m); *Mark 20,* 560mph at 10,000ft (910km/h at 3,048m). *Mark 15, 16 and 21* performances varied according to sortie requirement and are therefore not included.

Service Ceiling, Clean

Mark 1, 3, 11, 12 and 14, 40,000ft (12,192m); *Mark 4 early aircraft,* 52,000ft (15,849m); *Mark 4 and 7,* 45,000ft (13,716m); *Mark 8,* 43,000ft (13,106m); *Mark 9,* 41,000ft (12,433m); *Mark 10,* 44,000ft (13,411m); *Mark 11, 12, 14 and 20,* 40,000ft (12,192m); *Mark 13,* 36,000ft (19,972m); *Mark 15, 16 and 21,* dependent on range of guidance systems and are therefore not included.

Fuel, Maximum

Mark 1, 300 gallons (1,363 litres); *Mark 3, 4 and 7,* 500 gallons (2,275 litres); *Mark 8, 9 and 10,* 795 gallons (3,617 litres); *Mark 11, 12, 13, 14 and 20,* 600 gallons (2,730 litres); *Mark 15 and 16,* 500 gallons (2,275 litres).

Meteor Production and Serial Blocks

(New-build aircraft to Ministry contracts, including new-build aircraft diverted for export and private-venture prototypes.)

The following aircraft were manufactured in the United Kingdom by Gloster Aircraft Limited at Hucclecote, Gloucestershire and Sir W.G. Armstrong Whitworth Aircraft Limited at Baginton, Coventry, Warwickshire.

F.9/40 prototypes Hucclecote-built; Contract No. SB21179/C.23(2); DG202/G to DG209/G: 8 aircraft.

F.1 Hucclecote-built; Contract No. A/C1490/CB.7(b); EE210 to EE229: 20 aircraft.

F.3 Hucclecote-built; Contract No. 6/ACFT/1490/CB.7(b); EE230 to EE254; EE269 to EE318; EE331 to EE369; EE384 to EE429; EE444 to EE493: 210 aircraft.

F.4 Hucclecote-built; G-AIDC Private Venture prototype; Contract No. 6/ACFT/1490/CB.7(b); EE517 to EE554; EE568 to EE599; RA365 to RA398; RA413 to RA457; RA473 to RA493: 171 aircraft.
F.4 Hucclecote-built; Contract No. 6/ACFT/658/CB.7(b); VT102 to VT150; VT168 to VT199; VT213 to VT247; VT256 to VT294; VT303 to VT347: 200 aircraft.
F.4 Hucclecote-built; Contract No. 6/ACFT/1389/CB.7(b); VW255 to VW316; VW357; VW780 to VW791: 84 aircraft.
F.4 Baginton-built; Contract No. 6/ACFT/1389/CB.7(b); VZ386 to VZ429; VZ436 to VZ437: 46 aircraft.

T.7 Hucclecote-built; Contract No. 6/ACFT/1389/CB.7(b); VW410 to VW459; VW470 to VW489: 70 aircraft.

T.7 Hucclecote-built; Contract No. 6/ACFT/2430/CB.7(b); VZ629 to VZ649: 21 aircraft.
T.7 Hucclecote-built; Contract No. 6/ACFT/2982/CB.7(b); WA590 to WA639; WA649 to WA698; WA707 to WA743: 137 aircraft.
T.7 Hucclecote-built; Contract No. 6/ACFT/5044/CB.7(b); WF766 to WF795; WF813 to WF862; WF875 to WF883: 89 aircraft.
T.7 Hucclecote-built; Contract No. 6/ACFT/5621/CB.7(b); WG935 to WG950; WG961 to WG999; WH112 to WH136; WH164 to WH209; WH215 to WH248: 160 aircraft.
T.7 Hucclecote-built; Contract No. 6/ACFT/6066/CB.7(b); WL332 to WL381; WL397 to WL436; WL453 to WL488; WN309 to WN321: 139 Aircraft.
T.7 Hucclecote-built; Contract No. 6/ACFT/6410/CB.7(b); WS103 to WS117; WS140 to WS151; XF273 to XF279: 34 aircraft.

F.8 Hucclecote-built; G-AMCJ private venture 'Reaper'; Contract No. 6/ACFT/2430/CB.7(b); VZ438 to VZ485; VZ493 to VZ517: 74 aircraft.
F.8 Baginton-built; Contract No. 6/ACFT/2430/CB.7(b); VZ518 to VZ532; VZ540 to VZ569: 45 aircraft.
F.8 Baginton-built; Contract No. 6/ACFT/2983/CB.7(b); WA755 to WA794; WA808 to WA812; WA965 to WA969; WA981 to WA999; WB105 to WB112: 77 aircraft.
F.8 Hucclecote-built; Contract No. 6/ACFT/2983/CB.7(b); WA813 to WA857; WA867 to WA909; WA920 to WA964: 133 aircraft.
F.8 Baginton-built; Contract No. 6/ACFT/4040/CB.7(b); WE852 to WE891; WE895 to WE902: 48 aircraft.
F.8 Hucclecote-built; Contract No. 6/ACFT/4040/CB.7(b); WE903 to WE939; WE942 to WE976: 72 aircraft.

F.8 Baginton-built; Contract No. 6/ACFT/5043/CB.7(b); WF639 to WF662; WF677 to WF688: 36 aircraft.
F.8 Hucclecote-built; Contract No. 6/ACFT/5043/CB.7(b); WF689 to WF716; WF736 to WF760: 53 aircraft.
F.8 Baginton-built; Contract No. 6/ACFT/5621/CB.7(b); WH249 to WH263; WH272 to WH320; WH342 to WH386; WH395 to WH426; WH442 to WH484; WH498 to WH513: 200 aircraft.
F.8 Hucclecote-built; Contract No. 6/ACFT/6066/CB.7(b); WK647 to WK696; WK783 to WK827; WK849 to WK893; WK935 to WK955; WK966 to WK994; WL104 to WL143; WL158 to WL191: 264 aircraft.
F.8 Baginton-built; Contract No. 6/ACFT/6066/CB.7(b); WK906 to WK934: 20 aircraft.

FR.9 Hucclecote-built; Contract No. 6/ACFT/1389/CB.7(b); VW360 to VW371: 12 aircraft.
FR.9 Hucclecote-built; Contract No. 6/ACFT/2430/CB.7(b); VZ577 to VZ611: 35 aircraft.
FR.9 Hucclecote-built; Contract No. 6/ACFT/2983/CB.7(b); WB113 to WB125; WB133 to WB143: 24 aircraft.
FR.9 Hucclecote-built; Contract No. 6/ACFT/5621/CB.7(b); WH533 to WH557: 25 aircraft.
FR.9 Hucclecote-built; Contract No. 6/ACFT/6066/CB.7(b); WL255 to WL265: 11 aircraft.
FR.9 Hucclecote-built; Contract No. 6/ACFT/7252/CB.7(b); WX962 to WX981: 20 aircraft.

PR.10 Hucclecote-built; Contract No. 6/ACFT/658/CB.7(b); VS968 to VS987: 20 aircraft.
PR.10 Hucclecote-built; Contract No. 6/ACFT/1389/CB.7(b); VW376 to VW379: 4 aircraft.
PR.10 Hucclecote-built; Contract No.

6/ACFT/2430/CB.7(b); VZ620: 1 aircraft.
PR.10 Hucclecote-built; Contract No. 6/ACFT/2983/CB.7(b); WB153 to WB181: 29 aircraft.

NF.11 Baginton-built; Contract No. 6/ACFT/3433/CB.5(b); WA546, WA547 and WB543; WD585 to WD634; WD640 to WD689; WD696 to WD745; WD751 to WD800: 203 aircraft.

NF.11 Baginton-built; Contract No. 6/ACFT/6141/CB.5(b); WM143 to WM192; WM221 to WM270; WM292 to WM307; WM368 to WM404: 153 aircraft.

NF.12 Baginton-built; Contract No. 6/ACFT/6412/CB.5(b); WS590 to WS639; WS658 to WS700; WS715 to WS721: 100 aircraft.

NF.13 Baginton-built; Contract No. 6/ACFT/6141/CB.5(b); WM308 to WM341; WM362 to WM367: 40 aircraft.

NF.14 Baginton-built; Contract No. 6/ACFT/6412/CB.5(b); WS722 to WS760; WS774 to WS812; WS827 to WS848: 100 aircraft.

Meteor Assembly in the Low Countries

Belgium

Avions Fairey

F.4 Refurbished ex-RAF aircraft for Belgian, AF; EG-201 to EG-223: 23 aircraft.

F.8 Asssembly of Fokker-supplied components for Belgian AF; EG-151 to EG-180: 30 aircraft.

F.8 Assembly of Gloster-supplied components for Belgian AF; EG-224 to EG-260: 37 aircraft.

The Netherlands

N.V. Koninklijke Nederlandse Vliegtuigenfebriek Fokker

F.8 Supplied to Belgian AF; EG-1 to EG-150: 150 aircraft.

F.8 Supplied to RNethAF; I-101 to I-255: 155 aircraft.

F.8 Supplied by Avions Fairey, Belgium: 30 component sets.

Meteor Squadrons

Meteor F.1
No. 616.

Meteor F.3
Nos. 56, 63, 66, 74, 91, 92, 124, 222, 234, 245, 257, 263, 266, 500, 504, 541, 616.

Meteor F.4
Nos. 1, 19, 41, 43, 56, 63, 64, 65, 66, 74, 92, 222, 245, 257, 263, 266, 500, 600, 609, 610, 611, 615, 616.

Meteor T.7
Aircraft of this Mark served with nearly every squadron, in varying numbers.

Meteor F.8
Nos. 1, 19, 34, 41, 43, 54, 56, 63, 64, 65, 66, 72, 74, 85, 92, 111, 222, 245, 247, 257, 263, 500, 504, 600, 601, 604, 609, 610, 611, 615, 616.

Meteor FR.9
Nos. 2, 8, 79, 208.

Meteor PR.10
Nos. 2, 13, 81, 541.

Meteor NF.11
Nos. 5, 11, 29, 68, 87, 96, 125, 141, 151, 256, 264, 527.

Meteor NF.12
Nos. 25, 29, 46, 64, 72, 152, 153.

Meteor NF.13
Nos. 39, 219.

Meteor NF.14
Nos. 25, 33, 46, 60, 64, 72, 152, 153, 264, 527.

Meteor TT.20
Aircraft of this Mark served with several Royal Navy units and the 3/4 CAACU.

Meteor Conservation in the United Kingdom

Over fifty Meteors of various Marks still exist in the United Kingdom, nearly all as whole airframes. A very small number are airworthy, but the majority are held in museums or in storage for restoration. The following aircraft have been confirmed at the time of writing.

Present location

G.41 F.9/40
DG202/G Aerospace Museum, Cosford, Salop.

G.41C Meteor F.3
EE416   Science Museum, S. Kensington, London (nose section only).
EE425   Rebel Air Museum, Earls Colne, Essex (nose section only).

G.41G Meteor F.4
EE531   Midland Air Museum, Coventry Airport, W. Midlands.
EE549   Tangmere Military Aviation Museum, Chichester, W. Sussex. (Mark IV Special).

G.43 Meteor T.7
VW453   Musworth.
VZ634   Newark Air Museum, Newark, Notts.
VZ638/
G-JETM   Vallence Byway, Gatwick, Surrey.
WA634   Aerospace Museum, Cosford, Salop.
WA638   Martin-Baker Aircraft, Chalgrove, Bucks (spares for WL419).
WA662   South Yorkshire Aircraft Museum, Firbeck, Notts.
WF784   Gloucestershire Aviation Collection, Staverton, Glos.
WF825   Meteor Flight, Yatesbury, Wilts.

WF877/
G-BPOA   Kemble.
WH132   No. 276 Squadron ATC, Chelmsford, Essex.
WH166   Birlingham.
WL332   Jet Aviation Preservation Group, Long Marston, Worcs.
WL345   Bo-Peep Garage, Hastings, E. Sussex.
WL349   Gloucestershire Aviation Collection, Staverton, Glos.
WL360   Meteor Flight, Yatesbury, Wilts.
WL375   Dumfries & Galloway Aviation Museum, Dumfries, Scotland.
WL405   Martin-Baker Aircraft, Chalgrove, Bucks (spares for WL419).
WL419   Martin-Baker Aircraft, Chalgrove, Bucks (ejection seat trials aircraft).

G.41K Meteor F.8
VZ462   Second World War Aircraft Preservation Society, Lasham, Hants (Rear fuselage only).
VZ467/
G-METE   Air Support Aviation Systems, Cosford, Salop.
VZ477   Midland Air Museum, Coventry Airport, W. Midlands (nose section only).
WA984   Tangmere Military Aviation Museum, Chichester, W. Sussex (hybrid airframe).
WE925   Classic Jet Aircraft Group, Loughborough, Leics.
WF643   Norfolk & Suffolk Aviation Museum, Flixton, Suffolk.
WH291   Second World War Aircraft Preservation Society, Lasham, Hants.
WH301   Royal Air Force Museum, Hendon, London.

WH364   Gloucestershire Aviation Collection, Staverton, Glos (stored at Kemble).
WK654   Norwich Aviation Museum, Norwich, Norfolk.
WK914   Old Flying Machine Company, Duxford, Cambs (stored).
WK935   Aerospace Museum, Cosford, Salop (prone-pilot trials aircraft).
WK991   Duxford Aviation Society, Duxford, Cambs.
WL131   South Yorkshire Aircraft Museum, Firbeck, Notts (nose section only).
WL168   Yorkshire Air Museum, Elvington, Yorks.
WL181   North East Aircraft Museum, Sunderland, Tyne & Wear.

G.41L Meteor FR.9
VZ608   Newark Air Museum, Newark, Notts (Rolls-Royce RB.108 testbed aircraft).

G.47 Meteor NF.11
WD686   Muckleburgh Collection, Weybourne, Norfolk.
WD790   North East Aircraft Museum, Sunderland, Tyne & Wear (nose section only).
WM145   North Yorkshire Recovery Group, Chop Gate (nose section only).
WM167/
G-LOSM   Jet Heritage Limited, Hurn, Dorset.
WM224   No. 39 Squadron Association, North Weald, Essex (aircraft painted as WM311).
WM267   Blyth Valley Aviation Group, Walpol, Suffolk (nose section only).

WM292   Phoenix Aviation,
         Bruntingthorpe, Northants
         (stored for FAA Yeovilton).

G.47 Meteor NF.12
WS692   Newark Air Museum, Newark,
         Notts.

G.47 Meteor NF.13
WM366/
4X-FNA   Second World War Aircraft
         Preservation Society, Lasham,
         Hants.
WM367   South Yorkshire Aviation
         Museum, Firbeck, Notts
         (nose section only).

G.47 Meteor NF.14
WM261/
G-ARCX   Museum of Flight, East
         Lothian, Scotland.
WS726   No. 1855 Squadron ATC,
         Royton, Lancs.
WS739   Newark Air Museum, Newark,
         Notts.
WS760   Cranfield, Beds.
WS774   East Ross, Scotland.
WS776   Imperial Aviation Group,
         North Coates, Lincs.
WS788   Yorkshire Air Museum,
         Elvington, Yorks.
WS792   Brighouse Bay Caravan Park,
         Cumbria.

WS807   Gloucestershire Aviation
         Collection, Staverton, Glos.
WS832   Solway Aviation Society,
         Carlisle Airport.
WS843   Aerospace Museum, Cosford,
         Salop.

U.16
WH453   DRA, Llanbedr, Gwynedd.
WH800   DRA, Llanbedr, Gwynedd.

G.47 Meteor TT.20
WD646   No. 2030 Squadron ATC,
         Sheldon, Birmingham.

Index